A BASIC GUIDE TO BIBLICAL THEOLOGY

"Alan Thompson sets out to help the Bible reader understand how progressive revelation and the overall unity of the Bible provide the necessary reference points for the correct understanding of the scriptural message. His selection of major themes that are essential aspects of the progression of the message about Christ's saving work aptly enables us to appreciate both the unity and the diversity of Scripture. This book is a valuable addition to a growing body of literature that introduces both the technically trained theologian and the layperson to the discipline of biblical theology. To magnify the Christ-centeredness of the Bible is a worthy aim, which is the emphasis of this book."

—**Graeme Goldsworthy**, Moore Theological College, Sydney, Australia

"Understanding the Bible may seem daunting since it was composed over many centuries with an astonishing literary variety. Alan Thompson has provided an accessible, wise, clear, and faithful summary of some of the key themes in the biblical story. The length of the Bible and the diversity of historical situations addressed may hinder us from grasping where the story is going. Reading Thompson will help students, laypeople, and pastors see the larger framework and discern the overall structure and content of the Scriptures. It is a wonderful resource for a book club or for a small-group study or for a discipling relationship with another believer."

—**Thomas R. Schreiner**, The Southern Baptist Theological Seminary

"What a wonderful book on biblical theology! This volume is one of the most accessible, well-balanced, and engaging books on the subject. This project not only introduces readers to the major themes and structure of the Bible but also contains a splendid chapter on how to read Scripture responsibly. For anyone looking to dip their toes in the waters of biblical theology or to wade into the deep end, I heartily recommend Alan Thompson's *A Basic Guide to Biblical Theology*."

—**Benjamin L. Gladd**, The Carson Center for Theological Renewal

"Whenever a person hears someone do biblical theology—connecting the storyline of the Bible through its various parts according to themes written by the divine author—there's usually a deep resonance that generates a desire to be able to see these connections. Alan Thompson's *A Basic Guide to Biblical Theology* works through nine of the most important themes that span the Bible and presents them in a way that not only grounds the reader in these foundational themes but also trains the Bible student in how to search out additional themes with biblical integrity, leading to joyful discovery."

—**Nancy Guthrie**, Bible teacher and author of *Even Better than Eden: Nine Ways the Bible's Story Changes Everything About Your Story*

"I highly recommend this accessible, insightful introduction to biblical theology. Thompson provides sound guidance for readers seeking patterns and principles for how the whole Bible fits together."

—**Brian J. Tabb**, Bethlehem College and Seminary

"Knowing how the Bible fits together is foundational to the right interpretation and application of Scripture and to all theological formulation. Although the subject is vast, Alan Thompson has provided a wonderful, faithful, and helpful overview of the basic story and message of Scripture. This book is a must-read for those who want to know how to think God's thoughts after him and want to understand well the whole counsel of God. I cannot recommend this book enough; it will help both beginners and seasoned Christians learn how to understand and marvel at the glory of our triune God's redemptive plan centered in our Lord Jesus Christ."

—**Steve Wellum**, The Southern Baptist Theological Seminary

"Too often readers of the Bible don't see the forest for the trees. This engaging book will change that. It will open your eyes to a beautiful landscape in which all the paths lead to Jesus."

—**Sigurd Grindheim**, Norwegian Mission Society and Mekane Yesus Seminary, Addis Ababa, Ethiopia

A BASIC GUIDE TO BIBLICAL THEOLOGY

NINE THEMES THAT UNITE THE OLD AND NEW TESTAMENTS

ALAN J. THOMPSON

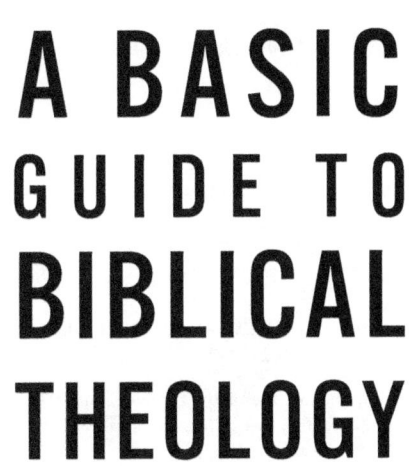

Baker Academic
a division of Baker Publishing Group
Grand Rapids, Michigan

© 2025 by Alan J. Thompson

Published by Baker Academic
a division of Baker Publishing Group
Grand Rapids, Michigan
BakerAcademic.com

All rights reserved. No part of this publication may be reproduced, stored in a retrieval system, or transmitted in any form or by any means—for example, electronic, photocopy, recording—without the prior written permission of the publisher. The only exception is brief quotations in printed reviews.

Library of Congress Cataloging-in-Publication Data
Names: Thompson, Alan J. author
Title: A basic guide to biblical theology : nine themes that unite the Old and New Testaments / Alan J. Thompson.
Description: Grand Rapids, Michigan : Baker Academic, a division of Baker Publishing Group, [2025] | Includes bibliographical references and index.
Identifiers: LCCN 2025013734 | ISBN 9781540969743 paperback | ISBN 9781540969750 casebound | ISBN 9781493452347 ebook | ISBN 9781493452354 pdf
Subjects: LCSH: Bible—Theology
Classification: LCC BS543 .T46 2025 | DDC 230/.041—dc23/eng/20250610
LC record available at https://lccn.loc.gov/2025013734

Unless otherwise indicated, Scriptures are taken from the Holy Bible, New International Version®, NIV®. Copyright © 1973, 1978, 1984, 2011 by Biblica, Inc.® Used by permission of Zondervan. All rights reserved worldwide. www.zondervan.com. The "NIV" and "New International Version" are trademarks registered in the United States Patent and Trademark Office by Biblica, Inc.®

Scripture quotations labeled CSB have been taken from the Christian Standard Bible®, copyright © 2017 by Holman Bible Publishers. Used by permission. Christian Standard Bible® and CSB® are federally registered trademarks of Holman Bible Publishers.

Scripture quotations labeled ESV are from The Holy Bible, English Standard Version® (ESV®), copyright © 2001 by Crossway, a publishing ministry of Good News Publishers. Used by permission. All rights reserved. ESV Text Edition: 2016

Scripture quotations labeled HCSB are from the Holman Christian Standard Bible®, copyright © 1999, 2000, 2002, 2003, 2009 by Holman Bible Publishers. Used by permission. Holman Christian Standard Bible®, Holman CSB®, and HCSB® are federally registered trademarks of Holman Bible Publishers.

Scripture quotations labeled KJV are from the King James Version of the Bible.

Scripture quotations labeled NASB are taken from the (NASB®) New American Standard Bible®, Copyright © 1960, 1971, 1977, 1995, 2020 by The Lockman Foundation. Used by permission. All rights reserved. www.lockman.org

Scripture labeled NKJV taken from the New King James Version®. Copyright © 1982 by Thomas Nelson. Used by permission. All rights reserved.

Scripture quotations labeled NRSV are from the New Revised Standard Version Bible, copyright © 1989 National Council of the Churches of Christ in the United States of America. Used by permission. All rights reserved worldwide.

Cover design by Studio Gearbox

Baker Publishing Group publications use paper produced from sustainable forestry practices and postconsumer waste whenever possible.

25 26 27 28 29 30 31   7 6 5 4 3 2 1

For Alayne,
Deborah, and Rebekah
with much gratitude for their love

CONTENTS

Preface xi
Abbreviations xiii

1. How to Put Your Bible Together   1
2. Creation and Rebellion   13
3. Covenant   25
4. The Exodus and the Tabernacle   43
5. Law (and Wisdom)   55
6. Sacrifice   73
7. Kingship   87
8. The Prophetic Hope   103
9. The Kingdom of God: "Now" and "Not Yet"   117
10. The Holy City: Complete Transformation at Last   133
11. Putting Your Bible Together: Patterns and Principles   149

Bibliography   163
Scripture and Ancient Writings Index   171
Subject Index   179

PREFACE

This book is an introduction to a subject so rich that it is worthy of a lifetime of joyful investigation—how the whole Bible fits together! The first chapter will elaborate more on my focus and rationale. At this point let me just say that my goal is to introduce you to a framework and pattern of reading that you will be able to integrate with everything else you do when you read and study God's Word. The book is designed for Bible readers at any stage of their Christian lives. Other classes (if one is beginning study at a college or seminary) or readings will supplement this introductory guide. At the end of each chapter are pointers to a few other resources for the beginnings of further study. I have learned from many others in the process of preparing and presenting this material over the years. The pointers to resources and occasional footnotes throughout show my indebtedness. Overall, I hope that there is enough in this introduction to spur you on to further study of God's Word.

I wish to thank Jim Kinney, Jennifer Koenes, and the editors at Baker Academic for their excellent assistance. I am especially grateful to Alayne Thompson, Nathan and Katie Batten, Derek Brotherson, Marwan Dwalibi, Sigurd Grindheim, Kirk Patston, Malcolm Reid, Todd Stanton, Brian Tabb, and Stephen Wellum, who all took time out of their busy schedules to read earlier drafts of this material, and to Paul Davies for help with the diagrams. I am also thankful for Sydney Missionary and Bible College (an affiliated college of the Australian University of Theology), the board, and the principal, Derek Brotherson, for the opportunity to complete this book during an action-packed study leave! I dedicate this book to my wife, Alayne, and our two girls, Deborah and Rebekah. They are truly expressions of God's kindness and grace to me.

ABBREVIATIONS

Secondary Sources

DNTUOT	G. K. Beale, D. A. Carson, Benjamin L. Gladd, and Andrew David Naselli, eds. *Dictionary of the New Testament Use of the Old Testament*. Baker Academic, 2023.
NDBT	T. Desmond Alexander, Brian S. Rosner, D. A. Carson, and Graeme Goldsworthy, eds. *New Dictionary of Biblical Theology*. InterVarsity, 2000.
NSBT	New Studies in Biblical Theology

Bible Versions

CSB	Christian Standard Bible
ESV	English Standard Version
HCSB	Holman Christian Standard Bible
KJV	King James Version
LSB	Legacy Standard Bible
NASB	New American Standard Bible
NIV	New International Version
NKJV	New King James Version
NRSV	New Revised Standard Version

1

How to Put Your Bible Together

Imagine the following scenarios. You move to a new city or country, and when you meet some Christians, you discover that they have a special interest in celebrating some of the feasts of the Old Testament, including the Feast of Tabernacles. They insist that if you want to be considered truly a member of God's people, you should continue to celebrate these festivals too—after all, they are biblical. Or perhaps you join a church that frowns on much activity on a Sunday. They argue that we should observe the Sabbath, since that is one of the Ten Commandments. Or perhaps you and your spouse are newly married, and in due course you find out that you are expecting a baby. Then one of you says that soon after birth the baby should be baptized, but the other one thinks that is something the child should have a say on if they later (hopefully) come to faith. How do you work through this? Or let's imagine a scenario in which someone wonders why we should read from or preach from the Old Testament. After all, don't we follow Jesus? Why bother with the Old Testament? All these, and many more, are questions related to how you put your Bible together.

The Bible is a big book! Indeed, it contains sixty-six books that span the history of Israel to the spread of the early church. More than that, the Bible begins with the creation of the world and concludes with the new creation that is yet to come. One of the most helpful ways to appreciate the message of this big book is to know how to piece together its major parts. In fact, as I will go on to explain, this is not only helpful; it is essential to your understanding of the whole Bible. Although many individual stories of the Bible are well known—such as Israel's exodus from slavery in Egypt, or David's defeat of Goliath, or some of Jesus's famous stories, like the parable of the sower—the key to understanding the Bible, and even these individual stories, is to know how the whole Bible fits together, and then how these individual stories fit into the overarching plan of the Bible. That's what this book will help you with.

This first chapter is a broad introduction to what we will be doing throughout this book—that is, the discipline that has come to be known as "biblical theology." In this chapter we will explain what biblical theology is, how it relates to other aspects of interpreting the Bible, how it is key to grasping the overall structure of the Bible, and then how we will develop this understanding of biblical theology throughout the rest of the book.

What Is Biblical Theology?

To understand what we will be doing in this book, it will be helpful to know what biblical theology is. I am using the phrase "biblical theology" to simply refer to the need to interpret any given passage or Bible book in the setting and timeline of where it lands—that is, in relation to what came before and what comes after.[1] This approach recognizes that God did not reveal everything at once but revealed his saving plan progressively, or gradually, over time. So, words like "temporal," "developing," or "unfolding" are often used to describe the way in which God has revealed himself and his purposes across the timeline of the Bible.

This is key, therefore, in approaching any given verse, chapter, or Bible book. Rather than thinking of the Bible as a collection of unconnected bits and pieces of information, we are to think of the Bible verses, chapters, and books as part of an unfolding plan in which more and more is revealed as time goes on. We are not to approach the verses or events and stories as though they appear in the Bible in a random, scattered way (see fig. 1.1). Rather, we approach the verses or events as they appear in a particular place in the unfolding timeline of the way God is revealing himself and his purposes (see fig. 1.2).

Figure 1.1

Not this:

---

1. The resources at the end of this chapter and throughout this book will point to a variety of ways of doing biblical theology and a variety of ways of structuring the development of themes through the Bible. A comprehensive book-by-book approach is Köstenberger and Goswell, *Biblical Theology*. A broad thematic approach is Grindheim, *Introducing Biblical Theology*.

Figure 1.2

But this:

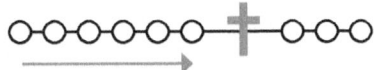

Thus, with any given passage, you need to ask where you are in the timeline of events. More than that, you need to ask, What came before, or led up to, this, and where does it lead? This is more than just understanding that you are reading a passage, say, in the middle of Israel's history, or while Israel is in exile, or during the period of the early church. This is a recognition that these are all connected and a part of the gradual unfolding of God's plan. So, the question is, How does this part that you are reading fit into that developing plan?[2] Recognizing the unfolding nature of God's saving plan, therefore, helps us better understand the place of the passage and connect it to earlier or later related passages.

There is, of course, much diversity in the Bible. There are many themes and various events impacting different people across hundreds of years. The contribution that biblical theology makes is to help us see that all these events and people are part of an overall unity of purpose and plan that runs through the whole Bible. As some commentators have said, we can think of the many authors across the Bible not as soloists, playing their own independent tunes, but rather as part of a symphony, all playing their part in a unified and coherent masterpiece.[3]

Two *prior* assumptions, therefore, that support this approach to the Bible are that

1. God is sovereign in history, and
2. the Bible is God's Word, his own revelation.

First, if God is sovereign in history, then he knows what will take place in the future. Thus, even in earlier events, he already has later events in view (this is easiest for Christians to see in the sacrificial system, for example—God already has in view the ultimate and final sacrifice through Jesus, and these earlier sacrifices anticipate and point to that final complete sacrifice). Second, if the Bible is God's Word, then God is providing his own interpretation of

---

2. I am not suggesting that the storyline must be found in every book (e.g., 2 John). I am merely saying that each passage or book must be understood in light of where it is in that timeline (e.g., in the context of the new covenant).

3. E.g., Strom, *Symphony of Scripture*.

those events through the human authors. We can expect there to be a unity and correspondence between earlier parts and later parts of his Word since ultimately he is the divine author behind it all. This also has in view what the Bible is (God's own revelation and explanation of his purposes and plan) as well as how the Bible comes to us. That is, unlike a textbook with topics listed in the table of contents, the Bible comes to us as an unfolding plan, with a beginning, development, and conclusion. So, basically, biblical theology is about "how to put your Bible together."[4]

Returning to our opening questions, this recognition of the unfolding nature of God's plan shows us how important biblical theology is to a whole host of questions and debates across different denominations. How do the covenants relate to one another? What is the role of the Old Testament law for believers today? How should we interpret the Old Testament in general, or Old Testament prophecy in particular? How should any given book of the Bible (e.g., 1 Kings or the book of Acts) be understood in its context and its setting and place in the unfolding plan of God? Sabbath observance, baptismal candidates, ethics, the place of Israel, and many more topics are all part of interpreting the Bible in this way, asking, How do earlier parts relate to later parts of the Bible? Or how does the Bible fit together? In other words, this is not an optional extra in learning how to read and understand the Bible; it is essential! As has often been said, the Bible is shallow enough for a child to play in and deep enough for an elephant to swim in. So, there is enough here to help new believers as well as seasoned readers of the Bible.

How Does Biblical Theology Relate to Other Interpretive Approaches?

Broadly speaking, we could speak of three terms that are often used for interpreting the Bible: (1) "exegesis," (2) "biblical theology," and (3) "systematic theology."[5] First, "exegesis" is the word used for what we do when we seek to understand the meaning of a particular verse or passage in its immediate context. Rather than pluck a verse out of its setting, we aim to understand what it means in that paragraph, chapter, and book. We seek to get out of the text what is intended in that context (associated with a little Greek preposition,

---

4. I first heard this phrase or a variation of it from Don Carson, although this is a common expression.

5. For an expanded discussion of this, drawing esp. on Carson, see DeRouchie et al., *40 Questions About Biblical Theology*, 119–29.

ek, which often means "out of"). The opposite of this is called "eisegesis" (associated with another little Greek preposition, *eis*, which often means "into"). That is, instead of reading *out* of the text what is there, eisegesis is reading *into* the text what is not there or what we want to be there. So, if someone says to you after a Bible study that what you did was remarkable "eisegesis," they are probably not complimenting you.

Second, biblical theology, as we have seen, is concerned with placing that text in the timeline of the Bible—what came before it and what comes after it. Third, after doing exegesis to find out what the text is saying and biblical theology to locate the meaning of the text in the unfolding plan of God, systematic theology focuses on logical (or systematic) relationships between all the texts on the same topic across the Bible. That is, systematic theology is *primarily* focused on not where the text fits in the timeline but how the text relates to and integrates logically with the other texts on that topic. For example, one text says Jesus is God, another says the Holy Spirit is God, and another says the Father is God. How do they relate to one another? What does the Bible teach about God? Thus, we have the doctrine or theology of the Trinity. Or, to take another example, one text says Jesus is fully human, and another text says Jesus is fully God. How do they relate to each other? Thus, we are thinking now about the doctrine or theology of the two natures—the humanity and deity—of Jesus.

We need all three of these approaches when we interpret the Bible: exegesis (placing the text in its immediate context), biblical theology (placing the text in the timeline of God's unfolding plan), and systematic theology (logically connecting the text to others on that topic). Many say, therefore, that whereas biblical theology is related primarily to temporal connections, systematic theology is related primarily to logical or atemporal connections.[6] In some ways, biblical theology is a mediating link, and systematic theology is culminating, putting everything together. Another related discipline is called "historical theology." This could be thought of as a subset of systematic theology, as it recognizes that these doctrines have been discussed and debated in councils and embedded in creeds throughout church history. We are not the first to try to put these texts together! Since none of us approach the Bible without our own prior understanding about matters like the nature of God, humanity, sin, and so on, we should aim to be shaped and corrected by the exegesis of the text in its immediate context. In this sense exegesis of the text should have the priority and should affect our biblical theology as well as our systematic theology.

---

6. E.g., Carson, "Apostolic Hermeneutics," 62.

Are There Any Examples of This Approach in the Bible Itself?

This approach of recognizing the importance of sequence, of a timeline, when interpreting the Bible can be illustrated briefly from three texts: Romans 4:9–12; Galatians 3:17–19; and Hebrews 4:6–10.[7] Although each passage makes a different argument, these examples illustrate how knowing historical sequence helps us understand the Bible.

First, in Romans 4 Paul uses a temporal argument to show that Abraham's circumcision wasn't a requirement for getting right with God. Paul asks the question, Under what circumstances was Abraham circumcised—was it before or after righteousness was credited to him? Then he answers his own question. Abraham was credited with righteousness by faith before, not after, he was circumcised (Rom. 4:3, 10, 22; referring to Gen. 15:6). Paul's simple point is that in light of this sequence of events, circumcision can't be a requirement to receive righteousness. Faith alone is all that is required!

Second, in Galatians 3:17–19 Paul argues along temporal lines that the law of Moses cannot be an essential requirement for believers today (we will explain this more in chap. 5). Then he lays out the sequence of events (see fig. 1.3).

Figure 1.3

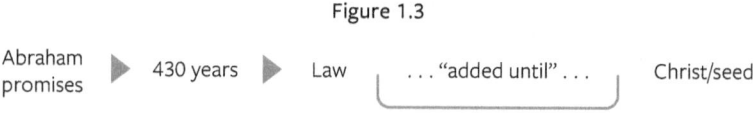

The law was a temporary arrangement. On the one hand, it came in at a certain point in time. On the other hand, it came for a specific period of time (hence the word "until" in Gal. 3:19). In this context, Paul argues against law keeping to gain favor with God on the basis of the sequence and timeline of events (elsewhere he argues against it on the basis of our sinfulness and inability to keep the law; e.g., Rom. 3:9, 20; Gal. 3:10).

Third, in Hebrews 3–4 the writer refers to the time Israel approached the promised land in Numbers 13–14. At that time, when Israel rebelled, the Lord said they would not enter the land—the "rest" that God had promised them. Hebrews 3–4, however, cites Psalm 95 (written, of course, many years after Numbers), in which the psalmist urges God's people that "today" they should not harden their hearts like they did when they failed to enter God's rest. In Hebrews 4:7 the writer states that this psalm was written "a long time later." Thus, if Psalm 95 refers to a "rest" that must still be entered after Israel was in the land, then the land can't be the ultimate meaning of

---

7. For these examples (and others) see Carson, *Collected Writings on Scripture*, 279–81.

God's promise for rest. "For if Joshua had given them rest, God would not have spoken later about another day" (Heb. 4:8). The "rest" must point forward to something else, something greater than God's presence in the land. This, says the writer to the Hebrews, is fulfilled in Jesus. However, the writer uses a temporal argument to make his case, highlighting the sequence along the timeline, as seen in figure 1.4.

Figure 1.4

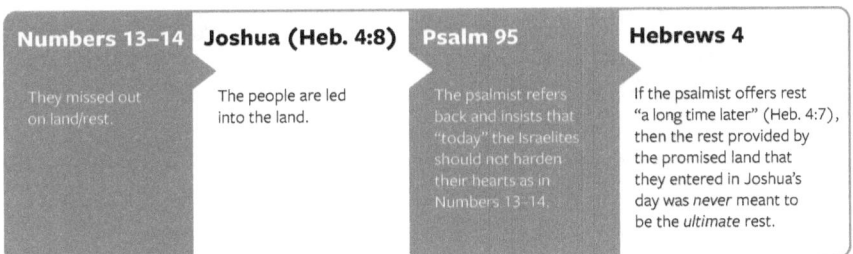

These arguments from biblical authors illustrate the importance of reading our Bible in light of the sequence of events. Since understanding the sequence of texts and events, and the relationship between these texts, helps us put our Bible together, grasping an overall structure of the unfolding plan of the whole Bible will also help.

What Are the Major Epochs (or Eras) in the Bible?

Many commentators have identified discernible major stages in the unfolding plan of God in the Bible. Usually, key events or people are identified along the storyline of the Bible. It is common, for instance, to recognize different stages in Adam (creation), Noah (flood), Abraham (promises), Moses (the law and the nation of Israel), Jesus, the church, and the second coming (new creation). Although these common divisions helpfully show the main stages and broad outline of the Bible, they don't necessarily help show the unity of God's unfolding plan, or how these various stages relate to one another. If, however, we take the arrival of Jesus and the writings of his apostles as key to identifying the goal, or the fulfillment, of the unfolding plan, then we can look for ways in which the New Testament can help us see not only a broad structure but also a structure that shows how the various parts or stages of the Bible relate to one another.[8]

---

8. I am not saying that what follows is the only way to identify the broad structure of the Bible, nor is this the only way to trace themes. However, I think the following broad structure

The Kingdom of God as a Broad Organizing Principle

Let us begin with Jesus's opening words in Mark's Gospel: "The time has come. . . . The kingdom of God has come near. Repent and believe the good news!" (Mark 1:15). This indicates that one way of looking at the whole Bible is that it is about the "kingdom of God." Because Jesus says that the kingdom of God has come, he implies that in one sense it wasn't here before, but it is here now. Psalm 103:19 declares that God's kingdom "rules over all." In that sense, *everyone* is in God's "kingdom" (under his universal, sovereign rule), whether they realize it or not. However, Jesus announces that the kingdom of God has arrived only with him, and it must be entered (e.g., Luke 18:17). Jesus's use of the phrase "kingdom of God," therefore, refers to something like God's saving rule, the kind of rule anticipated in the Old Testament when God's people would be restored, the enemies of God and of his people would be defeated, and God's righteousness would be seen (e.g., Isa. 24:23; 25:6–9; Dan. 2:44; Zech. 14:9).[9] This leads us to the second observation.

The Broad Structure of Promise and Fulfillment

When Jesus says, "The time has come," he implies not only that this saving rule has arrived but also that it must have been anticipated. This idea of promise and fulfillment is a major feature of how the New Testament writers view the broad plan of the Bible.[10] In Romans 1:2–3, for example, Paul says that the gospel was "promised beforehand through [God's] prophets" and that it was "regarding [God's] Son." Likewise, in 16:25–26 Paul says this gospel was "hidden for long ages past" but is now "made known through the prophetic writings." Similar references to the broad idea of promise and fulfillment are found throughout the New Testament (e.g., Matt. 11:13; John 1:16–17; Rom. 3:21; Gal. 3:17–19, 24; 1 Pet. 1:10–12). This simple observation has far-reaching consequences. First, it helps us see that there are discernible stages to God's unfolding plan—broadly speaking, there is a promise or anticipatory stage and a fulfillment stage. God's plan does not advance haphazardly. Second, this identifies Jesus and the good news about his saving life, death, and resurrection as the goal of the promise stage, the goal of the Old Testament. We will come back to this in the "So What?" section below. So far, we might

---

helps us put our Bible together. This section is indebted to Goldsworthy, *Preaching the Whole Bible*, 73–75, 82, 89–90; and Goldsworthy, *Christ-Centered Biblical Theology*, 20–27.

9. We will discuss this in more detail in chap. 9.

10. Of course, I don't mean that this is all there is to understanding the Bible. Chapter 11 will point to a range of ways to move from the Old to the New Testament. In this context, I'm looking at a big-picture way of seeing how the saving rule of God helps us put our Bible together.

visually represent this broad structure for how we put our Bible together as in figure 1.5. But can we be more specific than these two broad stages?

Figure 1.5

Kingdom of God

Promise ▶ Fulfillment

A More Specific Structure

There are a few places in the New Testament where an overview of the whole Bible is provided: Matthew 1:1–17; Acts 7:2–53; and Acts 13:16–41.[11] Let's briefly note the common stages and broad outline of these three passages. In Matthew 1:17 (summarizing 1:1–16), Matthew identifies the stages as in figure 1.6.

Figure 1.6

Similarly, in Acts 7 Stephen begins his history of Israel with Abraham (7:2) and concludes with David and Solomon (7:45–47), before pointing his audience to Jesus (and noting the exile in 7:43). In Acts 13 Paul begins with Israel's "ancestors" (13:17) and then summarizes Israel's history up to David (13:22), before concluding with John the Baptist and Jesus. These three outlines suggest that the high point of Israel's history was during the reigns of David and Solomon. This is not surprising when we read the Old Testament history of Israel and see how much space is given to David and Solomon (e.g., 1 Sam. 16–1 Kings 11). It is also not surprising when we remember what happened during their reigns. Israel was in the land, Israel was one nation under one king, the temple was built, everything was in place. The split of the nation and everything that followed eventually led to (as Matthew and Stephen highlight) the exile of both the Northern and Southern Kingdoms of Israel. Before, during, and after the exile the prophets explained the exile as God's judgment and pointed forward to a glorious transformation.[12]

So, the overall promise stage of God's unfolding plan could be seen in two stages—Israel's history (up to David/Solomon) and Israel's prophecy

---

11. See Goldsworthy, *Preaching the Whole Bible*, 73–75, 82, 89–90; and Goldsworthy, *Christ-Centered Biblical Theology*, 20–27.

12. We will look at the themes of kingship and the prophets in more detail in chaps. 7 and 8.

(surrounding the exile and pointing forward).[13] Since some fulfillment comes with Jesus and the fullness of the saving plan of God awaits the new creation, the fulfillment can also be seen in stages—a fulfillment begun in Christ and completed in the new creation (i.e., Jesus's first and second comings). So, we could visualize this as in figure 1.7.[14]

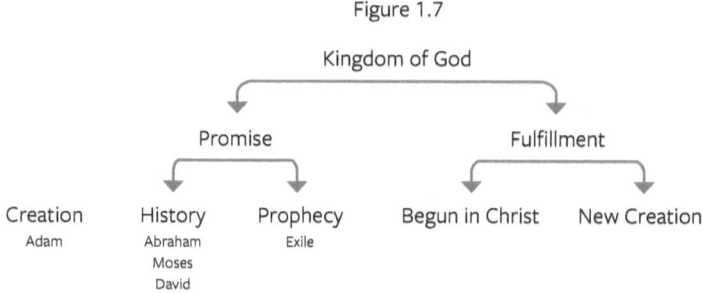

Figure 1.7

So What? Some Implications for How We Read Our Bible

What is the significance of this discussion about the overall structure of the Bible? There are significant implications for understanding the broad structure of the Bible as one of promise and fulfillment (i.e., the broad structure explained under the heading "The Broad Structure of Promise and Fulfillment" above). This affects how we approach each of these two major sections of the Bible. First, if Jesus and the good news about him are the fulfillment of what was written in the Old Testament, the goal to which the Old Testament was pointing, then this later stage of God's revelation (fulfillment) helps us interpret the earlier stage (promise). The later stage shows us what that earlier stage was anticipating. Likewise, if the earlier stage of God's revelation (the Old Testament) was pointing forward, anticipating the later stage (the arrival of Jesus and his rule), then that earlier stage is also necessary for us to be able to understand this later stage that came with Jesus. We need the New Testament to properly understand the Old Testament, and vice versa. This overall structure also helps us see that the unfolding plan of God is better understood not just as having different stages but as having stages that

---

13. I am using "history" here in broad terms to refer to the narrative accounts of Israel's life in the land. I recognize that what we call the "historical books" of Joshua to 2 Kings are called the "former prophets" in the Hebrew Bible.

14. Although, as we will see in the next chapter, the pattern of God's rule is found already in Eden, I have placed "Creation" to the side of the diagram, as I am using the phrase "Kingdom of God" above to refer to God's "saving rule" (i.e., the outworking of God's pattern and plan to restore and save his people, anticipated in Gen. 3:15, 21).

build on and relate to one another. We will see this as we unpack how major themes develop across the Bible.

The Plan for the Rest of This Book

For the rest of this book, we will show how major themes help us put our Bible together. In chapters 2–7, from creation to kingship, we will broadly follow this overarching structure of promise (in Israel's history and prophecy) and fulfillment (in and through Jesus) to see how each theme unfolds. At each stage we will aim to show first how the theme is introduced in the context in which it appears in the Old Testament (observing the emphases in that original context, showing that we are not reading back into that context something illegitimate) and then how that theme develops across the Bible in these broad stages (showing that we also need to read ahead to understand the theme fully). Then in chapter 8 we will show in broad terms how the writing prophets (e.g., Isaiah, Jeremiah, Ezekiel) take up each theme and how they help us put our Bible together. Since we treat these themes as they rise to prominence in their salvation-historical order, in chapters 9 and 10, having arrived at the fulfillment stage, we will break from our broad structure (of history-prophecy-fulfillment) to focus on how Jesus's teaching on the kingdom helps us put our Bible together (chap. 9) and then what the end of the Bible, especially Revelation 21–22, teaches us about the goal to which salvation history has been heading (chap. 10).[15] Finally, in chapter 11 we will take a step back and reflect on the broader question of how these themes help us move from the Old Testament to the New Testament.

How did we decide on the themes to follow? There are many more themes that we could develop (see chap. 11). What we will be looking at, however, are some of the themes that the Bible itself raises to prominence and that help us understand God's overarching and unfolding plan of redemption. The Bible highlights these themes as significant for understanding how the whole Bible fits together (e.g., covenants, sacrifice, kingship). We will also treat each theme in roughly the order in which it rises to prominence in salvation history (i.e., we look at the themes of covenants, the exodus, etc., before we reach the high point with David's and Solomon's kingships). Finally, each chapter concludes with a brief "So What?" section. These sections include brief reflections about some implications of the theme or what the theme teaches us about God.

---

15. Thus, the word "themes" in the subtitle for this book shouldn't be interpreted to mean that each chapter will follow the same structure (or development).

Because this book is an introductory basic guide to how to put your Bible together, there is obviously much more that could be said on each theme. Each chapter closes, therefore, with some books and articles that further explain the chapter and trace the theme in more detail. For readers who want to dig deeper, each chapter also closes with suggestions for other topics or debates that relate to the chapter, along with resources for those. These resources (such as dictionary articles and entire books on the theme) will also show that there are a variety of ways of tracing these themes and many more texts and topics that could be incorporated into each theme. There is more than enough here for an elephant to swim in! But let's begin at the beginning—creation.

FOR FURTHER READING

Goldsworthy, Graeme. *Gospel and Kingdom: A Christian Interpretation of the Old Testament*. Paternoster, 1981.

Goldworthy, Graeme. *Preaching the Whole Bible as Christian Scripture*. Eerdmans, 2000.

Roberts, Vaughan. *God's Big Picture: Tracing the Storyline of the Bible*. Inter-Varsity, 2003.

TO DIG DEEPER

- What are some differing approaches to biblical theology? See Klink and Lockett, *Understanding Biblical Theology*; Carson, "New Covenant Theology and Biblical Theology"; and DeRouchie et al., *40 Questions About Biblical Theology*.
- How do dispensationalists and nondispensationalists approach biblical theology? See Parker and Lucas, *Covenantal and Dispensational Theologies*.
- How does the New Testament use the Old Testament? See Beale and Carson, *Commentary on the New Testament Use of the Old Testament*; Beale et al., *Dictionary of the New Testament Use of the Old Testament*; and Tabb and King, *Five Views of Christ in the Old Testament*.

2

Creation and Rebellion

We said in the preceding chapter that we will focus on themes that the Bible itself raises to prominence, and the first three chapters of the Bible certainly highlight that the themes of creation and rebellion are significant! This sets the stage for understanding the rest of the Bible. Just as our Bible begins with "God created the heavens and the earth" (Gen. 1:1), so also it concludes with "Then I saw 'a new heaven and a new earth'" (Rev. 21:1). Before we begin to trace the themes of Genesis 1–3 through Israel's *history* and Israel's *prophets* and then to the arrival of *Christ* in the New Testament, we need to first orient ourselves to the main themes of these opening chapters of the Bible. In doing so, we can begin to see already God's commitment to and his purposes for his creation. Let's begin at the beginning.

God and Creation

The opening verse of the Bible tells us something immediately about God and his relationship to creation. Since he is the Creator, he is before everything, and everything exists because of him. There is only one God, not a god of the sea, and a god of the mountains, and a sun god, and so on. Furthermore, we are not masters of our own destiny. We are creatures, and we live in God's world. One of the repeated refrains of this opening chapter is that God creates by his word. Notice the repeated refrain "and God said . . . and God said . . . God called . . ." He speaks, and things happen. We might say he just "says the word" and "what he says goes." This tells us that nothing constrains or forces

God. He is free over his creation. He has power, and he rules effortlessly. He is the ruler, or king, or sovereign, over his creation, and he rules by his word.

In addition to the repeated refrain "and God said," phrases like "and it was so," "and God saw," and "there was evening/morning" are repeated throughout. This repetition suggests that God creates with order and intentionality; there is purpose to his creating activity. Many commentators observe a parallel pattern for the six days, with days 1–3 corresponding with days 4–6 (as seen in fig. 2.1). On day 1 light is created, whereas on day 4 the "lights" that govern day and night are created (see Exod. 10:21–23 for another example of light in the midst of darkness). On day 2 water and sky are separated, whereas on day 5 creatures for the water and sky (fish and birds) are created. On day 3 land and vegetation are created, whereas on day 6 living creatures for the land are created. These parallels fit with the opening description of God's creation as "formless and empty" (Gen. 1:2). Thus, days 1–3 correspond to the forming of creation, whereas days 4–6 correspond to the filling of creation.[1]

Figure 2.1

Genesis 1:1–2:3	
Forming	Filling
1. Light (1:3–5)	4. "Lights" (1:14–19)
2. Water and Sky (1:6–8)	5. Fish and Birds (1:20–23)
3. Land and Vegetation (1:9–13)	6. Living Creatures on Land (1:24–31)
7. Rest/Completion (2:1–3)	

My purpose here is not to engage in a detailed analysis of Genesis 1. What we can see from this, however, is that, as with our observations about repetition, there is design and intentionality; there is a deliberate pattern here. Therefore, when we read repeatedly that "God saw that it was good," this means, among other things, that it fits exactly with the purpose God had in making it. It is as if God looks at his creation and says, "Ahh, that's exactly what I was hoping for!"

Finally, we also see this emphasis on plan and order in the final day. When we notice the (general) correspondence across the days, day 7 stands out. This

---

1. There are enough anomalies in this correspondence to caution us about making too much of this parallel pattern. For example, the "lights" on day 4 are placed into the expanse that is described on day 2; and the water appears to have been created on day 1, gathered on day 3, and called "seas" on day 3, which does not precisely align with the creation of sea creatures on day 5. Our purpose here is to notice the overall pattern.

is confirmed when we read Genesis 2:1–3. The phrase "seventh day" is repeated three times in just two verses (vv. 2–3). The emphasis here is on completion. A goal has been reached; "God had finished the work he had been doing" (2:2). Thus, day 7 is the climax of these seven days.[2] All this shows that God is the sovereign ruler over creation and that he is committed to his creation, as seen in the detailed and deliberate purpose that went into creating the world. We will come back to this below.

Before we move on from these brief observations, we should also remember the wider context of the Bible's opening chapter. Genesis is the first book of the opening collection of books—Genesis to Deuteronomy—which is called the "Pentateuch" ("penta-" refers to the first *five* books of the Bible). The context of the Pentateuch is seen in the last chapters of Deuteronomy, where Moses prepares the people of Israel for their entrance into the land that God has promised them. Thus, Genesis 1 helps Israel understand how their God was able to rescue them from the gods of Egypt, and how their God is able to bring them into a land where Canaanite gods are worshiped.[3] Whereas "sun" and "moon" might be worshiped as gods in Canaan, Genesis 1:14–19 just calls them "lights" (a "greater light" and a "lesser light") that came about on one day of God's effortless creation. Furthermore, there is no battle here between the "gods." Rather, there is one God, who rules over all. Israel's Redeemer is the Creator of the universe! The opening chapter of the Bible also anticipates the broader plan of God for the salvation of the nations. Later promises to Abraham and the deliverance of Israel are set against this backdrop of the God who has created humanity (but we're getting ahead of ourselves).

God and Humanity

Given the amount of space devoted to the creation of and commission for humanity on day 6, humanity is the high point of the six days of creative activity. This is especially seen in Genesis 1:26–28, where humanity is described as made in God's "image." This means that although all creation belongs to God, humanity is set apart as having unique value, simply by virtue of being human. "Image" has the idea of likeness and representation. A relationship

---

2. My goal here is not to settle ongoing debates about the relationship between Gen. 1 and whether or not God created the world in six days, and if we have a relatively young earth or not. I think that the repetition of "evening and morning" and Exod. 20:11 support a six-day creation and that texts such as Luke 11:50, Matt. 19:4, and Rom. 1:20 support the location of humanity at "the beginning" of the world. However, I am focusing on the emphasis of Gen. 1 on God's sovereign purpose and plan in creation.

3. Cf. M. D. Williams, *Far as the Curse Is Found*, 40–62.

is established here, whereby humanity is blessed and granted a role and privileges. Everything is "given" to men and women, and they are to "rule" over the creatures. Since the preceding verses have highlighted God as the Creator of these creatures, humanity is in a privileged position of being responsible for looking after God's creatures. The role of "ruling" isn't what gives humanity value; it is a consequence of being made in God's image and therefore a representative ruler and accountable to God.[4]

This also has many consequences that we will not develop here.[5] The emphasis in this context, however, is that there is harmony and order—between God and humanity, between man and woman, and between humanity and the rest of creation. Harmony in relationship with God and accountability to him are also suggested later, in Genesis 3:8, when we read that the Lord God "was walking in the garden" of Eden. This refers to an experience of God's presence among humanity in the midst of his creation. In this context, Adam and Eve's (1) commission as image bearers to multiply, fill the earth, rule, and "subdue" the earth, together with (2) the command to guard the garden and (3) the restriction not to eat from the tree of the knowledge of good and evil, as well as (4) the promise of the tree of life, all imply that God's goal is for the knowledge of his glory to be enjoyed and spread through all the earth (1:26–28; 2:8–9, 15–17).[6] For now, however, we can see from the opening chapter of Genesis that God's commitment to and rule over his creation are seen in the purpose and plan he has for every part of it.

The Rebellion (Fall) of Humanity

If the emphasis in Genesis 1–2 has been on the rule of God over his creation by his word, and the perfect harmony between God and humanity and the rest of creation, then Genesis 3 shows the reversal of all this. The opening words of the serpent introduce suspicion toward God's word and his character with the question "Did God really say . . . ?" (3:1). The next words of the serpent question the reality of judgment with his assertion "You will not certainly die" (3:4). Thus, God's word is rejected, God is rejected as the one with ultimate authority, and independence from God and his rule is valued more than God. The real-life consequence of this rejection of God and his

---

4. That the "ruling" is a consequence of being made in God's image is seen in the phrase "so that they may rule" (Gen. 1:26).

5. E.g., that every human being has intrinsic value, regardless of their level of health or capacity, or age (whether they are at the beginning or nearing the end of life).

6. On Adam's "probation" and the goal of an eternal Sabbath rest in God's presence, see Fesko, *Last Things First*, 102–3.

word is seen in the following chapter with human conflict and the repetition of "and then he died" in Genesis 5. Judgment from God is seen, therefore, in the expulsion of Adam and Eve from the garden, from the place of harmony in the presence of God. This is the "spiritual" death that they experience, which is inevitably followed by physical death. Thus, the prospect of harmony forever in God's presence is forfeited.

A Glimmer of Hope

Genesis 1 has shown us, nevertheless, that God is committed to his creation and the people he created the earth for.[7] He calls his creation "good" and humanity "very good"; they are made for his purposes, and provision is given to them. This commitment of God to his people and his creation is seen in what has been called the first proclamation of the gospel in Genesis 3:15 (often called the "protoevangelion," from the Latin words for "first" [*proto*] and "gospel" [*evangelion*]). Although the verse is a little cryptic, and although not everything is explained here, there is enough to provide hope. The "seed" of the woman will "crush" the head of the serpent (see the NIV footnote). Rather than an anticlimactic description of how human beings will have ongoing trouble with snakes, this promise looks forward to a descendant who will deliver a fatal blow to the head of the one who brought this disastrous rebellion into the world. Later revelation clarifies that the "serpent" represents Satan (Rom. 16:20; Rev. 12:9; see also John 8:44). The idea of a coming "seed" or "descendant" develops through the line of Abraham, to one promised to David, and ultimately to Christ, the descendant or "seed" of Abraham and David who destroys the work of the devil through his victorious death and resurrection (Col. 1:13; 2:15; Heb. 2:14; 1 John 3:8).

Implications of Creation and Fall in the Unfolding of Salvation History

God's Plan for the Nations

The pointers to the implications of creation and fall presented here will be developed in later chapters, but for now we can see the significance of Genesis 1–3 for understanding the whole Bible. First, this is the starting point for understanding God's plan of salvation. Many interpreters rightly focus on God's promises to Abraham in Genesis 12 (see chap. 3) as crucial for

---

7. Goldsworthy, *According to Plan*, 112.

understanding God's plans for the nations. However, Genesis 12 comes after Genesis 1! That is, God's plans for all people stem from his rule over all creation. There is one God, so all people are accountable to him and must know him. This is why Paul begins with God as the Creator in his sermon to those who don't know the storyline of the Bible in Athens (Acts 17). These opening chapters explain both the predicament of humanity and why God's solution was always meant to extend to all creation and all nations. Thus, to anticipate what we will say below and throughout the rest of this book, God's commitment to his creation, his presence with and relationship with Adam and Eve, the description of the place of God's presence as Edenic, the role of humanity to represent God's rule over creation, and Adam's foundational role for all humanity—all these get picked up in the storyline of the Bible. The sequence of salvation history in large part moves from Adam, to Israel, to Christ, to all those who belong to Christ.

Glimpses of Eden in Israel's History

God's plan of salvation unfolds until we get to Christ with what Tremper Longman calls "glimpses of Eden" along the way.[8] These "hints" or "glimpses of Eden" point to God's ultimate goal of restoring his relationship with people who know him and enjoy his presence. Although there is more that can be said, we will observe just four developments in salvation history until the exile.

1. The account of the flood and the role of Noah include phrases that should ring some bells, reminding us of Genesis 1 (the next chapter will show how the covenant with Noah lays a foundation for the rest of salvation history). The instruction to Noah to "be fruitful and increase in number and fill the earth" (Gen. 9:1; cf. 9:7) recalls 1:28. The references to the animals of the earth and the "birds in the sky" (9:2) also recall 1:28 and the creation narrative. The description of humanity as in "the image of God" (9:6) recalls 1:26–27. While the judgment on all the earth with a flood signals a reversal of creation, Noah sounds like a new Adam, and the promises of blessing to him draw on the promises in Genesis 1 (more on this in the next chapter, on covenants).

2. The account of the exodus and the instructions for the tabernacle reflect "new creation" language in which God rescues his people and brings them back to enjoy his presence in his land. The language of light and darkness, with waters divided and dry land appearing, sounds like a new

---

8. Longman, *Immanuel in Our Place*, 13. The following discussion summarizes 28–61.

creation (see Exod. 14:20–21; 15:1–21; Ps. 74:13–14). The instructions for the tabernacle, following the exodus, show that this will be the place of God's presence, where he will "dwell among them" (Exod. 25:8). To show that this presence is a reminder of Eden, inside the tabernacle is a tree-shaped object, a menorah, which is described not only in terms of its branches and "flowerlike cups, buds and blossoms" but also in terms of "almond flowers with buds and blossoms" (25:31–36). The tent material is described as "finely twisted linen and blue, purple and scarlet yarn, with cherubim woven into them" (26:1; cf. 26:31, 36). Thus, when one walks inside, not only does the color appear to be sky-like but the tree and the cherubim also recall Eden. It also seems likely that the entrance to Eden from the east (Gen. 3:24) was the pattern for the entrance to the tabernacle, the temple of Israel, and the temple of Ezekiel 40:6.

3. Similar garden imagery characterized the temple design. "Cherubim, palm trees and open flowers" (1 Kings 6:29) were carved on the walls of the temple. At the top of the pillars were capitals "in the shape of lilies" with "two hundred pomegranates in rows all around" (7:19–20, 22) adding up to "four hundred pomegranates" for the two pillars (7:42). Then there was a basin of water called "the Sea" (7:23). All this is reminiscent of Eden, as the temple with its holy of holies represented the presence of God with his people in the land of Israel.

4. Finally, Israel's exile was more than mere expulsion from the land. Their exile was a removal, by God, "from his presence" (2 Kings 17:18, 20), reflecting again the banishment from Eden (Gen. 1:23–24).

The Prophetic Hope of a New Creation

When the prophets look forward, therefore, to a transformation of God's people after judgment, they speak in terms of a "new heavens and a new earth" (Isa. 65:17; cf. 66:22), or a new creation, in which harmony will be restored. Although it is likely symbolic language, the hope that "the wolf and the lamb will feed together" (65:25) recalls the harmony of the creation narrative to point ahead to the future. Similar language is used in Isaiah 11 to describe the time when "the earth will be filled with the knowledge of the LORD as the waters cover the sea" (11:9; cf. 35:1–10). Prophetic hopes for transformed Zion (51:3), Jerusalem (65:17–19), and Israel (Ezek. 36:35) and the universal rule of Israel's righteous king (Zech. 9:10; cf. Ps. 72:8) show that Eden is the pattern for Israel's hope for the new creation.

The river flowing out from Eden (Gen. 2:10) is reflected in the rivers that flow from the temple in Ezekiel 47:1–12 and Revelation 22:1–2. The location of a mountain connects Israel's temple on Mount Zion (e.g., Exod. 15:17) with the end-time temple (Ezek. 43:12; Rev. 21:10) and Ezekiel's description of Eden as located on a mountain (Ezek. 28:14, 16). Furthermore, Ezekiel 28:13–14, 16, and 18 seem to confirm the above connections between Eden and Israel's tabernacle and temple by referring to Eden as "the garden of God," "the holy mount[ain] of God," and containing "sanctuaries" (the plural "sanctuaries" was used to refer to Israel's tabernacle and temple; see Ezek. 7:24; cf. Lev. 21:23; Jer. 51:51).

Thus, as with the Adam-Israel-Christ pattern noted above, the prophets show that there is an Eden–Israel–temple–new-creation pattern. The opening chapters of Genesis, therefore, provide the pattern for the future hope of transformation, the hope of harmony in God's presence. And this hope has been maintained with "glimpses of Eden" along the way.

New-Creation Language in the New Testament

The opening chapters of Genesis help us understand language that is used to describe Jesus in the New Testament. On the one hand, Paul calls Jesus the "second Adam" (see 1 Cor. 15:47), meaning that in terms of salvation history, the actions of Adam and Jesus affect everything. On the other hand, Paul calls Jesus the "last Adam" (15:45), meaning that in terms of salvation history, no one comes after Jesus. Furthermore, Paul calls Adam a "type" of the one to come. That is, the effects of Adam's actions on all who belong to him set a pattern for how Jesus's actions will affect all who belong to him (Rom. 5:12–21). Adam's transgression brings death and judgment to all he represents (i.e., all humanity). But, by God's grace, Christ's obedience brings life and justification to all he represents (i.e., all who belong to him by faith). Jesus's death-defeating resurrection brings about a new beginning and a new humanity of those who belong to him (Col. 1:18). Thus, "new creation" language is used for those who belong to Christ. "If anyone is in Christ," says Paul, "the new creation has come" (2 Cor. 5:17). Or again, to be in Christ means that "neither circumcision nor uncircumcision means anything; what counts is the new creation" (Gal. 6:15). These verses indicate that because Christ's life, death, and resurrection overcame the effects of Adam's disobedience, all who belong to him receive life and his righteousness. Jesus's resurrection is the sign of the new life of the new creation; all who belong to him have life in him and belong already to the new creation that is coming.

Finally, as we have already noted, in the prophets ultimate salvation is described in terms of a "new heavens and a new earth" (Isa. 65:17; cf. 66:22;

Rev. 21:1). Peter says we look forward to "a new heaven and a new earth," which he adds is "where righteousness dwells" (2 Pet. 3:13). Thus, salvation is not so much a release from the body but a complete transformation, including a resurrection body in a new creation (1 Cor. 15). In keeping with what we observed about the prophetic hope (see above), the language that is used for the "inheritance" of the land in the Old Testament is used for the new creation in the New Testament (Matt. 5:5; Rom. 4:13–14; 8:17–19; Gal. 3:16, 18, 29; see, e.g., Josh. 18–19). Not only does Revelation 21:1 announce "a new heaven and a new earth"; 22:2 also describes the "tree of life" as ever fruitful, and 22:3 assures believers, "No longer will there be any curse." The key to this is the presence of God: "God's dwelling place is now among the people, and he will dwell with them" (21:3); "they will see his face" (22:4). This theme of God's purposes for the whole of his creation helps us understand why Revelation 21–22 sounds so much like the opening chapters of Genesis (more on this in chaps. 3, 4, and 10). However, the death-defeating resurrection of Jesus, the secure enjoyment of God's presence forever, the glorious transformation of God's people to glorify him forever, together with the complete removal of the threat of death and Satan forever (not to mention the removal of the effects of sin and the curse), ensure that the eternal consummation is even better than Eden.[9]

So What? Some Implications of This Theme of Creation and Rebellion

When we look back over the way this theme runs through the whole Bible, we are reminded of God's persistent commitment to his creation. He has never lost sight of this goal of restoring us to be able to enjoy his presence, and the "glimpses of Eden" along the way are a constant reminder of this. This theme also highlights for us that while we ought not separate the spiritual from the physical, the goal all along is for God's people to enjoy his presence and glorify him. The ultimate judgment for rebellion was expulsion from his presence, and our ultimate joy and salvation is to be restored to a relationship with him, enjoying his presence. All this comes through Jesus. Jesus is the one who undoes the effects of Adam's sin and the fall, restores us to a right relationship with God, and enables us to enjoy his presence forever. Jesus's resurrection body points to our future, incorruptible resurrection bodies that are no longer affected by death. The new creation comes in fullness when Jesus returns.

---

9. See Guthrie, *Even Better than Eden*, for more on this. See also chap. 10.

This also has implications for our understanding of who Jesus is. Just as Genesis 1 says that God created through his word, so Paul in Colossians 1 says that God created all things through the Son. The Son, therefore, is on the Creator side of the Creator-creation divide. In fact, "all things have been created through him *and for him*" (Col. 1:16; italics added)! This chapter, however, is not a discussion about everything we can learn from Genesis 1–3.[10] All we need to note here is that Genesis 1–3 shows the pattern, as Graeme Goldsworthy has famously said, of "God's people in God's place under God's rule."[11] We might add, "enjoying God's presence." The whole Bible points us forward to the prospect of enjoying God's presence forever, safe and secure through Jesus's death-defeating resurrection. But how does God bring about his saving purposes for humanity? That is the theme we turn to next.

FOR FURTHER READING

Carson, D. A. *The Gagging of God: Christianity Confronts Pluralism.* Zondervan Academic, 1996. (See esp. 193–252.)

Fesko, J. V. *Last Things First: Unlocking Genesis 1–3 with the Christ of Eschatology.* Mentor, 2007.

Goldsworthy, Graeme. *According to Plan: The Unfolding Revelation of God in the Bible; An Introductory Biblical Theology.* InterVarsity, 1991. (See esp. 90–111.)

Guthrie, Nancy. *Even Better than Eden: Nine Ways the Bible's Story Changes Everything About Your Story.* Crossway, 2018.

TO DIG DEEPER

- Was there a "covenant" with Adam? See the books on covenant in chapter 3.
- What is the relationship between Adam and us, and Adam and Christ? See Romans 5.

---

10. For example, the opening chapters of Genesis remind us that we are finite. The distinction between the Creator and his creation also helps highlight why idolatry is such folly. Worship of created things rather than the Creator occasions wrath (Rom. 1:23–25). Creation itself, however, is meant to be enjoyed (Acts 14:17; 1 Cor. 3:21–22; 1 Tim. 4:3–4; 6:17). Creation is often a pointer to God's sovereignty and power (Job 38–41; Isa. 40) and reminds us that God is to be worshiped (Rom. 1:21, 25; Rev. 4:11; see also Pss. 8; 19).

11. Goldsworthy, *According to Plan*, 99.

- Is Eden described as a temple? For a full discussion, see Beale, *Temple and the Church's Mission.* However, Daniel Block (*Covenant*, 27–30) disputes this (though he agrees that the tabernacle and the temple were later a miniature Eden).
- What are the similarities and differences between this creation and the new creation (and its arrival)? See chapter 10.

3

Covenant

This chapter is perhaps the most significant chapter in this book for putting our Bible together. The theme of covenant has a host of practical implications for matters as diverse as your own personal assurance of salvation to denominational distinctives about baptism. Before we go any further, let's briefly clarify what we're talking about. What is a "covenant"? Other English words that may come to mind include "agreement" or "contract." What is common to these words is they deal with relationships. "Covenant" is a relationship word. It refers to an agreement in which the terms of the relationship are defined. The parties in the relationship are identified, and the terms of their agreement are defined. That is, a covenant defines how the relationship will work and the consequences for keeping or failing to keep those terms. It is important to state that the theme or concept of a covenant may be present even if the specific word "covenant" isn't mentioned in the passage under consideration (e.g., 2 Sam. 7 and the Davidic covenant).[1]

We suggested in the opening chapter that God's saving plan unfolds throughout the Bible in discernible stages, with major markers or events along the way, rather than just as a continuous flow of incremental advancements. In this chapter we'll see that major stages or developments in God's saving plan are in large part linked to covenants. Indeed, some interpreters have argued that covenant, rather than kingdom, should be considered the major overarching theme of the whole Bible, under which other themes may be arranged. A good way to relate the two is that God maintains or administers his saving rule, his kingdom,

---

1. I.e., the Hebrew (*berith*) or Greek (*diathēkē*) word for the English word "covenant."

through or by covenants. Thus, "God's kingdom through God's covenants" is how one book succinctly puts it.² Figure 3.1 aims to convey the idea that the broad, overarching trajectory of the promise and fulfillment of God's saving rule is carried out through the various covenants. (The gaps between the arrows imply only that there are a number of covenants, not that they are unconnected.)

Figure 3.1

Kingdom of God

In what follows we will identify and summarize the main covenants that develop across salvation history between God and his people. These covenants are commonly named after the person most directly involved in each covenant, such as Noah, Abraham, Moses, and David. So, if you scan through the following headings, you will see that the names given to these covenants are "Noahic," "Abrahamic," and so on. In this chapter we will unpack each covenant in turn, showing how it relates to and develops God's saving purposes. In relation to the overall framework we introduced in chapter 1, Israel's *history* essentially covers the covenants with Abraham, Moses, and David, and Israel's *prophecy* is the context for the new covenant. Then we will see how all these covenants come together and find *fulfillment* in Christ.

Before we unpack the covenants, we need to make one more important observation about a statement that gets repeated (with slight variations) across the Bible. This statement is found with reference to each of the covenants that we will be summarizing. It has been called the "covenant formula." This formula is well known enough that if I begin with the words "You will be my people, and . . . ," I'm sure many would be able to complete the sentence with "I will be your God." This repeated formula expresses the essence of the covenant and shows, as we saw in Genesis 1–3, that a relationship with God is at the heart of his saving plan. It is found in the Abrahamic (Gen. 17:7), Mosaic (Exod. 6:7; 19:5; 20:2; 29:45–46), and Davidic (2 Sam. 7:14) covenants, as well as the new covenant (Jer. 30:22; 31:33; 32:38; see also Ezek. 34:30; 36:28; 37:23, 27). This hope for a restored relationship between God and humanity culminates in the new creation with the climactic declaration

---

2. Gentry and Wellum, *God's Kingdom Through God's Covenants*; this is a condensed version of Gentry and Wellum, *Kingdom Through Covenant*.

made by a loud voice from the throne saying, "Look! God's dwelling place is now among the people, and he will dwell with them. They will be his people, and God himself will be with them and be their God" (Rev. 21:3).

That this theme runs through all the covenants does not mean that there are no variations among the covenants; they are still distinct covenants with their own settings, contexts, and goals. So, we will work our way through these covenants, summarizing them briefly one at a time. Be prepared; this will be the longest, most complex chapter in the book, yet it is potentially one of the most rewarding! As we go, we will build a simplified visual picture with a key phrase for each covenant.

The Noahic Covenant

God's covenant with Noah lays an important foundation for the rest of salvation history as it shows God's continued commitment to his creation. In the last chapter we saw that God had intention and design in creating the universe and that there was harmony between God and his people and his creation. We saw that Adam and Eve were given the responsibility of representing God's rule and were given instructions to obey God's word—the word by which he rules his world.[3] We also saw that the rebellion against God's rule ruptured that harmony; Adam and Eve were expelled from his presence in judgment, and creation itself suffered the effects of this ruptured harmony. Nevertheless, God showed his continued commitment to his creation with the glimmer of hope provided in the promise of Genesis 3:15. The seed of the woman will crush the serpent's head. Mercifully, God does not forever punish and banish humanity or permanently rupture his good creation. He shows he is committed to his creation. God's commitment to his creation is especially seen in the promises associated with Noah. Let's first turn, therefore, to the Noahic covenant.

Although all of Genesis 6–9 is relevant for this covenant, the key text in view is 9:8–17. Genesis 9:8–11 especially highlights two key features of this covenant. First, there is an emphasis here on God's initiative. This covenant is not a contract between two equals. God is the one who announces that *he* will establish *his* covenant. The security of this covenant, therefore, rests with God alone. Even the sign of the covenant, a rainbow, is for God; it is a

---

3. Thus, we could begin this chapter with reference to God's arrangement with his creation through Adam as a covenant (see the resources that conclude the chapter). Our focus in this section is on the covenants that unfold through salvation history (covenants that develop God's plan to restore the harmony between humanity and himself, leading to a new creation).

reminder that he will never again "destroy all life" with floodwaters (9:15).[4] Second, the repeated emphasis in these verses is that this covenant is not only between God and Noah and all his descendants but also with "every living creature" (see 9:10 [x2], 12; cf. 9:15, 16). It is ultimately a covenant promise between God and "all life on the earth" (9:17).

As we noted in chapter 2, there are numerous allusions back to Genesis 1, with Noah functioning as another Adam. References to blessing (9:1; cf. 1:28a), the command to be "fruitful and increase in number and fill the earth" (9:1b; see also 9:7; cf. 1:28b), humanity's rule over the animals (9:2; cf. 1:26, 28), and the provision of food to humanity, which is made in God's image (9:3, 6; cf. 1:26–27, 29–30), all recall Genesis 1.

Similarly, many interpreters have also noted allusions to the creation account in Genesis 1. On the one hand, the flood account appears to be a reversal of creation. The separation and distinction of days 2 and 3 of Genesis 1 are reversed. The "springs of the great deep burst forth, and the floodgates of the heavens were opened" (7:11; cf. 1:6–8). On the other hand, the flood account also sounds like a "re-creation" account that draws on Genesis 1. The land is again separated from the water (8:1–3; cf. 1:9–10); living creatures are brought out, and animals are brought to Noah (7:15; 8:17–19; cf. 1:20–22, 24–25; 2:19); and days and seasons are mentioned again (8:22; cf. 1:14–18).

Thus, the covenant language in the flood account appears to show that God is reaffirming his original creation intent (the first occurrence of the word "covenant" in the Bible occurs in Gen. 6:18; this is then developed in 9:9–17).[5] All this indicates that this Noahic covenant could be called the "covenant of preservation."[6] This covenant shows that God's plan of salvation will proceed through salvation history on the certainty of God's continued commitment to his creation. The earth will not be destroyed, since God has a plan to redeem his people from all nations. This covenant is an "everlasting covenant" for "all generations to come" (9:12, 16; cf. 8:22; Isa. 54:9; Jer. 33:20, 25). The first installment of our visual (see fig. 3.2) shows the Noahic covenant as the backdrop (creation preserved) for the rest of salvation history.

---

4. Some suggest that the "bow" may symbolize a weapon of war, signaling that this is turned away (cf. Gen. 48:22; Josh. 24:12; 1 Sam. 2:4). Gentry and Wellum, *God's Kingdom Through God's Covenants*, 66–67; Williamson, *Sealed with an Oath*, 64.

5. See Gentry and Wellum, *God's Kingdom Through God's Covenants*, 59–61; Dumbrell, *Covenant and Creation*, 15–20. Though Williamson, *Sealed with an Oath*, 69–76, differs with Dumbrell (see the second item in the "To Dig Deeper" section below).

6. E.g., Robertson, *Christ of the Covenants*, 109.

Figure 3.2

Timeline of Salvation History

Noahic
(Preservation)

The Abrahamic Covenant

God's covenant with Abraham shows God's foundational promises to bring blessing to the nations. In Genesis 4–11, following the rebellion of Genesis 3, the problem of sin continues to spread, even after the flood (9:21), culminating in the rebellion of Genesis 11 and the people building a tower to "make a name" for themselves (11:4). What hope is there for humanity? When will this "seed" of the woman come? In Genesis 12 we encounter Abram (later called Abraham) and a cluster of promises that come to him. These promises are found in Genesis 12:1–3; 15:1–21; 17:1–16; and 22:15–18. Later passages of Scripture look back to these promises as part of one covenant with Abraham (see 2 Kings 13:23; 1 Chron. 16:15–16; Ps. 105:8–9). It is hard to overestimate the significance of these promises as they show that from now on, the hope for all human history is focused on one man and his "seed." In what follows we will focus on Genesis 12 as the heart of the Abrahamic covenant and Genesis 15 as the confirmation of this covenant with Abraham.

The Heart of the Abrahamic Covenant (Gen. 12)

The promises to Abraham focus on offspring, land, and blessing. Following the command for Abraham to go to the land that God will show him, there is a series of phrases that are followed by a significant concluding phrase.[7] This sequence occurs in verse 2 and again in verse 3. Let's lay the phrases out to see the significance of this:

> I will make you into a great nation,
>   and I will bless you;
> I will make your name great,
>   and you will be a blessing. (Gen. 12:2)

---

7. The following builds on M. D. Williams, *Far as the Curse Is Found*, 108.

The last phrase can be understood as a purpose statement (or perhaps a consequence). Thus, the last phrase could be translated as "so that you will be a blessing" (ESV, NRSV; see also LSB). That is, the preceding three promises lay the foundation for the final statement. They show what God will do for Abraham, and then the final phrase shows why he is doing this. A similar construction is found in verse 3:

> I will bless those who bless you,
>   and whoever curses you I will curse;
> and all peoples on earth
>   will be blessed through you. (Gen. 12:3)

The final phrase again shows the main point of these promises—they show God's plan for bringing blessing to the nations! The promise of blessing through Abraham to the nations is repeated again in 22:18, as well as in 26:3–4 (to Isaac; note "all these lands") and 28:14 (to Jacob).

The Confirmation of the Covenant (Gen. 15)

In Genesis 15:8–21 we have a dramatic ceremony that is designed to strengthen Abraham's faith, showing the security of these promises in God's plan. In this kind of covenant ceremony, the animals are cut in half, and then the parties to the covenant walk through the middle of this graphic scene (see Jer. 34:18). The message is essentially, "If I don't uphold my side of the agreement, then may I be as these animals are!" In Abraham's dream only a "smoking firepot with a blazing torch appeared and passed between the pieces" (Gen. 15:17). Since smoke and fire later represent God at Sinai (Exod. 19:18; 20:18) and in the wilderness (13:21), this is a symbolic way of referring to the presence of God. Therefore, God is the only one who passes between these animal pieces. In other words, God declares that he is the one who will ensure the fulfillment of these promises. They rest secure in him. It is true that Abraham had to follow God's instructions (just as Noah did). He was commanded to leave his country (Gen. 12:1), and he was later commanded to "walk before [God] faithfully" (17:1). Yet these are the means, or the how and when, for how God will bring about these promises for Abraham. They do not negate the fundamental promise and intention of God to bless Abraham and all nations through him. Later, Moses appeals to these promises in the golden calf incident (Exod. 32:13); God refers to these promises even in the midst of warnings of punishment for Israel's disobedience (Lev. 26:40–45); they form the basis for God's continued compassion toward Israel, since he is "unwilling to destroy them or banish them from his presence" (2 Kings 13:23);

and they form the basis of hope beyond judgment for Israel in the prophets (Mic. 7:14–20; esp. 7:20).

The covenant sign of circumcision (Gen. 17) especially highlights the importance of physical descent for the fulfillment of these momentous promises. It is, after all, through Abraham's descendants that blessing will come to the nations. Thus, the Abrahamic covenant forms the basis for the rest of salvation history! We will soon see that these promises are repeated for the Davidic covenant and the new covenant, and they are significant for understanding the blessing that comes to the nations through Jesus. This leads to the next installment of our visual (see fig. 3.3).

Figure 3.3

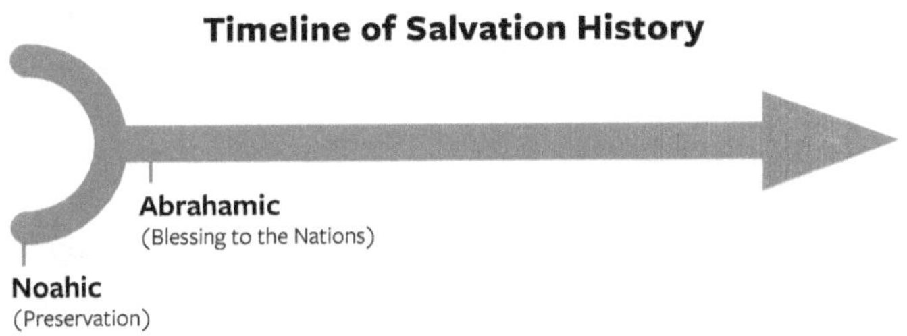

Timeline of Salvation History

Abrahamic
(Blessing to the Nations)

Noahic
(Preservation)

The Mosaic Covenant

God's covenant through Moses focuses on the descendants of Abraham who became the nation of Israel. It shows God's desire for an obedient people and his gracious provision for their sin so that he may dwell among them. Following the pattern highlighted by Graeme Goldsworthy (which we noted in chap. 1 regarding God's people, place, rule), the covenant with Abraham in Genesis demonstrates God's plan to have a people who enjoy his rule in the place he will give to them. The book of Exodus then shows God's faithfulness to his promises as he rescues his people from the rule of the Egyptians to bring them to the land he promised. So, with the giving of the law at the time of the exodus, there are both continuities and new developments with the Mosaic covenant.

On the one hand, continuity with the Abrahamic covenant is seen in the references to the promises to Abraham as the basis for the exodus (Exod. 2:24; 6:4; see also Deut. 7:7–9; Ps. 105:8–11, 42–45; Jer. 11:2–5) and in the repetition of the covenant formula as the heart of the covenant (Exod. 6:7; Deut. 29:13). Thus, the Abrahamic covenant remains in view and is not replaced by the Mosaic covenant (see Exod. 32:13; Lev. 26:42; Num. 24:9 ["Those who bless you be blessed and those who curse you be cursed!"]; Deut. 1:8; 4:31; and Jer. 4:1–2 ["The nations will be blessed," CSB]).

On the other hand, the Mosaic covenant introduces significant developments. Our focus here is especially on Exodus 19–24. The first main development takes into consideration that the people have grown from just Abraham and his immediate family to a much larger group of people. Thus, the covenant through Moses focuses on the people of Israel as a nation. They are a "holy nation" (Exod. 19:6). Thus, one main feature of this covenant is that it provides structures and laws that enable the people to function as a nation, and the people express their relationship to God through these laws and structures. One primary purpose for this was to maintain the distinctiveness or the preservation of Israel as a nation (e.g., Lev. 20:22–26). This was important, of course, because of the promise that it would be through Abraham's "seed" that blessing would come to all nations. This implies, therefore, a built-in obsolescence to this covenant. It is in place until that seed comes (Gal. 3:19).

The second main development is that this covenant especially defines and marks out sin. Depending on whether or not we group some laws together, there are either 611 or 613 laws in this covenant. Of course, their function is not only to highlight sin, but there are a lot of laws! It is also true that the Hebrew word *torah*, which we translate as "law," often merely means "instruction." There is much instruction in the Mosaic covenant—instruction about how to live, instruction about the character of God and his gracious provision, instruction about how to love both God and neighbor. Nevertheless, the nature of this instruction is codified in many laws. Thus, in the New Testament this covenant is often just simply called the "law" (Rom. 5:20; Gal. 3:17). The sign of this covenant, the Sabbath, was also a command for Israel to keep, focusing on the cessation of work and marking Israel as a nation belonging to God (see Exod. 31:13–17; Ezek. 20:12, 20).

The ultimate effect of this law covenant is that the sinfulness of Israel (and by extension all humanity) was highlighted, even as it also pointed forward to the need for an ultimate provision for sin. Although the giving of the Ten Commandments begins with a reminder of God's deliverance of his people from Egypt (and thus a reminder that obeying these laws did not earn Israel their status as God's people), and although the provision of laws for sacrifices and instruction about how to approach God through priests was God's gracious revelation enabling his people to know his presence, and although the laws were also God's gracious revelation of his character so his people may know how to live in his presence, nevertheless, the focus of this covenant arrangement was on laws to obey. Thus, the inclusion of laws for sacrifices and priests, for the tabernacle, and for every matter related to their life as a nation of people all ultimately revealed the trait of human sinfulness (cf. Rom. 3:19; 5:20; 7:7; Gal. 3:19).

Even with a gracious sacrificial system, Israel's priests became corrupt, and Israel itself didn't even obey the purpose of the sacrificial system (see, e.g., Jer. 7). The repetitive nature of the sacrifices year after year showed the perennial problem of sin (Heb. 10:1–3). The lists of curses for disobedience also accentuate this (Lev. 26:14–44; Deut. 27:15–26; 28:15–68 [esp. 28:45]; 31:29; Josh. 24:19–20; 2 Kings 17:15; 18:12). Israel's only hope was found in the foundational promises to Abraham (Lev. 26:42–45; 2 Kings 13:23). The Israelites' inability to keep the law suggests that this law covenant points beyond itself to a solution to come, a descendant to come.[8] We will come back to this in chapter 5, on law. But for now, figure 3.4 presents the next installment of our visual.

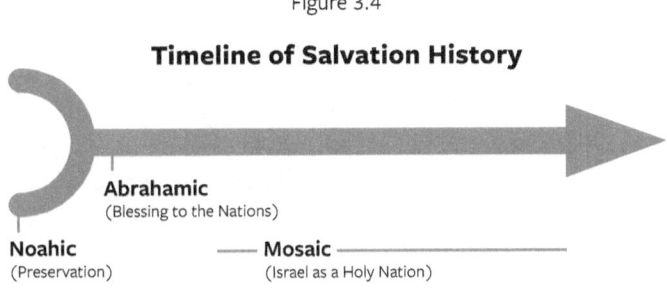

Figure 3.4

Timeline of Salvation History

The Davidic Covenant

The covenant with David builds on the promises to Abraham and shows how God's blessing will be mediated through David and his line. The key text for this covenant is 2 Samuel 7:11–17 (cf. 1 Chron. 17:10–14). Our focus here is on the significance of this arrangement with David for understanding the development of the covenants in God's saving plan (for more, see chap. 7, on kingship). With the appointment of Saul, and then the installation of David as king, the institution of kingship brings a new development in God's saving plan. This institution of kingship will now display God's pattern for the redemption of the world more fully as God formally establishes kingship as the means by which he will rule his people.[9] With David's kingship, Israel as a nation has

---

8. In this sense the law was also a temporary expression of God's grace until Christ came (John 1:16–17), a testimony to God's provision of righteousness through Christ (Rom. 3:21), and a "prophecy" of God's ultimate saving plan through Christ (Matt. 11:13).

9. Robertson, *Christ of the Covenants*, 229.

a stability it has not had to this point, and the entire nation is united under his rule. This is the context in which these amazing promises come to David.

The promises to David unfold with a play on words that the Lord makes in his message to David through Nathan. On the one hand, David is not going to build a "house" for God (i.e., the temple, 2 Sam. 7:5). On the other hand, the Lord will establish a "house" for David—meaning a "household" or "dynasty" (7:11). The promises of an everlasting dynasty and throne are clearly identified as a covenant by the biblical writers, even though the word "covenant" does not appear in 2 Samuel 7 (see, e.g., 2 Chron. 21:7; Pss. 89:3–4, 28, 34; 132:11–18).

As many commentators have pointed out, the covenant promises to David pick up on the promises to Abraham, such as the promise of a great name (2 Sam. 7:9; cf. Gen. 12:2), security in the land (2 Sam. 7:10; cf. Gen. 12:7), and rest from enemies (2 Sam. 7:11; cf. Gen. 22:17; Ps. 89:23). Furthermore, these promises will be fulfilled through David's "seed/offspring" (2 Sam. 7:12; cf. Gen. 17:4–8; 22:18), kings will descend from David (2 Sam. 7:12–16; cf. Gen. 17:6, 16), and the covenant formula of a special divine-human relationship is reiterated (2 Sam. 7:14; cf. Gen. 17:7–8; Ps. 89:26). All this is likewise summarized as God's blessing (2 Sam. 7:29; cf. Gen. 12:2).[10] These links between the promises to Abraham and David indicate that God's plan to bring blessing to the nations through Abraham's descendants is now going to be channeled through David and his line.

Does David grasp the significance of these momentous promises to him? There is one text that especially indicates David's wonder at these events—2 Samuel 7:19. Although the NIV translates the verse as though David was amazed that these promises could come to him as a mere human being ("This decree . . . is for a mere human"), the NIV footnote indicates that another way of translating this verse recognizes this promise of blessing through David as a reference to humanity in general ("This decree . . . is for the human race"). This way of translating the verse is the approach taken by the ESV ("This is instruction for mankind") and the CSB ("This is a revelation for mankind"). These translations better express the significance that David grasps here—that these promises show the way that blessing will come to all people.[11] That these promises have in view all nations, echoing the Abrahamic covenant, is clearly picked up in the concluding declaration of hopes for the Davidic king in Psalm 72:17: "All nations will be blessed through him" (see 72:8–11).

---

10. For these connections, and more, see McComisky, *Covenants of Promise*, 21; Williamson, *Sealed with an Oath*, 144.

11. See esp. Kaiser, "Blessing of David," 298–318; see also McComiskey, *Covenants of Promise*, 22–23; Gentry and Wellum, *God's Kingdom Through God's Covenants*, 195–96.

Thus, the hopes for humanity and all creation reinforced in the covenant promises to Noah, to Abraham, and to Israel are now focused on the promises to Israel's King David. Just as Israel was called God's son in Exodus 4:22–23, so the descendant of David will be called God's son (2 Sam. 7:14). Psalm 2 likewise speaks of the enthronement of the Davidic king in the language of sonship. In biblical times sons followed in the footsteps of their father; if their father was a farmer, then they would be a farmer.[12] So, to be a "son" of someone or something often meant a resemblance or likeness to that person or quality. To be a "son of wickedness," for example, meant that you were characterized by wickedness. A "son of peace," likewise, was characterized by peacemaking. Thus, the Davidic king will be a "son of God," representing God's rule over his people and bringing God's rule and blessing to Israel and the nations, fulfilling and mediating the promises to Abraham.

With these amazing promises, the reigns of David and Solomon (the son of David), over a united Israel in the land with Jerusalem as Israel's capital, and the construction of the temple point to this period as the high point of Israel's history. Yet the threat of punishment for wrongdoing (2 Sam. 7:14), the subsequent developments with David and Bathsheba and then with Solomon, and the division of Israel show that there must be more to come. With the exile, the prophets look forward to a greater David to come—a Davidic king who will be a faithful covenant partner, an obedient and righteous king who will reign in righteousness and lead his people in righteousness. Although we will develop this more in the chapters on kingship (chap. 7) and the prophets (chap. 8), at this point we need to see the significance of the new covenant in the unfolding plan of God. The next installment of our visual (see fig. 3.5) shows the Davidic covenant picking up on the intent of the Abrahamic covenant, mediating the promise of blessing to the nations through the "seed"/descendant of David, even as the Mosaic covenant continues to be in operation for Israel.

Figure 3.5

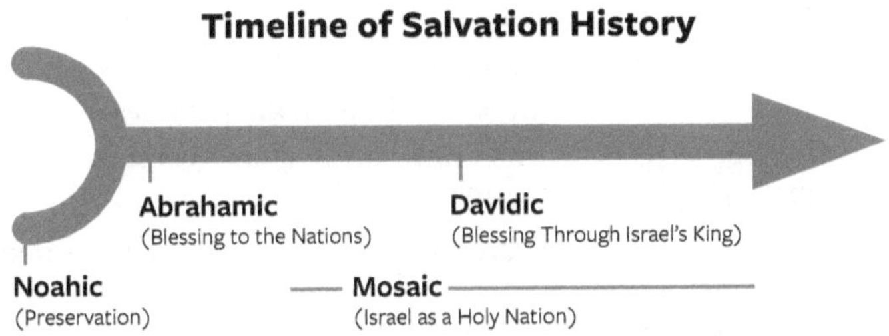

Timeline of Salvation History

Abrahamic
(Blessing to the Nations)

Davidic
(Blessing Through Israel's King)

Noahic
(Preservation)

Mosaic
(Israel as a Holy Nation)

---

12. See Carson, *Jesus the Son of God*, 14.

The New-Covenant Hope of the Prophets

The new covenant shows that Israel's ultimate hope must be for God to provide the forgiveness of sin and the transformation of heart that Israel (and by extension all humanity) needs. With the new covenant we move from covenants instituted in Israel's *history* to the prospect and reality of exile and the hope of Israel's *prophets*. Our key text for examining the new covenant is Jeremiah 30–33, especially 31:31–34 (see also Isa. 40–66; Ezek. 34; 36–37). In this new covenant, the promises contain both continuity and discontinuity with the preceding covenants.[13]

First, what *isn't* new about the new covenant? In continuity with the Abrahamic covenant, the new covenant promises blessing to the nations, ultimately through a servant who will be a "light for the Gentiles" (Isa. 42:6; 49:6; cf. Jer. 33:9; Ezek. 36:36; 37:28). Although the new covenant is set in contrast with the Mosaic covenant, God's plan for an obedient people remains (Jer. 31:33; see below on the "law" in the heart). In continuity with the Davidic covenant, the arrival of the new covenant is accompanied by the coming of a new, ideal Davidic king who will rule over a united Israel (Ezek. 37:24–27; see also Isa. 55:3–5).

Second, what *is* new about the new covenant? The discontinuity apparent in the new covenant is that the problem evident throughout all the previous covenants needs to be dealt with—that is, the problem of sin and the wrath and judgment that sin brings. The problem all along has been the inability of Israel—and Israel is merely exhibit A of the problem for all humanity—to keep God's commands. The Noahic covenant showed this with Noah's sin soon after the end of the flood (Gen. 9:21). The Mosaic covenant showed Israel's inability to obey and their constant sin throughout their history, culminating in their removal from the land and from God's presence (2 Kings 17). This is exemplified in the Davidic covenant with the continual sin of the kings, leading Israel into more and more sin, more judgment, and ultimately the exile. So, the new covenant deals with the ultimate problem that none of the earlier covenants were able to deal with.

How is this done? (1) There will be an "inner transformation" of the heart, enabling God's people to obey his commands (Jer. 31:33; 32:39–40; Ezek. 36:26; 37:14). Therefore, (2) there will be an "intimate relationship with God" (Jer. 31:33–34; Ezek. 36:27–28).[14] "No longer will they teach their neighbor, or

---

13. For the following, see M. D. Williams, *Far as the Curse Is Found*, 210–15; Williamson, *Sealed with an Oath*, 180–81; Gentry and Wellum, *God's Kingdom Through God's Covenants*, 229–36.

14. The quoted words in the preceding two sentences, and the summary in this paragraph, though arranged differently, are from Williamson, *Sealed with an Oath*, 180.

say to one another, 'Know the LORD,' because they will all know me, from the least of them to the greatest" (Jer. 31:34). They will know the Lord because (3) there will be complete forgiveness of sins (31:34; 33:8; 50:20; Ezek. 16:63; 36:33). The statement "I will forgive their wickedness and will remember their sins no more" (Jer. 31:34) recalls (and contrasts with) earlier texts in Jeremiah where the Lord says he will "remember their wickedness and punish them for their sins" (14:10).

The Lord's promise in Jeremiah 31 that everyone in this covenant will "know the LORD" means that there will no longer be the need for covenant mediators among the people of God to mediate between them and God—a structural change is coming. There won't be a special class of people in the new covenant who have an inside track, so to speak. Under the Mosaic covenant, priests, prophets, and kings were all covenant mediators between God and the rest of the people. The revelation of how to know the Lord came through these mediators. In the broader context of Scripture, this change will be due to the ultimate prophet, priest, and king, who will be righteous. Ultimately the new covenant will be mediated through this righteous servant.[15]

Furthermore, although provision was made for foreigners to join the nation of Israel (e.g., Exod. 12:48–49; Ruth 2:12), the primary means for belonging in this nation was by birth (hence, e.g., the laws related to tribal inheritance and priestly activity). Because membership in the nation was primarily by birth, it was possible to be in the Mosaic covenant as a member of the nation of Israel and not know the Lord. So, some in that Mosaic covenant (i.e., in the nation of Israel) would have to say to others in that same covenant, "Know the LORD!" (Jer. 31:34; cf. Heb. 8:11). Indeed, many of the covenant mediators—priests, prophets, kings—didn't know the Lord. Thus, this promise in Jeremiah 31 also recalls (and contrasts with) earlier texts in Jeremiah where the Lord says that "those who deal with the law did not know me" (Jer. 2:8) and that "my people . . . do not know me" (4:22). Throughout Jeremiah the Lord frequently condemns the prophets and priests of Israel.[16] This terminology is also reminiscent of the description of the sons of Eli who "did not know the LORD" (1 Sam. 2:12 ESV). According to Jeremiah, therefore, a major change is coming in the structure of the covenant community—they will all "know the LORD."

This means that there is also another significant change with this new covenant—a shift in the scope or the extensiveness of those who know the

---

15. Thus, Gentry and Wellum, *God's Kingdom Through God's Covenants*, 233, describes the shift from "faulty mediators" in the old covenant to a mediator without sin in the new covenant.
16. E.g., Jer. 2:8; 5:31; 13:13; 14:14–15; 23:9–31; 26:8–16; 32:32.

Lord in the covenant people. Now, not some but "all" in this covenant will "know the Lord." Figure 3.6 shows the significance of this shift. The two formerly distinct circles (where one was much smaller than the other) are now overlapping.

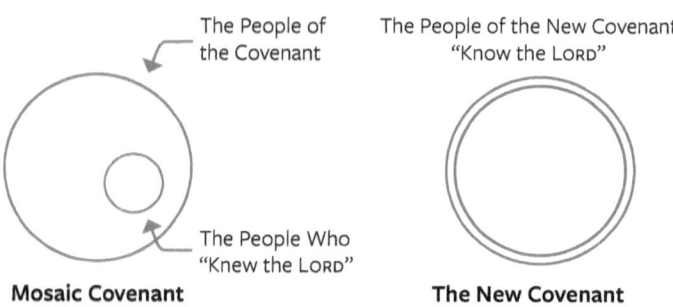

Figure 3.6

Finally, because the goal of all the covenants will be reached—the goal of personal relationship between God and his people—this new covenant (4) will be "everlasting" in the fullest sense (Isa. 55:3; 61:8; Jer. 32:40; 50:5; Ezek. 16:60; 37:26).[17] It is unlike the Mosaic covenant in that it is indestructible (as the Lord says in Jer. 31:32). In bringing all the earlier covenants to an ultimate fulfillment, this covenant also points ahead to eternity, to the new creation, when those who are in the new covenant will experience the fullness of that new-covenant knowledge of the Lord (1 Cor. 13:12). The new-covenant gift of the Spirit is a "deposit" anticipating and guaranteeing our full inheritance (2 Cor. 1:22; 5:5; Eph. 1:14).

Having already pointed ahead a little, let us now turn to the way the New Testament describes the fulfillment of these covenants. Figure 3.7 is the final installment of our visual for covenants.

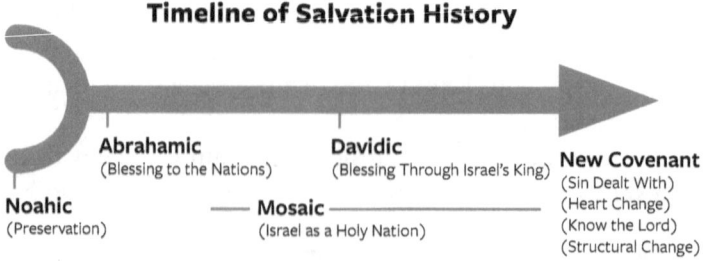

Figure 3.7

---

17. Williamson, *Sealed with an Oath*, 180–81.

New Testament Fulfillment

Jesus the Messiah is proclaimed in the New Testament as the one who enables all God's promises to be fulfilled. Astonishingly, Paul says that "no matter how many promises God has made, they are 'yes' in Christ" (2 Cor. 1:20). Gentiles, Paul says, were "foreigners to the covenants of the promise, without hope and without God in the world. But now in Christ Jesus you who once were far away have been brought near by the blood of Christ" (Eph. 2:12–13; see also Isa. 42:6; 49:8). The opening verse of the New Testament identifies Jesus as "the son of David, the son of Abraham" (Matt. 1:1; see also 1:17). We will see this again and again as we continue to work through these major themes of the Bible, but for now let's briefly observe how the New Testament writers identify Jesus with each of the covenants we have been summarizing.

Regarding the *Abrahamic covenant*: The New Testament writers make numerous connections between Jesus and Abraham (e.g., Matt. 3:9; Luke 1:55, 72–73; Rom. 9:6–8; Gal. 4:21–31). Paul argues that the promises made to Abraham find their ultimate fulfillment in Jesus. He is the "seed" of Abraham through whom the nations are blessed (Gal. 3:16). Therefore, those who believe in Christ are also "Abraham's seed, and heirs according to the promise" (3:29; see also 3:7, 8, 14; cf. Acts 3:25–26).

Regarding the *Mosaic covenant*: Jesus lived under the regime of the Mosaic administration (Gal. 4:4) and is the one who both sinlessly obeyed God and therefore uniquely kept the obligations of the law (John 8:29; Rom. 5:19; 2 Cor. 5:20–21; Heb. 4:15; 7:26), yet he also redeemed us from the curse of the law by taking the punishment for our disobedience on himself in our place (Rom. 3:25; 8:3–4; Gal. 3:13). Furthermore, since Jesus is the promised "seed" of Abraham, he is the one who brings an end to the law covenant as an administration (Matt. 5:17; Luke 16:16; Rom. 10:4; Gal. 3:19, 24; Heb. 7:12). Jesus himself declared that the law pointed to him (Matt. 11:13) and that Moses wrote about him (John 5:46; cf. Heb. 3:5).

Regarding the *Davidic covenant*: As we noted above, the very first verse of the New Testament describes Jesus as "the son of David" (Matt. 1:1). Jesus is the long-awaited royal son of David who will shepherd God's people (Luke 1:32–33, 69–70). Furthermore, by his resurrection he shows how the promise made to David, that there will always be one of his descendants on his throne, can be eternal—Jesus is risen, enthroned, and reigns forever (Acts 2:29–35)!

Regarding the *new covenant*: Jesus states at the Last Supper that his death will institute the new covenant. Thus, Jesus's death and resurrection enable his people to have the new-covenant blessings of complete forgiveness and the presence of the Holy Spirit and transformed hearts, enabling them to respond to him in faith and obey his teaching (Luke 22:20; cf. 1 Cor. 11:25; 2 Cor. 3:6; Heb. 8:6–13; see also 1 John 2:20, 27). To know Jesus is to know God, the heart of the new-covenant promise (John 17:3). In keeping with the indestructible nature of the new covenant, the writer to the Hebrews argues that Jesus, as the sinless mediator of the new covenant (9:15; 12:24), brings the guarantee of a better covenant (7:22; 8:6), with an eternal redemption (9:12) and an eternal inheritance (9:15).

The Nature of the New-Covenant People of God

Let's pause here briefly to note the significance of this discussion about the new covenant for understanding the nature of the people of God in the New Testament. My summary above of the developments in the new covenant is consistent with the view that there is significant discontinuity in our understanding of what the people of God look like in the shift from the nation of Israel (under the old Mosaic covenant mediated through prophets, priests, and kings) to the nature of the people of God in the new covenant (mediated through Christ). As noted above, physical descent in the nation of Israel was the primary way people entered the Mosaic covenant. Therefore, only some of the nation "knew the LORD." In the new covenant, however, if you are in the new covenant, you "know the LORD."

Those who see more continuity in the people of God across the Testaments argue that the covenant community in both Testaments is made up of a mixed community, including the children of believers. Thus, they argue that baptism should be administered to infants, as circumcision was administered to (male) children in the old covenant. They might respond to the presentation of the new covenant above by saying that either (1) "know" isn't salvific (i.e., that the major change is just the removal of mediators) or (2) because the full experience of this transformation will not be experienced until eternity, there is a "not yet" element to this in the New Testament, meaning there will still be some who are only outwardly in the new covenant (hence, e.g., the warning passages in Hebrews against apostasy).[a] Both suggestions support the argument that infant baptism can be administered under the new covenant, just as circumcision was administered to (male) infants in the nation of Israel in the Old Testament.

In response, we note again the references to "know" cited in the discussion of the new covenant above that were used earlier in Jeremiah. The "knowledge" in

Jeremiah 31 is also understood to be salvific because of the connection made in Jeremiah 31:34 itself: "They will all know me.... *For* I will forgive their wickedness." The "for" explains why they "know" the Lord; they have been forgiven. This forgiveness is a present reality for those who are in the new covenant. Indeed, forgiveness of sin is an essential element of the new covenant (Luke 22:20; Heb. 10:16–17). Furthermore, in the New Testament, those who apostasize (i.e., abandon the faith) do so because they were never really in the new covenant (1 John 2:19). Those who have genuinely come to "share in Christ" hold firmly to "the very end" (Heb. 3:14).[b] Certainly the people who meet together in a church building may not always be believers, and some may falsely profess to be believers and even get baptized (e.g., Simon in Acts 8). Yet those who know the Lord are those who are in the new covenant because their sins have been forgiven. Thus, my presentation of the new covenant is consistent with those who reserve baptism for those in the new covenant—that is, those who confess their sin and who profess faith in the Lord Jesus, the mediator of the new covenant, through whom they receive the new-covenant promise of the Holy Spirit and complete forgiveness of sins (Acts 2:33, 38–39, 41) and therefore "know the Lord" (cf. Jer. 31:34; Ezek. 36:26; John 3:3).[c]

[a] For more on the "now and not yet" framework, see chap. 9.
[b] See Grudem, "Perseverance of the Saints," 133–82.
[c] In the New Testament, those who belong to Christ by faith are Abraham's seed (Gal. 3:7, 26–29); they are the true circumcision (Phil. 3:3; Rom. 2:29). Although debates about circumcision occur regularly in the New Testament (e.g., Acts 15; Gal. 2; Rom. 4), the only place where baptism is mentioned in the same context as circumcision is Col. 2:11–12. However, in that context, circumcision refers to the internal spiritual transformation and new life accomplished by Christ and received through faith (see Thompson, *Colossians and Philemon*, 106–9). The New Testament occasionally refers to the baptism of a "household." In these instances it is because the members of the household have responded to the gospel (e.g., Acts 16:32 ["spoke the word ... to all"], 34; 18:8 ["entire household believed"]; 1 Cor. 1:16; 16:15 ["the household of Stephanas were the first converts"]; the apparent exception in Acts 16:15 is deliberately parallel to 16:31–34; see also John 4:53; Acts 11:14).

So What? Some Implications of This Theme of Covenant

The interconnectedness of these covenants across the Scriptures reminds us again of the unity and coherence of God's Word and the faithfulness of God. God is a faithful, promise-keeping God. His commitment to rescue and renew a people who reflect his character magnifies his wisdom, patience, righteousness, and grace. With the arrival of the new covenant and with Jesus being the Lord of the covenant as well as the ultimate obedient covenant partner for us, there is great assurance and certainty in this theme. As those who through Jesus know the Lord and whose sins are remembered no more, we can think of ourselves as God's new-covenant people! Praise God for all that he has done, and will do, through Christ for us as his people.

FOR FURTHER READING

Dumbrell, William J. *Covenant and Creation: A Theology of the Old Testament Covenants.* Paternoster, 1984.

Gentry, Peter J., and Stephen J. Wellum. *God's Kingdom Through God's Covenants: A Concise Biblical Theology.* Crossway, 2015.

Gentry, Peter J., and Stephen J. Wellum. *Kingdom Through Covenant: A Biblical-Theological Understanding of the Covenants.* 2nd ed. Crossway, 2018.

Robertson, O. Palmer. *The Christ of the Covenants.* Presbyterian and Reformed, 1980.

Schreiner, Thomas R. *Covenant and God's Purpose for the World.* Crossway, 2017.

Williamson, Paul R. *Sealed with an Oath: Covenant in God's Unfolding Purpose.* NSBT 23. InterVarsity, 2007.

TO DIG DEEPER

- Is there a "covenant of works" with Adam (Hosea 6:7)? See Belcher, *Fulfillment of the Promises of God*; Gentry and Wellum, *Kingdom Through Covenant*, 79–84; Fesko, *Adam and the Covenant of Works*.
- How does the Noahic covenant relate to creation? In the books above, see the contrast between Dumbrell, *Covenant and Creation*, and Williamson, *Sealed with an Oath*; see also Gentry and Wellum's discussion in *Kingdom Through Covenant*, 179–258.
- Who are the members of the new covenant? For implications for baptism, apostasy, and so on, see Gentry and Wellum's books for summaries of the discussion of and support for a Baptist position (e.g., *Kingdom Through Covenant*, 556–63, 812–24); see Belcher, *Fulfillment of the Promises of God*, 244–47; Swain, "New Covenant Theologies," 551–69, for responses from an infant baptism position.
- Should covenants be categorized as conditional/unconditional (or grant/treaty)? See Williamson, *Sealed with an Oath*, 17–43; Gentry and Wellum, *God's Kingdom Through God's Covenants*, 254–56.

4

The Exodus and the Tabernacle

The exodus was not only the foundational and most significant saving event in Israel's *history*; the exodus would also shape Israel's life and the hope of the *prophets* for the future. It also pervades the New Testament's description of *fulfillment* in and through Jesus. In fulfillment of God's promises to Abraham, his descendants had grown into a nation. Yet they were oppressed in Egypt. What happened to God's promises? The great deliverance that came through Moses reverberates throughout the rest of the Bible. It is one of the major themes that helps us put our Bible together. As we noted in chapter 1, in God's unfolding plan earlier events often anticipate later events, and later events are better understood in light of earlier events. Although God orchestrated the exodus and instituted the tabernacle system, these events anticipated much more to come! Since the exodus was a rescue from slavery so that Israel might worship God, we will look at both exodus and tabernacle together in this chapter. We will first observe the original context in which these themes are introduced in salvation history before tracing the development of these themes in Israel's *history* until the exile. We will then briefly summarize the *prophetic* hope before turning to the way these themes are picked up and find *fulfillment* in the New Testament.

The Exodus

In the storyline of the Bible, the pattern was set in Eden, in which God created his world for his people so that they might enjoy his presence. The setting of the exodus is one in which, as we noted above, the descendants of Abraham who have become the nation of Israel are yet to enter the land in which they will serve and worship God. In one sense, therefore, the exodus is described in language that reflects a "new creation" type of rescue from life outside the garden of Eden to life in God's presence. As in Genesis 1, God establishes a new humanity and brings them into a new, Eden-like land, where they can enjoy his presence as he dwells among them. The sea is parted, dry land appears, and there is light in the midst of darkness (Exod. 14:20b–21; cf. Gen. 1:2–4, 9–10; 8:3–4). The Song of Moses combines Yahweh's defeat of the sea with Yahweh "shepherding his people . . . to his Edenic holy mountain (Exod. 15:1–21; Pss. 74:13–14; 78:53–54)."[1]

The more immediate basis for the exodus, however, is the covenant with Abraham (repeated to Isaac and Jacob)—in particular, the promises of descendants and land so that God will have a people who belong to him and enjoy his presence in the place he graciously gives to them. The rest of Genesis highlights God's faithfulness to his promises, despite repeated apparent threats to those promises to these descendants. The slavery and captivity in Egypt highlight these threats, as his people are in danger and far from this land. Thus, although Abraham's descendants are now many, they are "in the wrong place and under the wrong rule."[2] The following verses explain the context for the exodus: "The Israelites groaned in their slavery and cried out, and their cry for help because of their slavery went up to God. God heard their groaning and *he remembered his covenant* with Abraham, with Isaac and with Jacob. So God looked on the Israelites and was concerned about them" (Exod. 2:23–25).[3] The key here is that God "remembered his covenant with Abraham." This doesn't mean that God had forgotten about it or that he had something else on his mind. Rather, this way of speaking is idiomatic for saying that God called it to mind and acted on it. That is, the basis of his actions in rescuing Israel from slavery was his covenant promises to Abraham. It is in this context, then, that God announces to Moses what he will do for Israel.

> Therefore, say to the Israelites: "I am the LORD, and *I will* bring you out from under the yoke of the Egyptians. *I will* free you from being slaves to them, and *I will* redeem you with an outstretched arm and with mighty acts of judgment. *I will* take you as my own people, and *I will* be your God. Then you will know

---

1. This summary and quoted words are from Watts, "Exodus," 478–80.
2. Goldsworthy, *According to Plan*, 131.
3. Unless otherwise indicated, italicized words in Scripture quotations have been added by the author.

that I am the LORD your God, who brought you out from under the yoke of the Egyptians. And *I will* bring you to the land I swore with uplifted hand to give to Abraham, to Isaac and to Jacob. *I will* give it to you as a possession. I am the LORD." (Exod. 6:6–8)

In these few verses there are seven "I will" statements.[4] This emphasizes that the fulfillment of these promises rests on God alone. He is declaring what he will do. These "I will" statements also seem to be framed. If we lay them out in a way that highlights this frame, it might help us make the observations that follow.

I will bring you out.
I will free you.
I will redeem you.
   I will take you as my own people.
   I will be your God. (Then you will know . . .)
I will bring you to . . .
I will give it to you.

The first three emphasize the "bringing out." That is, they focus on the redemption or rescue from slavery. The last two emphasize the other side of this, the "bringing in." That is, they focus on the gracious provision of the land. The exodus is more than just rescue from slavery. The middle two promises center on the goal, which is essentially the covenant formula again: that God would be their God, and they would be his people. The goal is once again the relationship in which God's people enjoy God and his presence in the place he provides for them. Thus, in the immediately preceding verse, God says, "I have remembered my covenant" (Exod. 6:5).

In these events Israel will come to know God especially as Yahweh, the gracious covenant-keeping God who is committed to his relationship to his people. The Passover, which is instituted in Exodus 12, shows that Israel's redemption has come through a substitutionary sacrifice (see chap. 6, on sacrifice). Israel was, after all, an idolatrous people like Egypt (Ezek. 20:7). The giving of the law in Exodus 20, therefore, begins with this declaration: "I am the LORD your God, who brought you out of Egypt, out of the land of slavery" (20:2). The context for the giving of the law is God's gracious initiative in rescuing his people, and that rescue is based on his covenant promises (see chap. 5, on law).

---

4. See M. D. Williams, *Far as the Curse Is Found*, 33–39, for the following observations.

In summary, the exodus shows that God redeems his people from an alien rule by his own power and brings them to himself so they may enjoy his presence. God does this by judging his enemies and supernaturally rescuing his people through sacrifice. Before we see how significant this exodus rescue is for the rest of Scripture, we must note the place of the tabernacle in God's purposes.

The Tabernacle: The Dwelling of God with His People

Israel is not just rescued from slavery; the exodus culminates in the dwelling of God with his people. At the beginning of the exodus account, when God is offering reassurance to Moses about approaching Pharaoh, the Lord says, "When you have brought the people out of Egypt, you will worship God on this mountain" (Exod. 3:12). Thus, Israel's identity is found not in their independence and freedom but rather in Yahweh's presence with them and their worship of him.[5] The significance of this is easily seen when we look at the rest of the book of Exodus, from 24:12 to 39:31. First, 24:12 to 31:18 provides instructions for God's sanctuary, the tabernacle and related structures. Then, after the golden calf incident, 36:8 to 39:31 essentially repeats most of this material about the tabernacle as the tabernacle is constructed. This repetition, detail, and length (about twelve chapters) highlight the importance of the tabernacle in God's deliverance of Israel from slavery—that is, it highlights the significance of God's dwelling in the midst of his people.

God's Dwelling

There is more that we can mention about the details of the tabernacle, and we will cover a little more in chapter 6, on sacrifice, but for now let us observe the main emphasis of this account. The key is given in Exodus 25:8: "Have them make a sanctuary for me, and I will dwell among them." Again, in 29:45–46 the Lord says, "Then I will dwell among the Israelites and be their God. They will know that I am the LORD their God, who brought them out of Egypt so that I might dwell among them. I am the LORD their God." The dwelling of God "among" his people is visually represented in the arrangement of the tribes around the tabernacle (see Num. 2). The twelve tribes are arranged evenly around the tabernacle, with three on each side (the tribe of Levi is spread around the tabernacle, so the tribe of Joseph is split into two—Ephraim and Manasseh; see fig. 4.1).

---

5. Watts, "Exodus," 479.

Figure 4.1

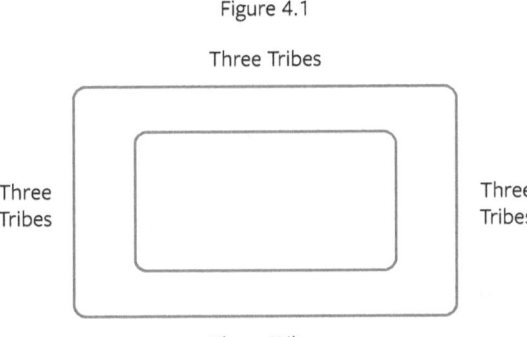

Furthermore, the ark with its "seat" or "cover" symbolizes God's throne in the midst of his people (cf. Ps. 80:1). Since the ark contains the terms of agreement between God and his people, the ark symbolizes the presence of the King of the covenant; he is to be at the center of Israel's life. See figure 4.2 for a basic outline of the tabernacle furnishings.

Figure 4.2

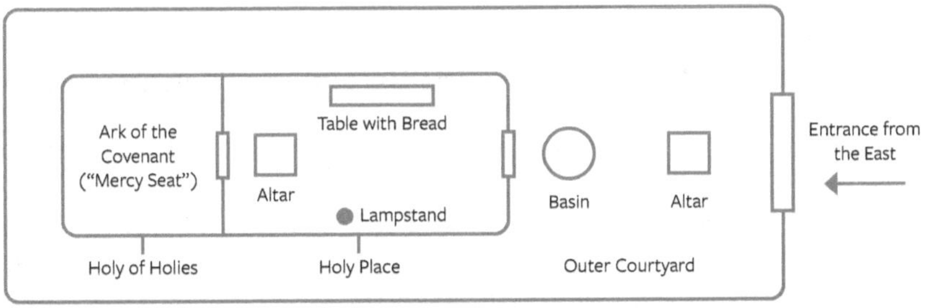

A place that has a seat, a table, a lampstand, and some bread sounds like a home. This doesn't mean that God physically lives there, nor is the bread for him. The idea is that God is in the midst of his people. The holiness of God amid a sinful people means that this can be possible only with sacrifice (again, see chap. 6).

The Tabernacle as a "New Eden"

In keeping with the foundational pattern of Eden as the place of God's presence, much of the description of the tabernacle and its furnishings recalls the description of Eden as God's sanctuary.[6] The description of God walking

---

6. The following summarizes Beale, *Temple and the Church's Mission*, 66–80; Longman, *Immanuel in Our Place*, 29, 35; Watts, "Exodus," 480–81. See chap. 2 on Eden for more (e.g., the lampstand and the garden imagery in the temple).

back and forth in the garden (Gen. 3:8) is also used for God's presence in the tabernacle (Lev. 26:12; Deut. 23:14). Similarly, the instructions for Adam to "work . . . and watch over" the garden (Gen. 2:15 CSB) are also used for the priestly service in the tabernacle (Num. 3:7–8; 8:25–26; 18:5–6; 1 Chron. 23:32; Ezek. 44:14). The guarding cherubim in the tabernacle recall the cherubim guarding the way to the tree of life (Gen. 3:24; Ezek. 28:14, 16; see also 1 Kings 6:29–35; Ezek. 41:17–20). The lampstand with its branches outside the holy of holies may reflect the tree of life. The reference to gold and onyx in Genesis 2:12 is likely the backdrop for the descriptions of the tabernacle furniture and decorations as well as the high priestly garments (Exod. 25:7, 11–39; 28:9–12, 20; 1 Kings 6:20–22; 1 Chron. 29:2). The entrance to Eden from the east (Gen. 3:24) is likely the pattern for the entrance to the tabernacle, the temple of Israel, and the temple of Ezekiel 40:6.

In summary, the exodus and the tabernacle system must be viewed together. Together they highlight God's rescue of his people from oppressive rule so that they might worship him and enjoy his presence. The pattern in Eden is picked up in the promises to Abraham and brought about by God, who powerfully and graciously keeps his promises.

The Implications of the Exodus in the Unfolding of Salvation History

The significance of the exodus and the tabernacle in the unfolding of the rest of salvation history cannot be overstated. Having summarized the setting of the exodus and the tabernacle, we will better understand why the exodus shaped the prophetic hope and why it pervades the New Testament if we first grasp how influential it was in Israel's history.[7]

The Significance of the Exodus in Israel's History

The exodus comes to pervade every area of Israel's life.

1. The nation counts the years of its existence from the exodus.[8] Indeed, the building of the temple and the placement of the ark in the temple look back to the exodus as if this was the intended goal of the ark from that time (1 Kings 6:1; 8:21).

---

7. In addition to the observations we made in chap. 2 on Eden, we will also briefly trace the development of the tabernacle–temple–Jesus–church–Holy City theme in later chapters (e.g., in chap. 8 on the temple and the prophetic hope; chap. 9 on Jesus as the place of God's presence; chap. 10 on the Holy City; and chap. 11 in the summary of the theme of worship).

8. M. D. Williams, *Far as the Curse Is Found*, 22.

2. The exodus is spoken of as "the most spectacular example of God's redemption."⁹ The institution of the Passover includes provision for the events of the exodus to be recited again and again for each generation every year (Exod. 12:21–28; see 12:26: "When your children ask . . ."). Likewise, the Israelites are instructed to recite a summary of the events surrounding the exodus whenever they present the firstfruits of their produce to the priest: "My father was a wandering Aramean, and he went down into Egypt . . . " (Deut. 26:5–10). When a writer wants to think of something incredible or beyond the ordinary, the exodus is drawn on as both the beginning of Israel's history and the most astonishing event imaginable (e.g., in the horrible events of Judg. 19:30: "Such a thing has never been seen or done, not since the day the Israelites came up out of Egypt").

3. The exodus shapes Israel's national calendar and life.¹⁰ The new year is determined by the exodus (Exod. 12:2). Sabbath days and years recall the exodus (Deut. 5:15: "Remember that you were slaves in Egypt"). The yearly feasts remind Israel of the exodus (Exod. 23:14–15: "For in that month you came out of Egypt"; Lev. 23:42–43: "When I brought them out of Egypt"; Deut. 16:9–12: "Remember that you were slaves in Egypt"). The food laws are understood in the context of the exodus (Lev. 11:45: "I am the LORD, who brought you up out of Egypt to be your God; therefore be holy"). Israel's social relationships are to be affected by it: their care for strangers (Exod. 22:21; Lev. 19:33–34; Deut. 10:17–19: "For you yourselves were foreigners"); their care for the vulnerable (Deut. 24:18: "Remember that you were slaves in Egypt and the LORD your God redeemed you from there"; cf. 24:22); and their treatment of slaves (Lev. 25:42, 43; Deut. 15:13–15: "Remember that . . .").

4. The exodus is recalled at the end of Israel's life in the land, when they are approaching the exile. Solomon and Rehoboam's oppression (1 Kings 12:8–11; cf. Exod. 1:14; 5:1–21), burden on builders (1 Kings 9:15–19; cf. Exod. 1:11), and hardening (1 Kings 12:15) recall similar descriptions of Pharaoh. Jeroboam becomes like Aaron and makes golden calves "who brought [Israel] up out of Egypt" (1 Kings 12:28–33; cf. Exod. 32:4, 8). Ultimately, like Adam and Eve, Israel is exiled from God's presence, and their removal is attributed to their rejection of the exodus and Mosaic/Sinai covenant (2 Kings 17:7–23).

---

9. M. D. Williams, *Far as the Curse Is Found*, 22.
10. This paragraph and the next follow Watts, "Exodus," 481–82.

The Significance of the Exodus for Israel's Prophetic Hope

The exodus was not just something that Israel looked back to as the foundational highlight of their *history*. With the exile and removal from the land on the horizon, the exodus was so significant that it shaped the language and hopes of the *prophets* for Israel's future. Although there are many texts that we could look at here, we will quote just two from Isaiah and one from Jeremiah to get the idea.[11] Basically, the point is that the exodus was the model for a future redemption. The italics added in the verses below draw attention to the language that shows the exodus became a pattern for understanding the hope of restoration to come.

> There will be a highway for the remnant of his people
>   that is left from Assyria,
> *as there was for Israel*
>   *when they came up from Egypt*. (Isa. 11:16)

> *Was it not you who dried up the sea,*
>   *the waters of the great deep,*
> *who made a road in the depths of the sea*
>   *so that the redeemed might cross over?*
> Those the LORD has rescued will return.
>   They will enter Zion with singing;
>   everlasting joy will crown their heads. (Isa. 51:10–11)

"So then, the days are coming," declares the LORD, "when people will no longer say, 'As surely as the LORD lives, who brought the Israelites up out of Egypt,' but they will say, 'As surely as the LORD lives, who brought the descendants of Israel up out of the land of the north and out of all the countries where he had banished them.' Then they will live in their own land." (Jer. 23:7–8; cf. 16:14–15)

The broad pattern of history-prophecy-fulfillment that helps us put our Bible together, as explained in chapter 1, is evident again here. The foundational saving event of the exodus in Israel's history is picked up in the prophets as they point forward to an even greater deliverance to come.

The Significance of the Exodus for the New Testament

The exodus was so significant that it shaped not only Israel's life, calendar, and prophetic hope but also much of the New Testament's portrayal of the fulfillment that Jesus brought. Again, there are too many connections to cover here; some will be developed in chapter 6 when we discuss sacrifice, and in

---

11. Cf., e.g., Isa. 40–55 (esp. 44:24–28); Ezek. 45:21–24; Hosea 1:10–2:1, 14; 11:1, 10–11.

chapter 9 when we discuss the arrival of the kingdom in the ministry of Jesus. The following brief observations simply show the pervasiveness and influence of this exodus pattern throughout the New Testament.

1. The introduction to Mark's Gospel cites Isaiah 40:3, which points to the fulfillment of Isaiah's prophecy of a new exodus (Mark 1:1–3).
2. In a less direct way, the opening chapters of Matthew's Gospel show that the pattern of Israel's exodus is lived out and embodied in Jesus. He spends time in Egypt (Matt. 2:13–15), he is baptized in the Jordan (3:1–17), he spends forty days in the wilderness (where he does not succumb to temptation; 4:1–11), and he appears to be a new-but-greater Moses as he gives his teaching on a mountain (5:1–7:29).
3. The significance of Jesus's death is especially understood in light of the Passover. At the transfiguration, Jesus's death is referred to as an "exodus" (Luke 9:31; see the NIV footnote). Jesus is described as our Passover lamb (1 Cor. 5:7; 1 Pet. 1:19). The Gospels describe the Last Supper, in anticipation of his death, as taking place within a Passover meal (Matt. 26; Luke 22).
4. The accomplishment of our salvation by Jesus's death is described with language that recalls the exodus. Our salvation is described in terms of redemption from slavery into adopted sonship (Rom. 3:24; 1 Pet. 1:18; cf. Exod. 4:22–23; Hosea 11:1) through Jesus's death as a "sacrifice of atonement" (Rom. 3:25).
5. The description of Jesus as God's presence among his people is presented in terms that recall the purpose of the tabernacle. When John 1:14 says that the Word "made his dwelling among us," the Greek could be translated as "he tabernacled among us."[12] Similarly, John 2:19 describes Jesus as the temple (cf. 4:20–24).
6. Finally, the dwelling and presence of God among his people are ultimately fulfilled in the new creation. Revelation 21–22 describes this ultimate goal in terms of the holy of holies—that is, God's presence—doing away with the need for a temple (we will elaborate on this in chap. 10).

So What? Some Implications of This Theme of the Exodus and the Tabernacle

Once again, as we've seen with the themes of creation/rebellion and covenant, the exodus/tabernacle theme highlights God's desire for relationship and

---

12. See LSB footnote.

presence with his people. The theme also draws attention to God's faithfulness to his promises—the pattern and promises of a deliverance from alienation and a return to God are not forgotten but fulfilled. The theme also points to the cost and extent to which God will go to rescue his people, and our helplessness to get ourselves out of our predicament.

The theme also points to the similarities and differences across the Old and New Testaments. On the one hand, the pattern of the exodus shapes the language of the New Testament for our salvation with the repeated language of redemption, slavery, sacrifice, and dwelling all picked up in the New Testament. Yet, on the other hand, our deliverance is not across a geographical plot of land—our deliverance is from Satan, from slavery to sin, and from alienation from God so that we may have fellowship with God. The presence of God with us is not a tent or a building but God himself—through Jesus and by his Spirit.

We noted above that God's gracious exodus deliverance of Israel through sacrifice was so significant that it shaped the pattern of Israel's life (e.g., the references above such as "Remember that you were slaves in Egypt"). In a similar way, the New Testament also repeatedly shows that believers' lives are to be shaped by the gospel of God's deliverance of us through Christ's sacrifice. Jesus commands us to love just as he has loved us (John 13:34). Husbands are to love their wives "as Christ loved the church and gave himself up for her" (Eph. 5:25). Believers are to forgive one another "just as in Christ God forgave" them (Eph. 4:32). Paul transitions to more specific application in his letter to the Romans, after outlining the provision of righteousness by grace through Christ's wrath-bearing death, with the words "Therefore, . . . in view of God's mercy" (Rom. 12:1). In other words, just as the Israelites' behavior was to be shaped by the gracious deliverance of the exodus, so our lives are to be shaped by the good news of the new exodus of God's deliverance of us, by grace, through Christ. True freedom is found in what we were made for—knowing God and enjoying his presence as he enables and empowers us to serve and worship him, as we look forward to the ultimate redemption of our bodies and the enjoyment of his presence forever.

FOR FURTHER READING

Longman, Tremper, III. *How to Read Exodus*. InterVarsity, 2009.
Piotrowski, N. G. "Exodus, The." In *DNTUOT*.

Rosner, B. S., and P. R. Williamson, eds. *Exploring Exodus: Literary, Theological and Contemporary Approaches*. Apollos, 2008.

Watts, R. E. "Exodus." In *NDBT*.

TO DIG DEEPER

- This chapter has shown that the language of the geographical exodus was picked up in the prophets to point ahead to a future deliverance for God's people, and this pattern culminated in the deliverance through the redeeming sacrifice of Christ to bring us from slavery to sin to the knowledge of and relationship with God. What are the implications of this "foreshadowing" of our ultimate deliverance for interpreting the Old Testament in light of the New Testament? What does this teach us about God's purpose in recording the events in the Old Testament? What implications does this have for understanding the similarities and differences across the Testaments?
- As we noted in chapter 2, some dispute the tabernacle/temple language in Eden (though without disputing the later Edenic language of the tabernacle/temple). See again Block, *Covenant*, 27–30 (see "To Dig Deeper" in chap. 2), and compare this with the discussion in Beale, *Temple and the Church's Mission*, 66–80; Longman, *Immanuel in Our Place*, 29, 35; and Watts, "Exodus," 480–81, summarized above under "The Tabernacle as a 'New Eden.'"
- The possibility of broader new exodus themes throughout the New Testament has been an area of ongoing study. To investigate this further, you could start with the articles by Piotrowski ("Exodus") and Watts ("Exodus").

5

Law (and Wisdom)

We come now to one of those topics that is at the heart of the real and practical implications for how we put our Bible together. What are Christians supposed to do with the laws given to Israel—in particular, the laws at the heart of the Mosaic covenant that we looked at in chapter 3? This topic could be said to have more immediate relevance to the "So what?" question and the difference that this book might make to everyday Christian living and our view of the Bible. What should you do if you read the following verse in your regular Bible reading? "When you build a new house, make a parapet around your roof so that you may not bring the guilt of bloodshed on your house if someone falls from the roof" (Deut. 22:8). Is this still applicable to Christians today? If not, then what about the rest of the laws, and what use would they be? Have you sinned by disobeying this law? What would "guilt of bloodshed" mean? The death penalty? What about those who aren't Christians? Should this law be lobbied for so that builders and architects would be guilty of violating this building code if they didn't follow this law? We will come back to this passage briefly at the end of this chapter to see how we might view this and other passages like it.[1]

First, however, let's briefly review. We have seen God's purposes being worked out in his continuing commitment to his creation after Adam and Eve's rebellion. God's gracious saving promises to humanity are expressed through covenants, and his goal is to have a people who belong to him, who

---

1. We will also focus below on the Sabbath, as it is often seen as a test case that reveals how we put our Bible together.

enjoy his presence and his gracious rule in the place that he provides for them. This pattern was seen in the garden, and it is the backdrop to the promises to Israel, through whom God will bring blessing to the nations. As we noted in chapters 3 and 4, on covenants and the exodus, the exodus highlights God's plan to have obedient people who reflect his character and enjoy his presence. Broadly speaking, then, with the exodus and the establishment of the Mosaic covenant we encounter two more significant developments in the unfolding plan of God—law and sacrifice. For a visualization, see figure 5.1.

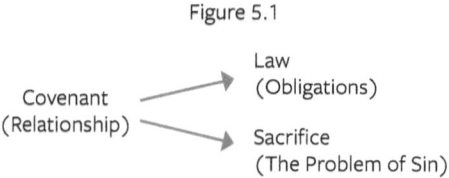

Figure 5.1

At this stage in salvation history, we see that covenant is the means by which God establishes a relationship with his people. The goal is always that he will be their God and they will be his people. We also learn at this stage in salvation history that, on the one hand, within the Mosaic covenant relationship there are obligations (i.e., law). On the other hand, this side of the rebellion (fall) of humanity, sin needs to be dealt with for one to be in a covenant relationship with God (i.e., sacrifice). We will look at sacrifice in the next chapter. Although, as we mentioned in chapter 3, on covenants, the Hebrew word for "law" (*torah*) often means "instruction," and although sacrifices were incorporated into the Mosaic covenant, we will focus on the command aspect of the law in this chapter. Due to the unique nature of this topic in its applicability to Christian living, this chapter on law will break a little from the pattern we have generally followed so far (history-prophecy-fulfillment). We will briefly note the broad place of the law in Israel's history and prophecy. However, we will then focus our attention on the place of the law in the life of the Christian—that is, what does the New Testament say about how we relate to the laws of Moses?

The Mosaic Law in Israel's History and Prophecy: A Brief Overview

The Giving of the Law: Some Reminders

As we noted above, God's desire has always been to have his people enjoy his presence and obey him. The Mosaic law gives expression to this pattern in a particular context. As we noted in chapter 3, the law was given to the nation of Israel in the context of God's covenant relationship with Israel. The law came, therefore, to people whom God had already graciously rescued from slavery in fulfillment of his promises, not as a means to enter into or earn this relationship (Exod. 20:1–2). The law was also given in the context of the Mosaic covenant, which stipulated how Israel was to live as a nation in the land. It therefore has a focus on Israel as a national entity. This also means that the law has a focus on the distinctiveness of Israel compared to the nations around it, so that it would be a holy nation devoted to the Lord rather than to the gods of the nations and also preserve Abraham's seed. This distinctiveness was also meant to enable Israel to serve as a model nation to the nations around it (Deut. 4:6–8; 26:19).

Turning to the Ten Commandments themselves, we see that the law also reveals God's character and purposes for his people. The first commandment, following the declaration "I am the LORD your God," is "You shall have no other gods before me" (Exod. 20:2–3). That is, the law begins with the Lord's exclusive claim over his people, and the laws continue to unpack the implications of this exclusive claim.[2] Thus, the demands of the law aren't arbitrary. They reflect the character of a holy God, reveal his purpose for his people to reflect his character, and enable his people to enjoy the harmony of their relationship to him in his world (cf. Lev. 26:1–13). As in the pattern of the garden, obedience to the law was the means by which Israel would experience preservation in the land (cf. Ps. 44:13–14; Jer. 24:9; Ezek. 5:14–15; 22:4–5; 23:10).

The Mosaic Law and the Exile

When we move from the beginning of Israel's history to the exile, we find that the law played a vital role in explaining why Israel went into exile. Second Kings 17 describes why the Northern Kingdom of Israel went into exile. In 17:7–8 the writer looks back to the beginning when Israel was brought out of Egypt and explains that the exile took place because "they worshiped other gods and followed the practices of the nations the LORD had driven out before them." The writer then states that this idolatry and wickedness took place even though the Lord repeatedly warned both Israel and Judah through the prophets, who said, "Turn from your evil ways. Observe my commands and decrees, in accordance with the entire Law that I commanded your ancestors to obey and that I delivered to you through my servants the prophets" (17:13). Then the writer describes Israel's response to these warnings: "They rejected

---

2. Goldsworthy, *According to Plan*, 142–43.

his decrees and the covenant he had made with their ancestors and the statutes he had warned them to keep. . . . They imitated the nations around them. . . . They forsook all the commands of the LORD their God" (17:15–16). These repeated references to the law at the end of Israel's life in the land show Israel's inability to keep the laws God had given them. Israel is exhibit A of the human predicament. Like Adam and Eve, therefore, Israel is removed from God's presence (17:20). The promise of life in God's presence can be fulfilled only by God's grace.

The Mosaic Law and the New Covenant

This inability of Israel to obey the law shows one of the main features of the new covenant that the prophets look forward to. Two of the key passages here are Jeremiah 31:32–33 and Ezekiel 36:26–27 (see also Jer. 32:39–40; Ezek. 37:14). In chapter 3 we noted the emphasis on forgiveness of sin in the new covenant. At this point, however, we want to observe just one key element of the new covenant. Jeremiah 31:32 says that the new covenant will not be like the covenant God made with Israel when he took them out of Egypt. That is, it won't be like the Mosaic covenant. Why will it not be like that covenant? "Because they broke my covenant" (Jer. 31:32). A new covenant is needed because of the inability of Israel to obey the demands of the law covenant. So, in the next verse the Lord says that in the new covenant he will put his law "in their minds and write it on their hearts" (31:33). Thus, there will still be "law" in some sense in the new covenant (we will see in what sense when we turn to the New Testament). The difference is that God's people will have a new ability to obey him. Ezekiel 36:26–27 speaks of this as a new heart and the enablement of the Spirit so that God's people will follow God's decrees and keep his laws. So, the law given to Israel was unable to be kept by them due to their sinful hearts; this resulted in their exile from the land (like Adam and Eve from the garden). So the prophets look forward to a time when the fundamental inability of God's people to obey will be changed.

But what will this law look like? Bible-believing Christians have come to different conclusions about the place of the Mosaic law in the life of the believer. Are we still under obligation to obey the law of Moses? If not, why not? If so, are we obligated to obey all of it or just parts of it? How do we decide which parts we are obligated to obey? An additional factor here is the shift to the new covenant of a people who know the Lord with a transformed heart, made up of Jews and gentiles—all whom the Lord calls and grants his Spirit to. So, let's turn now to address this question: How should the New Testament believer approach the Mosaic law?

The Mosaic Law in the New Testament

Before we address the question of how we as New Testament believers should approach the Mosaic law, we must state a foundational and crucially important truth. There is a sense in which all the righteous demands of the law have been met for us in Christ. The Lord Jesus is regularly described in the New Testament as sinless (e.g., 1 Pet. 2:22; 1 John 3:5). But the New Testament also highlights Jesus's obedience to the law as the basis for how believers in him can be declared righteous. On the one hand, through trust in the Lord Jesus we receive forgiveness of sins because of his death on the cross (see chap. 6). On the other hand, God credits righteousness to us when we place our faith in the Lord Jesus. This righteousness is the righteousness of the Lord Jesus. More specifically, it is Jesus's obedience that is counted as ours. This topic is beyond the scope of this chapter, but you can look into the following passages for more on this wonderful truth: Romans 5:17, 19; 8:4; 2 Corinthians 5:21; and Philippians 2:8; 3:9.

As we noted above, even though Christians agree on God's desire for an obedient people, they come to different conclusions about the place of the Mosaic law in the life of the believer. Therefore, before we look at the key passages that refer to whether the believer is under obligation to obey the Mosaic law covenant, let's briefly summarize three common approaches to this question. The first two views approach the question with a framework that groups the Mosaic laws into three categories:

- The ceremonial law (i.e., laws related to sacrifices, offerings, feasts, festivals, dietary and clothing requirements, etc.).
- The civil law (i.e., laws related to disputes and restitution, property, negligence, interest on loans, etc.).
- The moral law (i.e., laws related to marriage and family, murder, idolatry and worship of God—many see these as essentially encapsulated in the Ten Commandments).

In broad terms these general categories are helpful. However, we will soon come to some challenges to grouping the laws of Moses as a way to determine which laws New Testament believers are obligated to obey. One challenge worth noting from the outset is that the categories are not easily separated. For example, Exodus 22:25 forbids taking interest. Is this part of the moral or the civil law? It probably belongs to both categories, as do many other laws. But for now this framework helps us understand two common approaches to determining which parts of the law of Moses New Testament believers are still obligated to follow. If we visualize the three groups of laws as in figure 5.2, the question the first two views below ask is, Which of the boxes continue through to the New Testament?

Figure 5.2

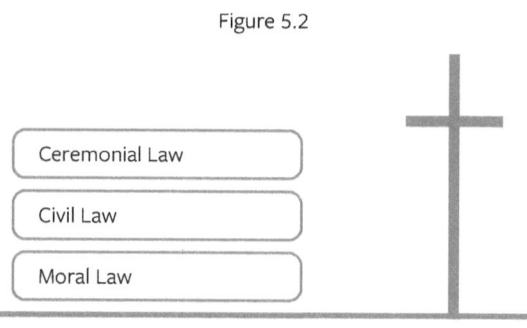

Mosaic Law Covenant

View 1: The Three Divisions of the Law and Theonomy

One approach to the application of the law today has been called "Theonomy" (sometimes called "Reconstructionism"). The word comes from two Greek words, *theos* and *nomos*—"God" and "law" or "God's law." Of the three divisions of the law noted above, this position argues for the continuity of the moral and civil laws. Since Jesus's sacrificial death fulfills the ceremonial laws, this view does not argue for the continuity of the priesthood or sacrificial system. Rather, this view argues that we should seek to implement the moral and civil laws, and the punishments of the Mosaic law, in society today. Some forms of Christian nationalism are recent expressions of this view.[3]

We will come to some challenges that this view faces from the New Testament below, but one significant weakness is its failure to adequately deal with the context of the Mosaic law for the nation of Israel in their land. The "political" aspects of the law were directly tied to the setting of Israel as a nation determined and defined by God. Laws related to property and inheritance were necessary for the preservation of the physical descendants in their

---

3. I say "some forms" because those who merely advocate for the goodness of the Bible's teaching on, say, marriage and life might be labeled Christian nationalists by others, but they do not advocate for a Christian-only government. See a summary of seven views on religion and government in Naselli, "What Is the Spectrum of Major Views on Political Theology?" For a critique of Theonomy and related recent forms of Christian nationalism, see DeRouchie, *Delighting in the Old Testament*, 213–28; cf. also Poythress, *Shadow of Christ in the Law of Moses*, 311–61; Barker and Godfrey, *Theonomy*.

promised land. In the new covenant, people from many nations around the world make up God's people and live under the rule of Christ.[4] For now, however, this view may be visualized as in figure 5.3.

Figure 5.3

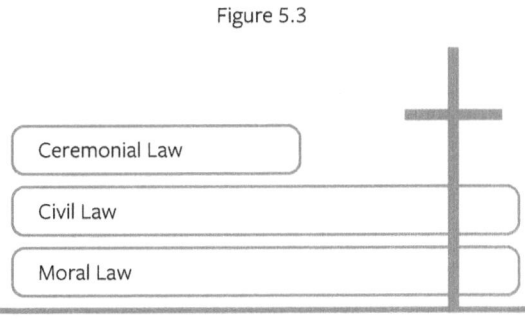

Mosaic Law Covenant

View 2: The Three Divisions of the Law and the Continuity of the Moral Law

Another, more common approach to determining which aspects of the law are still binding on believers today (which also follows this threefold division of the law) might be called the "Reformed" view. This view is associated with the Westminster Confession of Faith or the 1689 Baptist Confession of Faith—both excellent Reformed confessions that summarize biblical teaching. Unlike the preceding view, this view does not advocate for the continuing authority of the civil law, due to the shift in salvation history from the people of God being the nation of Israel to the people of God being people from all nations. Like the preceding view, however, this view sees the continuing authority of the moral law for believers today—especially the succinct summary of the moral law in the Ten Commandments.

Since nine of the Ten Commandments are repeated in the New Testament, there is not a lot of functional difference between those who hold to this view and those who hold to the view we will discuss next. One of the Ten Commandments, however, has been a point of debate among Bible-believing Christians—the Sabbath. Traditionally, in churches that hold strongly to one of the confessions noted above, there may be expectations around what one should or shouldn't do on a Sunday, since they understand Sunday to be the

---

4. Cf., e.g., the description of the believers in the church at Antioch (Acts 13:1) or the recipients of Peter's first letter (1 Pet. 1:1). There is no hint in the New Testament that replicas of Israel's land-based theocracy will now be set up in every nation.

Christian "Sabbath." So, in one sense, your view of the Sabbath can be a kind of test case for working out your view of how your Bible fits together. Once again, we will come to some critique of this below, but for now, this view may be visualized as in figure 5.4.

Figure 5.4

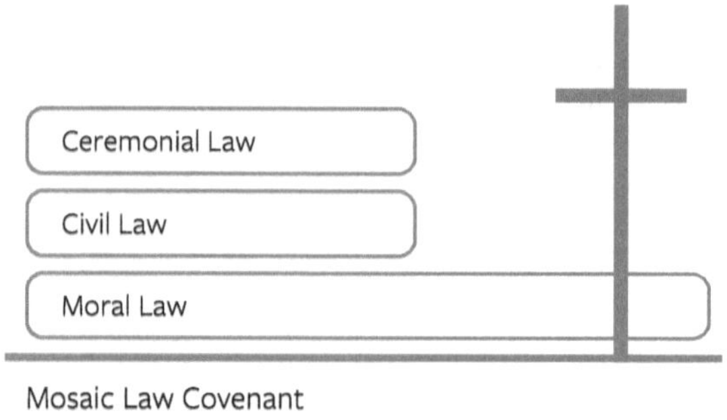

Ceremonial Law
Civil Law
Moral Law

Mosaic Law Covenant

View 3: Fulfillment of the Law of Moses in the "Law of Christ"

The third view, although ending up with much in common with the preceding view, has a different approach. Rather than distinguishing between ceremonial, civil, and moral aspects of the law of Moses as a basis for determining which aspects of the law are still binding on believers, this view sees the law as part of the entire law covenant that has been brought to its fulfillment, goal, and conclusion in Christ.[5] The entire law, therefore, is forward pointing, anticipating fulfillment. The rest of this chapter will briefly summarize four of the key passages for this discussion and in defense of this third view, before drawing some conclusions (and adding another diagram!).

Matthew 5:17

In the Sermon on the Mount, Jesus declares, "Do not think that I have come to abolish the Law or the Prophets; I have not come to abolish them but to fulfill them" (Matt. 5:17). After reading the first line, our Theonomy brothers and sisters (view 1) say, "Amen, see, Jesus didn't come to abolish the law!" The key to interpreting this verse, however, is what Jesus says next. On the one hand, yes, Jesus did not come to do away with or destroy (i.e., "abolish") the law (or

---

5. The view that I argue for here follows the chapter by Doug Moo ("The Law of Christ as the Fulfillment of the Law of Moses: A Modified Lutheran View") in Strickland, *Five Views on Law and Gospel*, 319–76.

the prophets). On the other hand, notice what he says he *has* come to do—"to fulfill them." That is, Jesus doesn't say he has come to "enforce," "keep," or even "confirm" them in the sense that they remain exactly the same. He has come to "fulfill" them.

What does this mean? It always helps to look at the context of a passage for the meaning of a word. In this case the word "fulfill" has been used numerous times in the immediately preceding chapters. Each time the word "fulfill" is used in Matthew 1:22; 2:15, 17, 23; 4:14, the passage indicates that what took place "fulfilled" something that was said by the prophets. Similarly, in Matthew 11:13 Jesus says that "all the Prophets and the Law prophesied." That is, they all looked forward. To "fulfill" the law in this context, therefore, means that Jesus is the one to whom the law pointed. He is not against the law. How could he be? He is the goal to which the law was pointing. In the rest of the Sermon on the Mount, Jesus repeatedly says, "But I say to you" (see 5:22, 28, 32, 34, 39, 44 ESV). There are various contrasts that Jesus notes here, some of which clarify or deepen Old Testament teaching (perhaps in contrast to rabbinic debates), and some of which go beyond their Old Testament settings (e.g., 5:33–37). But whatever the basis for the contrast that Jesus draws, the repeated refrain is "I say to you" (not "Moses says"). The emphasis throughout the sermon is on Jesus's authority and what he says. That is why at the conclusion the crowds are "amazed at his teaching, because he taught as one who had authority" (7:28–29).

This passage, therefore, indicates that a shift has come in salvation history—not in God's continuing goal for an obedient people but in what the direct authority over the believer now is. Since the law and the prophets pointed to Jesus, and since Jesus has now come, the way we view the law and the prophets and what they mean for our lives now is through Jesus and what he says. Jesus is the direct authority for our lives. The law and the prophets are now understood only in light of him and his coming. Let's proceed with what the apostle Paul says about this.

1 Corinthians 9:20–21

In 1 Corinthians 9:20–21 Paul sets out two alternatives with respect to the law, and then he identifies his own position as between these two positions. We may visualize Paul's stance like this:

Not "under the law"
    But "under Christ's law"
Not "free from God's law"

Paul says that he is not "under the law." What he means by this is clarified in the preceding discussion about becoming "like a Jew, to win the Jews." That is, "to those under the law" Paul has become like one under the law (9:20). To be "under the law" in this context means something like being under the jurisdiction of the law, or under the law's regime (see Gal. 4:4–5, which describes Jesus as born "under the law"). Yet Paul is also quick to add in the next verse that even though he is not "under the law," he is not "free from God's law" (1 Cor. 9:21). That is, just because he is not under the law covenant doesn't mean that he is free from all moral constraint, or free from God's demands. Nevertheless, this reference to "God's law" must be something that is not quite the equivalent of "the law" of Moses, since Paul has just said that he is not under that law. On the one hand, this implies that the Mosaic law was a temporary expression of God's desire for an obedient people, evident since Eden. On the other hand, Paul adds that he is "under Christ's law" (9:21). That is, he is bound by the teaching of Jesus, his Messiah and Lord. Thus, in summary, Paul does not view himself as a Jew "under the law" who adjusts to win gentiles, nor does he view himself as outside of God's law entirely. Instead, he is bound first and foremost to Christ. He is free to adopt aspects of Jewish life or gentile life to avoid creating stumbling blocks and to win each person to Christ.

Romans 10:4

In Romans 10:4 Paul simply states that "Christ is the end of the law" (ESV). The word used for "end" has the sense of "goal." Some commentators use the example of a finish line to represent the cluster of ideas being communicated here. Imagine that you are in a running race, a sprint. Now, imagine the finish line ahead of you. What is the function of that finish line in the race? In one sense it is the "goal." That's what you are running toward. Yet in another sense it is also the "end." Once you reach your goal, you have reached the end of the race. Perhaps for these reasons the NIV translates this verse as "Christ is the culmination of the law."

Galatians 3:19, 24, 25

In Galatians 3 Paul describes the place of the law in salvation history. First, Paul states that the law was "added . . . until the Seed to whom the promise referred had come" (3:19). This tells us three things: (1) The "law" that Paul is speaking about is the law covenant, the Mosaic covenant; (2) Paul is not separating the law into distinct sections that end or continue but referring to the Mosaic law as a whole; and (3) this law was given for a specific time period—until Christ.

In Galatians 3:24 Paul adds that "the law was our guardian until Christ came." Although some translations have "our guardian to lead us to Christ" (NASB), Paul is not referring to individuals who come to trust in Christ but speaking in broad salvation-historical terms. Thus, recent translations better express the phrase here as "until Christ came" (NIV, ESV; or "until Christ," CSB). Furthermore, the term "guardian" here translates the Greek word *paidagōgos* (similar to our English word "pedagogy"), which refers to someone who might mind children, lead them to school, or look after them until school age. Again, the idea is a temporal one—the "guardian" was needed only until a certain point in time. So, in the next verse, Paul states that with the arrival of Christ as the object of our faith, "we are no longer under a guardian" (3:25). These verses could be represented visually like in figure 1.3, which was introduced in chapter 1.

Figure 1.3

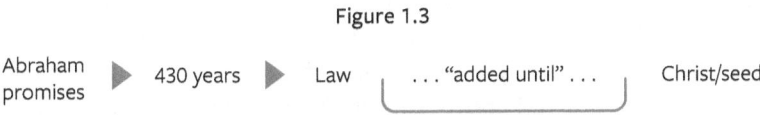

The same three points that we made about Galatians 3:19, therefore, could be made about 3:24–25: (1) The law guardian is the Mosaic covenant; (2) Paul is referring to the law as a whole rather than distinct sections of it; and (3) the specific time frame culminates with Christ. Before we draw some conclusions, however, there is another theme in the New Testament that we must note.

Fulfilling the Law

There are a number of passages in the New Testament that summarize the whole law in relation to what believers must do, but the word used is "fulfill." In Galatians 5:14 Paul says that "the entire law is fulfilled in keeping this one command: 'Love your neighbor as yourself.'" Likewise, in Romans 13:9 Paul lists the commandments against adultery, murder, stealing, and coveting, and then he adds, "And whatever other command there may be, [they] are summed up in this one command: 'Love your neighbor as yourself.'" Paul then specifies, "Love does no harm to a neighbor. Therefore love is the fulfillment of the law" (13:10). The idea is that love for neighbor includes all that the law demands of Christians in their relationships with other people. This does not mean that we get to define "love" however we want, nor does it mean that "love" is simple affirmation of what other people want. There are plenty of places where "love" gets defined in the New Testament (see, e.g., Eph. 4:25–5:2, which is summed up as "walk in the way of love" in 5:2;

see also, of course, 1 Cor. 13:1–13, esp. 13:6). What Paul says here is derived from Jesus's summary of the entire Bible (the "Law and the Prophets") in Matthew 22:37–40 (cf. 7:12), which is also cited by James (James 2:8). The key point here is that when Paul mentions the law with reference to Christians, he doesn't say that Christians "keep" or "obey" the law; he says that Christians "fulfill" the law.[6] This means that when New Testament believers follow the goal of the law to love their neighbors as understood in light of Christ, his teaching, and the teaching of his apostles, Christians find that they are not opposed to the Mosaic law; they "fulfill" the intention, the goal, of the law.

Concluding Summary

Let's conclude with just two main observations. (1) On the one hand, we can say from the passages above that we are no longer under the jurisdiction of the Mosaic law *directly*. The Mosaic law as a whole was a temporary arrangement. We are more immediately under the "law of Christ." That is, we are under the lordship and teaching of Christ and, we might add, the teaching of his authorized apostles in the New Testament. (2) On the other hand, if the law (and the prophets) pointed forward to Christ and his teaching, anticipating the goal to which the law pointed, then we should still read those laws as providing instruction for us (note the terminology relating to instruction in Rom. 15:4; 1 Cor. 10:11). The law can now be understood in light of the new situation that Christ has brought. Thus, these laws apply to us, but not "directly." Let's illustrate this again.

On the one hand, I am not saying that we relate directly to the law of Moses as in figure 5.5.

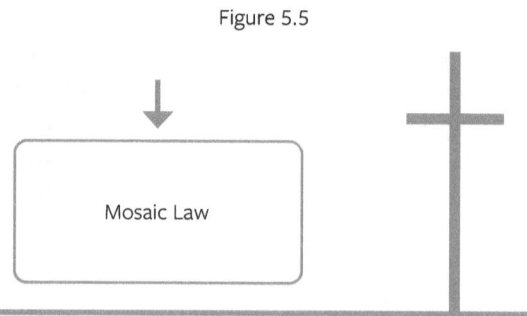

Figure 5.5

---

6. Rosner, *Paul and the Law*, 121. Some interpreters say that Paul's claim in Rom. 3:31 shows his ongoing commitment to "keep" the law ("Do we, then, nullify the law by this faith? Not at all! Rather, we uphold the law"). However, the preceding verses show that Paul refers here to the righteous standard of the law that is upheld through Christ's sacrificial death so that those who place their faith in him can be declared righteous (3:22–26).

On the other hand, I am not saying that we divide up the law into categories to work out which laws continue to apply to us, as in figure 5.4.

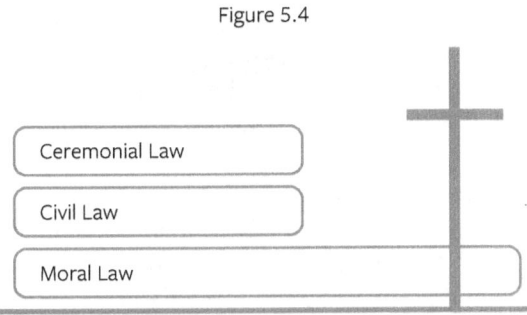

Figure 5.4

Mosaic Law Covenant

Instead, I am saying that the law both points to and culminates in the Lord Jesus and his teaching, and also that now in light of Jesus and his teaching we can go back to those laws and see how they could apply to us, even though we are no longer bound by the laws that were given so the nation of Israel could live in the promised land. This can be visualized as in figure 5.6.

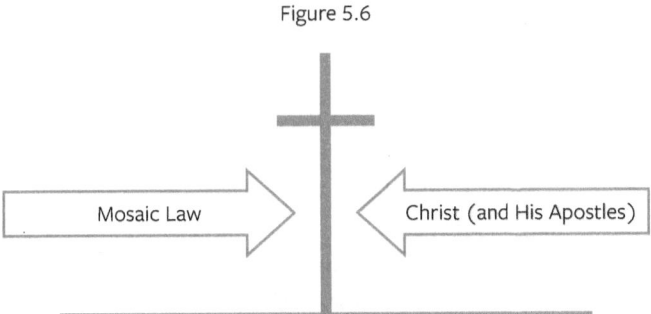

Figure 5.6

Let's return briefly to the passage we began this chapter with, Deuteronomy 22:8, and relate it to our view of the Mosaic law in the life of the Christian today. On the one hand, we are not under obligation to investigate and report whether we or fellow believers have railings around the top of our roofs. Nor do we need to advocate for railings around the top of roofs to our local government. We also don't need to try to figure out if this is merely a civil law or whether it is also moral. Of course, we can recognize that the context of the command is the flat-roof structure of ancient houses. On the other hand, the passage has moral implications, for a lack of care could result in someone falling to their death or sustaining severe injury. So, we can conclude that we are not directly obligated to this law such that pastors need to instruct their congregations about roofing requirements. Yet we can also see that the passage shows a concern for the well-being of others and therefore falls within the broad category of love for neighbor. "Love" in the Bible means a concern for the good of the other person. It is loving, therefore, to follow the building codes of the local government or to build a safety fence around a swimming pool, for example. In ways such as this, a believer "fulfills" the goal of this command.[7]

Or to take the example noted under view 2 above, is a Christian obligated to cease from work on a Christian Sabbath—that is, Sunday? View 3 would approach this through the lens of the New Testament. Two key passages here are Romans 14:5–6 and Colossians 2:16–17. Can you imagine Moses saying the following? "One person considers one day more sacred than another; another considers every day alike. Each of them should be fully convinced in their own mind" (Rom. 14:5). Or this? "Therefore do not let anyone judge you by what you eat or drink, or with regard to a religious festival, a New Moon celebration or a Sabbath day" (Col. 2:16). As with the passages on the law cited above, Paul then says, "These are a shadow of the things that were to come; the reality, however, is found in Christ" (2:17). In other words, according to Paul, the new-covenant believer is no longer obligated to obey the Sabbath command and cease from work on Saturday (or Sunday) as a special day. The Sabbath pointed forward to an ultimate rest, a rest that is found when one trusts in Christ (Matt. 11:28; Heb. 4:3, 9–10; see the brief discussion of Heb. 3–4 in chap. 1). Should a believer still rest from work? Of course. The Sabbath was a good reminder that Israel should trust God, that they were finite, that they were made for God, that he accomplishes his good purposes, and that he is not dependent on his people. We, too, need to rest, remembering our creatureliness. But the (new-covenant) believer in Christ is no longer obligated to obey, say, Exodus 35:3 or Numbers 15:32–36, because the Sabbath was a sign of Israel's Mosaic covenant with God (Exod. 31:12–18; cf. Jer. 17:21–27).[8]

---

7. This is an example in which all views discussed above can end up with similar applications of some specific texts. For example, Bahnsen applies this law in a similar way in his argument for Theonomy (e.g., "The Theonomic Reformed Approach to Law and Gospel," in Strickland, *Five Views on Law and Gospel*, 101–2). In doing so, however, he merely recognizes the cultural change in housing structures. He inconsistently adapts and applies this law to settings that are vastly different. His application is done without fully integrating the framework and pattern established by the New Testament and the salvation-historical and covenantal move from Israel as a nation in their land with civil laws (and penalties) for living in that land to the nature of the new-covenant community. New-covenant believers "fulfill" this command to protect life when they love others in such a way as to do "no harm to a neighbor" (Rom. 13:8–10). See also DeRouchie, *How to Understand and Apply the Old Testament*, 443–44.

8. See also our summary of "worship" in chap. 11.

What About the Wisdom Literature?

There is a set of books in the Old Testament that is often thought difficult to fit into a biblical theology of God's unfolding plan in salvation history—that is, books associated with the theme of wisdom, such as Job, Proverbs, Ecclesiastes, Song of Solomon, and some of the Psalms (e.g., Pss. 1; 37; 49; 112). Since we are focusing on themes that help us put our Bible together, some may wonder why we don't have a whole chapter devoted to the theme of wisdom in this book. Part of the reason is that we are looking at developments in salvation history, such as the tabernacle or kingship, that help us understand the saving plan of God in Christ. We are focusing on events and institutions that are put in place in Israel's history and picked up in Israel's prophets. Where, then, does wisdom fit into all this? I will suggest below that wisdom, like the law, fits into the broad category of living well in God's world. Yet the theme of wisdom has its own distinct contribution.

First, let's define what we are talking about. Wisdom is associated with the language of "knowledge" and "understanding," but it is more like what we would think of as skill or know-how (cf. Exod. 28:3; 31:3, 6; 35:10). It is also associated with righteousness and justice, so the "skill" in view is more than just how to negotiate life; it has a moral dimension. Wisdom is associated with God's activity in creation (Prov. 3:19–20; 8:22–31; Job 28). So, wisdom has to do with living in God's world and knowing how to navigate the order and the complexities of this world.

Second, even though many of the insights of the Wisdom books are gleaned from keen observations of how to live in God's world, they come in the context of Israel's covenant with God through Moses. Therefore, even though many of the insights seem more directly relevant to all people in all times, I suggest that we approach the Wisdom books the same way we approach the Mosaic law. In the two diagrams above where "Mosaic law" is placed either in a box before the cross or in an arrow pointing toward the cross (figs. 5.5 and 5.6), we could place "Wisdom" in those boxes too. That is, to fully understand the theme of wisdom, we do not enter it directly apart from the flow of history; we enter it in light of Christ. We do not have space to develop this fully here, so the following main points will summarize some key passages, and the chapter will conclude with some resources to study this further.

1. Wisdom is connected to the law of Moses in the following ways:

   - The "fear of the Lord" (i.e., of "Yahweh," the covenant God of Israel) is the key to wisdom. Since Yahweh is wise (cf. Job 12:13) and is the source of wisdom (Prov. 2:6; 8:22), to "fear the Lord" is to recognize this, listen to him, submit to him, and trust him. This fear of (or reverence for) the Lord is the purpose of the law according to Deuteronomy 4:10. This phrase is also repeatedly mentioned throughout the Wisdom books. It is the conclusion of Ecclesiastes (12:13), it is the framework for Proverbs (e.g., 1:7; 9:10), and it is paralleled with "turn from evil" in Job (28:28; cf. 1:1, 8; Prov. 3:7; 16:6).

- Observing the law is wisdom according to Deuteronomy 4:6, and this, too, is repeated throughout the Wisdom books (e.g., Pss. 19:7; 37:30–31; cf. Jer. 8:8–9).
- The Mosaic law covenant is often the assumed framework in Proverbs, with references to features of the Mosaic covenant such as the land (Prov. 2:21–22; 10:30), boundary markers (22:28; cf. Deut. 19:14; 27:17), sacrifices (Prov. 15:8; 21:27; Job 1:5; 42:7–8; Eccles. 5:1–7), obedience (Prov. 4:4, 10; 6:21–23; cf. Lev. 18:5; Deut. 6:1–3, 6–9; 11:18–21), and more (e.g., Prov. 3:9–10).

Wisdom literature often applies the framework of the law and the reality of God's sovereignty and providence to the complexities and patterns of life and death. In his introduction to his commentary on Proverbs, Derek Kidner says it well: "There are details of character small enough to escape the mesh of the law and the broadsides of the prophets, and yet decisive in personal dealings. Proverbs moves in this realm, asking what a person is like to live with, or employ; how he manages his affairs, his time and himself."[a] Jason DeRouchie's summary for Proverbs, Job, and Ecclesiastes is helpful here. Proverbs: "Fear God, turn from evil, live in light of the future." Job: Fear God "for who he is, not for what he gives or takes away." Ecclesiastes: Fear and follow God "despite life's enigmas."[b]

2. Wisdom is also associated with kingship in Israel, especially Solomon and his rule (1 Kings 3:12, 28; 5:7; esp. 4:34). The wise king embodies wisdom as he mediates God's rule (see Prov. 8:15–16). Thus, the book of Proverbs is associated with "Solomon son of David, king of Israel" (1:1; cf. 10:1; see also 1 Kings 4:32). The book of Ecclesiastes is likewise described as "the words of the Teacher, son of David, king in Jerusalem" (1:1; cf. 1:12; see also 1 Kings 8). Thus, the prophetic hope was for a king to come in the line of David with "the Spirit of wisdom and of understanding, the Spirit of counsel and of might, the Spirit of the knowledge and fear of the Lord" (Isa. 11:1–2; cf. Jer. 23:5).

3. Jesus is the embodiment of wisdom (1 Cor. 1:24; Col. 2:3). His teaching in parables is proverb-like wisdom. As a child he "grew in wisdom" (Luke 2:52;

cf. 2:40). His teaching is characterized by wisdom (Matt. 13:54). He is "greater than Solomon" (Luke 11:31). Indeed, he is the source of wisdom (Luke 21:15).

4. In conclusion, if Jesus is the ultimate embodiment of wisdom and the source of wisdom, then the wise person is the one who builds their life on Jesus (Matt. 7:24). Wisdom's "children" are those who respond to and follow Jesus (Luke 7:35). The gospel message about Christ is wisdom, in contrast to the apparent "wisdom" of the world (1 Cor. 2:6-7; Eph. 3:10; Col. 1:28; 2:23; 2 Tim. 3:15). In Christ we have wisdom from God. By the Spirit and through Scripture, the Word of Christ, we grow in wisdom through prayer (Col. 1:9; 3:16; 4:5; James 1:5). The theme of wisdom, therefore, fits broadly into the category of living well in God's world with fellow fallen image bearers as a believer and with all the complexities and challenges of life and death. Since the original setting for much of this was the Mosaic covenant and Israel's kingship, we best understand what it means to be "wise" in God's world when we read this literature in light of the new covenant in Christ.

[a] Kidner, *Proverbs*, 13.
[b] DeRouchie, *What the Old Testament Authors Really Cared About*, 323.

So What? Some Implications of This Theme of Law

This theme shows that God's consistent plan is for obedient people who reflect his will and character. The law of Moses articulated God's will for the nation of Israel. Yet Israel's failure led to exile from God's presence—like Adam and Eve. Israel was indicative of the failure of all humanity to obey God's will. The ultimate goal expressed in this law can be seen only in the perfectly obedient Son, the Lord Jesus. God has graciously provided for us a perfectly righteous, obedient, and wise Savior. Our standing and relationship with God are based not on how many laws we obey but on the obedience and righteousness of Christ. In his sacrificial death he took the punishment for our disobedience in our place—we rely on him. With the new-covenant gift of the Spirit, God's people are transformed by his grace to reflect the character of this Son—the one who embodied love for God and love for people, the goal of the law. This theme, therefore, points to God's righteous and gracious character and our need for him.

FOR FURTHER READING

Law

Barker, William S., and W. Robert Godfrey, eds. *Theonomy: A Reformed Critique*. Academie Books, 1990.

Rosner, Brian S. *Paul and the Law: Keeping the Commandments of God*. NSBT 31. InterVarsity, 2013.

Schreiner, Thomas R. *40 Questions About Christians and Biblical Law*. Kregel, 2010.

Strickland, W. G., ed. *Five Views on Law and Gospel*. Zondervan, 1993.

Wisdom

Kaiser, Walter C. "Wisdom Theology and the Centre of Old Testament Theology." *Evangelical Quarterly* 50 (1978): 132–46.

Longman, Tremper, III. *The Fear of the Lord Is Wisdom: A Theological Introduction to Wisdom in Israel*. Baker Academic, 2017.

Robertson, O. Palmer. *The Christ of Wisdom: A Redemptive-Historical Exploration of the Wisdom Books of the Old Testament*. P&R, 2017.

Schultz, Richard L. "Unity or Diversity in Wisdom Theology? A Canonical and Covenantal Perspective." *Tyndale Bulletin* 48 (1997): 271–306.

Waltke, Bruce K. "The Book of Proverbs and Old Testament Theology." *Bibliotheca Sacra* 136 (1979): 302–17.

TO DIG DEEPER

- For guidance on applying the whole range of laws found in the Mosaic law covenant, see, for example, Averbeck, *Old Testament Law for the Life of the Church*; DeRouchie, *How to Understand and Apply the Old Testament*; DeRouchie, *Delighting in the Old Testament*; and Poythress, *Shadow of Christ in the Law of Moses*.
- For differing perspectives on a range of issues related to discontinuity or continuity between the Old and New Testaments, see Feinberg, *Continuity and Discontinuity*.
- For more on Christ's obedience and righteousness credited to believers (see Rom. 5:19; 8:3–4), see Piper, *Counted Righteous in Christ*.

6

Sacrifice

Of all the themes covered in this book, the theme of sacrifice is probably the most well known among Christians in at least one sense. Most Christians understand that the sacrifices in the Old Testament are somehow fulfilled in Jesus's death. Since I'm a New Zealander by birth (and since New Zealand is known for having a lot of sheep), I sometimes say (tongue in cheek) that most Christians don't take a sheep to church now, even in New Zealand! This theme reveals that we know intuitively, whether we fully realize it or not, that we are meant to read the Bible as an unfolding story from promise to fulfillment. Thus, this theme perfectly illustrates that the New Testament, as later revelation, enables us to understand what the Old Testament was pointing to and that the Old Testament helps us understand what the New Testament proclaims as fulfilled in Jesus. We know that the animal sacrifices in the Old Testament weren't the permanent and abiding plan of God. Why do we know that? Because of what we know about Jesus's sacrifice. We know that the animal sacrifices pointed to something similar yet vastly better.

Yet this relationship between sacrifices and Jesus is also illustrative of how we are meant to put our Bible together. This theme especially highlights the continuity across the Testaments as well as the discontinuity between them. On the one hand, this theme illustrates continuity by showing us that Jesus's sacrificial death didn't occur in a vacuum, unconnected to anything that came before. On the other hand, this theme illustrates discontinuity in the radical newness that is seen in Jesus and his sacrifice. In other words, we need Jesus himself and the teaching of his apostles to fully grasp the message of the Old Testament. But now we are getting ahead of ourselves!

Before we proceed, let's briefly review. When we discussed the tabernacle, we saw that, following the expulsion of Adam and Eve from God's presence in the garden, the tabernacle highlighted the significance of God dwelling with his people. At the same time, however, distance between God and his people was also highlighted, as Israel lived in tents outside the tabernacle. Sacrifices, therefore, show that God had designed a way for this distance to be minimized, enabling a holy God to dwell in the midst of a sinful people. As we noted in the previous chapter, on law, the institution of the Mosaic covenant shows that this side of the fall and rebellion of humanity, while there are obligations for God's covenant people (law), the problem of sin needs to be dealt with (sacrifice). This chapter will begin with a summary of the initial institution of the sacrificial system in Israel's *history*, briefly summarize the *prophetic* hope, and then zero in on two key *New Testament* descriptions of Jesus's death, before concluding with some "So what?" reflections.

The Institution of Sacrifice in Israel's History: Some Key Themes

Although sacrifices appear early in the Bible (e.g., Gen. 8:20–21; 15:9–17; Exod. 24:4–8), the rationale, details, and instructions for the variety of sacrifices come into focus in the Mosaic covenant. There is much to be gained from a deep dive into the various sacrifices and festivals, but in this chapter, we will focus on the big picture and the main points.

Substitution and Punishment

As we saw in chapter 4, the exodus and tabernacle must be understood together. The people of Israel are rescued so they can worship God, enjoying his presence in the place he provides. Following the account of the exodus and the giving of the law, therefore, the rest of the book of Exodus focuses on the tabernacle, God's dwelling with his people. The book of Leviticus continues this account by describing how a holy God can dwell in the midst of a sinful people—through sacrifice. Although there are many passages we could focus on, two key chapters highlight the main themes related to sacrifices: Exodus 12 and Leviticus 16. Exodus 12 explains the most significant deliverance in Israel's history—the exodus and the Passover sacrifice. Leviticus 16 describes the Day of Atonement sacrifice at the heart of the book of Leviticus.[1] The concepts

---

1. Many commentators have noted that in the structure of Leviticus, Lev. 16 is at the heart of the book (and perhaps even the center of the Pentateuch!).

of substitution and punishment for sin (or "substitution" and "wrath") are significant features of these sacrifices.

The Passover account in Exodus 12 explains that the lamb's blood is there so that when the Lord sees it, he will "pass over" that household (12:3–4, 12–13). When the Lord passes through Egypt that night, he brings judgment on the gods of Egypt and on the idolatry of the Israelites (12:12; cf. Ezek. 20:4–10). So, the blood of the lamb symbolizes both substitution and punishment—the lamb dies in place of the judgment that otherwise would have come. The exodus, therefore, is a deliverance from the tyranny of Pharaoh as well as the judgment of God.

Similarly, following the exodus, Leviticus shows how a holy God can dwell with a sinful people. In the Day of Atonement instructions of Leviticus 16, the deadly effects of sin and the significance of the Lord's provision are highlighted in this once-a-year ceremony in which Aaron enters the holy of holies. In addition to Aaron's own "sin offering to make atonement for himself and his household" (16:6), Aaron is to take two male goats "for a sin offering" for the people (16:5). One goat is sacrificed for this sin (or purification) offering, cleansing the holy of holies so that the Lord may continue to dwell among his people (16:9, 15–17, 20).[2] The other goat, however, is sent away. Aaron is instructed to confess over a live goat "all the wickedness and rebellion of the Israelites—all their sins" with both hands placed on the goat's head (16:21). Then the goat is sent away into the wilderness, symbolically carrying "on itself all their sins to a remote place" (16:22). The goat is "cut off" from the people, symbolizing God's punishment (cf. 20:3). Thus, the theme of substitution is especially highlighted as atonement is made, providing cleansing and the removal of the offense against God (16:30, 34).

Averting God's wrath is also a key context for Leviticus 16.[3] The opening verse of the chapter describes this as the time when "the LORD spoke to Moses after the death of the two sons of Aaron who died when they approached the LORD" (16:1). That is, the context is the deaths of Nadab and Abihu in Leviticus 10:1–2. After their deaths, Moses quotes the words of the Lord: "Among those who approach me I will be proved holy" (10:3). Moses then warns Aaron to follow the Lord's instructions for approaching him, "or you will die and the Lord will be angry with the whole community" (10:6–7; cf.

---

2. The "cleansing" of everything here shows the defiling effect of (even unintentional) sin. Sigurd Grindheim notes that cleansing can also take care of the effect that our sins have on God (e.g., defilement led to God's judgment and departure from the temple, Ezek. 8:1–10:22; see also 5:11; 24:13; 36:17–18; and the promise of Jer. 33:8). Grindheim, *Hebrews*, 458–59. As we will note below, "uncleanness" may be ritual and not always moral or sinful.

3. Jeffery et al., *Pierced for Our Transgressions*, 46–50.

Num. 18:32). Thus, the deaths that 16:1 refers to in the context of the Day of Atonement are deaths that came as a result of God's judgment on their rebellion, when they thought they could approach a holy God on their own terms.[4]

Within this concept of substitution there are three main emphases: (1) perfection (Exod. 12:5; Lev. 22:17–25; symbolizing the absence of the effects of sin); (2) identification (Lev. 1:4; 16:21–22; symbolizing the placement of sin on the animal on behalf of the sinner); and (3) acceptance by God (Lev. 1:4).[5] We will come back to these three features below when we get to the prophetic hope. For now we can note some basic observations. Obviously, these instructions for atonement were effective. The Lord accepts these offerings to "make atonement," to provide forgiveness (Lev. 1:4; 4:35). He is, after all, the one who instituted them. Yet there is a built-in way to recognize that sacrifices can't be the ultimate solution to the problem of sin.[6] What is that? Their regularity. There is a Day of Atonement every year, not to mention the many, many sacrifices that occur on a whole array of occasions.[7] Furthermore, surely a thoughtful Israelite might wonder how the death of an animal could be sufficient for their own death for sin? Micah recognizes this dilemma: "With what shall I come before the Lord and bow down before the exalted God? Shall I come before him with burnt offerings, with calves a year old? Will the Lord be pleased with thousands of rams, with ten thousand rivers of olive oil?" (Mic. 6:6–7). Before we develop this further, however, let's unpack two more key elements: the operation of the sacrifices and the role of priests.

The Operation of the Sacrifices

The opening chapters of Leviticus list the various sacrifices twice—first grouped by association (Lev. 1–6), then grouped by administrative procedures

---

4. The link between "making atonement" and averting God's wrath is, of course, not just limited to these two passages. In Num. 16 Moses instructs Aaron to hurry to make atonement for the people to avert God's wrath (16:46–47). In chap. 25 the Lord says to Moses that Phinehas "turned my anger away from the Israelites . . . and made atonement for the Israelites" (25:10–13). The psalmist declares, in Ps. 85, "You forgave the iniquity of your people and covered all their sins. You set aside all your wrath and turned from your fierce anger" (85:2–3). Likewise, Micah asks, "Who is a God like you, who pardons sin and forgives the transgression of the remnant of his inheritance? You do not stay angry forever but delight to show mercy" (Mic. 7:18).

5. Motyer, *Look to the Rock*, 55.

6. See our discussion of Hebrews below. The author of Hebrews points to the necessity and effectiveness of Christ's sacrifice for repentant sinners under the old covenant as well as the new covenant (Heb. 9:15; 10:11–14; 11:40). Thus, we might say that the "effectiveness" of these sacrifices was ultimately because of God's purposes in Christ.

7. E.g., morning and evening (Exod. 29:38–42; Num. 28:2–8), Sabbaths (Num. 28:9–10), new month (28:11–15), Passover (28:19–25), day of firstfruits (28:26–31), Feast of Trumpets (29:1–6).

for the priests (Lev. 6–7; cf. 6:8).[8] Without going into detail, we will briefly note the main sacrifices before we proceed. The *burnt offering* (sometimes called the "ascension offering" because of the ascending smoke) seems to express a wholehearted offering to "make atonement," for the animal is completely consumed on the altar (Lev. 1:4; 9:7; 16:24; cf. Gen. 8:20–21; 2 Chron. 29:7–8; Job 1:5). The *grain offering* (or meal or tribute offering) expresses thankfulness for the firstfruits of the harvest (though it often accompanies burnt offerings, often in atonement contexts; Lev. 14:20–21, 31). The *peace offering* (or fellowship, thank, or freewill offering) expresses thankfulness in celebration of restored fellowship. The *sin offering* is for purification (not always for sin but sometimes for ritual uncleanness; Lev. 15:13–15, 28–30). The *guilt offering* (or trespass or reparation offering) offers reparation for guilt for sin (Lev. 6:1–5; 19:20–22).[9] Broadly speaking, these sacrifices show that every area of life matters to God and that he intends to deal with both sin and the effects of sin (as seen in the decay and death that follow Gen. 3) so that his people can enjoy his presence and express their thankfulness to him.

Following the summaries of Leviticus 1–7, Leviticus 9:8–21 provides a window into the operation of the sacrifices and into the significance of the sacrifices for the Israelites. First, in 9:8–12 the priest offers sacrifices for himself—a sin (or purification) offering (9:8) and a burnt offering (9:12). Then, in 9:15–21 the priest offers sacrifices for the people—a sin/purification offering for the people (9:15), a burnt/ascension offering for the people (9:16–17; the accompanying grain offering is for thanksgiving), and finally a peace/fellowship offering for the people (9:18–21). Thus, the sequence shows that sin is dealt with and then reconciliation is celebrated. The amount of space given to explain each offering increases each time so that the greatest amount of space is given to explain the last offering—the celebration of restored fellowship—as if to highlight that the goal, fellowship with God, has been achieved and is cause for celebration!

Then Leviticus 9:22 concludes with a summary—referring again to the three sacrifices and to the blessing that Aaron announces to the people. The

---

8. The discussion in this paragraph summarizes Dumbrell, *Covenant and Creation*, 112–13. Note that these are not all blood sacrifices, and they are not all for atonement. There is a rich variety here. Nevertheless, the blood highlights death in place of the Israelite. For a succinct summary of the offerings, see Longman, *Immanuel in Our Place*, 77–101.

9. Although there is some debate about what sins are forgiven, it seems that both "unintentional" and "intentional" sins require sacrifices and are forgiven. Sin with a "high hand," or perhaps defiant, unrepentant sin that rejects God, is not forgiven (as in the New Testament). See, e.g., Lev. 4; 6:1–7; Num. 15:22–36 (esp. 15:30–31); Deut. 29:19–21; Mark 3:28–30; Heb. 10:26. Dumbrell, *Covenant and Creation*, 111.

content of this blessing is not given here, but it is likely that which is found in Numbers 6:24–26. This blessing emphasizes the blessings of being in a covenant relationship with God, knowing his grace and favor, and the peace that comes from being in a right relationship with him.

The Priests

God provides not only a way of reconciliation through sacrifice but also a mediator between him and his sinful people. In one sense the role of priests varies enormously. They serve in the sanctuary by offering sacrifices (for the people as well as for themselves) and transporting the tabernacle, they pray for the people, they teach the law, they find out God's will for the people, and they keep and guard the sanctuary (Num. 3:7–8; 18:5–7; see Adam's role in Gen. 2:15). Essentially, however, their role is to represent the Israelites as a nation. The key chapter here is Exodus 28. In 28:11–12 Aaron as high priest wears two shoulder pieces with the names of the tribes of Israel engraved on them—six on one and six on the other. As Aaron goes about his priestly duties before the Lord, therefore, he bears "the names on his shoulders as a memorial before the LORD." Likewise, in 28:29–30 Aaron wears a breastpiece with four rows of three precious stones so that "whenever Aaron enters the Holy Place, he will bear the names of the sons of Israel over his heart . . . as a continuing memorial before the LORD." In other places the priest is said to "bear the guilt" of the people before God in the sanctuary (28:38; cf. Lev. 10:17; Num. 18:1). Thus, the priest represents Israel before God and embodies the covenant relationship.

However, even though the sacrificial system shows that God has provided a means by which sin can be removed and his wrath turned away, still the problem of God's righteous wrath against Israel as an unrepentant and idolatrous people persists throughout their history (see, e.g., 2 Kings 22:13, 17; 23:26; 2 Chron. 24:18; 29:8; 34:25; 36:16). Ultimately, as with Adam and Eve, God's wrath against Israel culminates in exile (e.g., Jer. 11:7–8; 25:4–7; 32:30–33).

Sacrifice and the Prophetic Hope

Following the institution of the sacrificial system in Israel's history, and yet the persistent disobedience of Israel and the impending judgment of exile from the land, the prophets point forward to a renewal of God's people. But does sacrifice feature in this hope?

Do the Prophets Critique the Sacrificial System?

Some commentators have concluded, because of some statements in the prophets, that the prophets are against the sacrificial system. Isaiah quotes the Lord as saying, "I have no pleasure in the blood of bulls and lambs and goats. . . . Stop bringing meaningless offerings! . . . Your New Moon feasts and your appointed festivals I hate with all my being" (Isa. 1:11–14). In Hosea the Lord says, "I desire mercy, not sacrifice, and acknowledgment of God rather than burnt offerings" (6:6). In Amos the Lord says, "I hate, I despise your religious festivals. . . . Even though you bring me burnt offerings and grain offerings, I will not accept them" (5:21–27). Does this mean the Lord is against the sacrificial system (which he himself appears to have provided according to the law), or that the prophets somehow have advanced from a primitive view?[10] No. Each of these prophets is decrying Israel's false assumption that they could offer sacrifices without repentance, as if the temple alone were all they needed, not a heart turned toward the Lord (see Jer. 7:21–23). It is their abuse of the system, not the system itself, that the prophets denounce (cf. 1 Sam. 15:22–23). Nevertheless, this still highlights a weakness of the sacrificial system. On the one hand, the repetition (and use of animals) points to the temporary nature of the remedy. On the other hand, the very abuse of the system and God's hatred of their sinful misuse of the system point to an inherent weakness—obviously it does not change the heart or prevent Israel from exile, judgment, and rejection by God. What is needed is a new-covenant arrangement in which sin is fully and finally dealt with.

Sacrifice in the New-Covenant Hope

The prophets, therefore, not only denounce Israel's abuse of the sacrificial system of the Mosaic covenant but also point forward to a new-covenant hope. As we saw in chapter 3, on covenants, the *basis* of the new-covenant hope for a covenant in which all who are in the covenant "know the LORD" is that God "will forgive their wickedness and will remember their sins no more" (Jer. 31:34).[11] The word "for" introduces this promise, giving the basis for this "knowledge" of the Lord in the new covenant. The new covenant looks forward to a comprehensive dealing with sin, and also a transformation of heart, so that this covenant, unlike the Mosaic one, will not be broken (31:32).

---

10. For an older example of this approach, see Whitley, *Prophetic Achievement*, 63–92. For a summary of approaches like this, see Anderson, "Sacrifice and Sacrificial Offerings," 881–82.

11. See also the promise of Jer. 33:8: "I will cleanse them from all the sin they have committed against me and will forgive all their sins of rebellion against me."

The Servant of the Lord: The Ultimate Sacrifice

This prophetic hope for a full and final dealing with sin picks up on the language of the sacrificial system and focuses on the Servant of the Lord. The "servant" in Isaiah represents Israel and yet also restores Israel from blindness and disobedience and brings salvation to the gentiles (Isa. 49:3, 5–6). As we noted above, the sacrificial system focuses on substitution and punishment. For example, the sacrificed Passover lamb averted God's judgment so that the Lord "passed over" the house. Within this concept of substitution and punishment there is perfection, identification, and acceptance. The portrait of the Servant of the Lord in Isaiah 53 shockingly applies sacrificial language to a person—he is an "offering for sin" (53:10; i.e., a guilt or reparation offering; he "bore the sin" and was "cut off," 53:4–12; see on Lev. 16 above). Thus, he is the ultimate substitute: "He was pierced for our transgressions, he was crushed for our iniquities; the punishment that brought us peace was on him" (Isa. 53:5). Like in the sacrificial system, this substitute would be characterized by (1) perfection (53:9; no violence, no deceit); (2) identification (53:5–6; "the punishment that brought us peace was on him"; note the contrasts between "us," "we," "our" and "he," "him"); and (3) acceptance (53:11–12; he "will justify many").[12] The servant, therefore, embodies the covenant relationship—he would himself be "a covenant for the people" (42:6; cf. 54:10; 55:3).

Sacrifice and the New Testament

The New Testament does not abandon the principles of sacrifice, punishment, and substitution. There is no hint that the move from the Old Testament to the New is a move from wrath to love, or a kind of "evolution" from primitive ideas of sacrifice to more enlightened concepts. Rather, we move from promise to fulfillment, and fulfillment in an even greater way than could be imagined. The New Testament draws on a range of sacrificial language to describe Jesus and his saving death. As mentioned in chapter 4, on the exodus, Jesus is our Passover lamb (1 Cor. 5:7); his death is identified with the Passover (Matt. 26; Luke 22); he is the sinless, spotless lamb (1 Pet. 1:19; see Exod. 12:5; Lev. 1:10; 3:6); he is a sin offering (Rom. 8:3; 2 Cor. 5:20–21; Heb. 13:12; see Lev. 16:27) and a burnt offering (Eph. 5:1–2; see Lev. 1:9, 13, 17; i.e., as acceptable); and he has borne the curse of the law (Gal. 3:10; see Deut. 27:26). However, we will focus on just two key descriptions of Jesus's death—from Romans and Hebrews.

12. Motyer, *Look to the Rock*, 55.

Jesus's Death as an Atoning Sacrifice (Rom. 3:24-25)

In Romans 3 Paul draws on exodus language to describe our salvation—we are "redeemed" from "slavery" to sin through Jesus's death, which was a "sacrifice of atonement" (Rom. 3:24–25). However, there are three significant details about this sacrifice from the opening phrase of Romans 3:25—two that are similar to the Old Testament context and one that is dramatically different.[13] First, as in Leviticus, this sacrifice is at the initiative of God the Father—"God presented . . ." (cf. Lev. 17:11). This is not a case of a loving Son convincing a wrathful Father. No, this is a loving provision from the Father and a gladly obedient Son. Second, this sacrifice bears God's wrath. The NIV translation for the Greek word *hilastērion*, "sacrifice of atonement," could be translated as "propitiation" (ESV, meaning "to bear or turn aside God's wrath"). The word itself is used to refer to the place of atonement (i.e., the "mercy seat" or "atonement cover," Heb. 9:5; cf. Lev. 16:2), but context determines the nature of that atonement. Words related to the one used here are often used in contexts where God's wrath is averted, and this is the case here in the context of Romans 3:25 (1:18; 2:5; 5:9).[14] Third, the NIV translation "presented" should be understood as a public presentation (hence "displayed publicly," NASB). The place of atonement (or mercy seat) was in the holy of holies in the tabernacle or temple. Who would see this sacrifice? Just the high priest. Amazingly this ultimate sacrifice is one that is "displayed publicly." In Christ's death God "demonstrates his own love for us" (5:8). In the storyline of the Bible, therefore, the language of sacrifice and a wrath-bearing substitute culminates in an even greater display of God's grace in Christ.

Covenant, Law, and Sacrifice in Hebrews

The Letter to the Hebrews especially develops and ties together the themes of covenant, law, and sacrifice. One word dominates this letter's description of the comparison between the old-covenant sacrificial system and what Jesus accomplished, and that word is "better." Everything about what Jesus accomplished is better. Hebrews comments on what we noted above about the sheer repetition of the sacrifices (not only "once a year" on the Day of Atonement

---

13. For a comprehensive discussion of this verse, see Moo, *Romans*, 252–57.
14. The Greek translation of the Old Testament (LXX) uses similar words in contexts where wrath is averted. E.g., the verb *hilaskomai*: Exod. 32:14 (cf. 32:11–12); 2 Kings 24:4 (cf. 23:26; 24:20); Ps. 78:38 (LXX 77:38; cf. 78:31); Lam. 3:42 (cf. 3:43). And the verb *exilaskomai*: Num. 16:46 (cf. 16:47); 25:13 (cf. 25:11). "Wrath" is God's settled opposition to sin, due to his righteousness and holiness. Note, too, that Rom. 1:32 identifies death as punishment for sin, and Rom. 3:25 and 5:9–10 identify Jesus's death as the means by which believers are forgiven, reconciled, and declared righteous.

[9:7] but "day after day" and "again and again" [10:11]). The effect of this, says the writer, is that the sacrifices were more of a reminder than a remedy (10:1–3). In this new-covenant sacrifice, however, sins will be remembered no more (see 8:12). Thus, Jesus is the mediator of a better covenant (7:22; 8:6; 9:15; 10:16–18; 12:24). This makes Jesus a better high priest (2:17; 4:14–5:10; 8:1–6; see 5:3; 7:23–27) who provides a better hope (6:18–19; 7:19) based on better promises (8:6) because his was a better sacrifice (9:11–14, 23–28).[15] This means that believers in Jesus have infinitely better access. Note the way the author highlights this better access in the frame of Hebrews 9–10. The section begins by discussing the access under the old-covenant sacrificial system: only the high priest and only once a year (9:7–8). Then, after discussing Christ's better sacrifice, the writer concludes this section by extolling the confidence we have to access the holy of holies, drawing near with full assurance (10:19–23). Through Jesus's effective and final sacrifice, sins are remembered no more (8:12; 10:17).

Hebrews nicely illustrates what we have been saying in this book about the need to read the Old Testament to understand the New Testament, but also that the New Testament shows what the Old Testament was ultimately pointing to and is therefore our interpretive lens for understanding the Old Testament. For example, there is much in Hebrews about the sacrificial system, so one needs to know what the Old Testament, especially Leviticus and Numbers, teaches about it to understand the significance of what Hebrews says about Jesus's sacrificial death. Otherwise references to the holy of holies, entrance once a year, sacrifices, and so on are hard to grasp. Leviticus and Numbers, of course, especially highlight the holiness of God, the problem of the stain and guilt of sin, and God's gracious provision through the mediation of priest and sacrifice so that a holy God could dwell among a sinful people.

While Hebrews draws on themes found in Leviticus and Numbers, it also introduces developments and differences. For example, Hebrews describes Jesus's priesthood as that of Melchizedek—the mysterious priest-king that Psalm 110 refers to (looking back to Gen. 14:18)—rather than of the line of Aaron, within the tribe of Levi (Heb. 7:11). So significant is this change of priesthood that the writer says it requires a change of law (Heb. 7:12). Jesus was of the line of Judah (not Aaron). The Levitical priesthood is so intertwined with the law of Moses (e.g., Leviticus) that much of that law can't apply because Jesus's priesthood is different! As Hebrews says regarding the line of Judah, "No one from that tribe has ever served at the altar," and as if

---

15. Hebrews 9:9–10, 13–14, and 15 describe the old-covenant "gifts and sacrifices" as providing cleansing that is external, temporary, and anticipatory of the greater cleansing of the conscience accomplished in the new covenant through Christ's sacrifice.

to reinforce the difference adds, "In regard to that tribe Moses said nothing about priests" (7:13–14). Although kings sometimes acted in priestly ways and the roles were not always kept entirely distinct (2 Sam. 6:17–18; 1 Kings 8:63; 1 Chron. 16:1–2; though cf. 2 Chron. 29:27), the combination in one person of a king in the line of Judah and a priest who was supposed to be of the line of Aaron was avoided (2 Chron. 26:16–18; Heb. 7:14). One only needs to read the denunciations of Israel throughout the Old Testament whenever Israel appointed priests who were not Levites to see the significance of the claim that Jesus was a priest from the line of Judah (e.g., 1 Kings 12:31; 13:33–34; 2 Kings 17:32; 2 Chron. 11:14–15; 13:9; 23:6; cf. Exod. 29:9; Num. 3:10; 18:7).

To be sure, the priest-king pattern runs through Scripture. It is seen in Eden (Gen. 1:28; 2:15; see the role of "ruling" and "guarding" in the sanctuary of Eden, noted in chap. 2), in the "kingdom of priests" description of Israel (Exod. 19:6), in the occasional priestly acts of kings noted above, and in the hope of a priest-king to come in Psalm 110 (cf. Zech. 6:9–15). This pattern points to a priest-king to come who is greater than the Levitical priesthood. Nevertheless, the Mosaic covenant as a whole and the Levitical priesthood in particular are not sufficient to understand Jesus's priesthood since there are no priests from the line of Judah in Leviticus. But that is not the only major difference between Hebrews and Leviticus. No priest in Leviticus is also the sacrifice. No priest in Leviticus is sinless, having no need to offer sacrifices for himself. No priest in Leviticus is able to live forever, having no need to be replaced. Realizing that the author of Hebrews begins with Jesus rather than Leviticus for his understanding of the significance of Jesus's sacrifice keeps us from misunderstanding Hebrews by expecting everything in Hebrews to line up on a one-to-one correspondence with Leviticus.[16] Instead, while Leviticus and Numbers help us understand Hebrews and the significance of Jesus's atoning sacrifice, Jesus himself and his teaching and accomplishments are the interpretive lens through which we see everything in the old covenant fulfilled in an even greater and "better" way (anticipated in the priest-king pattern noted above).

Sacrifices Applied to the Christian

In keeping with a key feature of Leviticus and following the completion of the sacrificial system in Christ and his sacrificial death, the New Testament

---

16. For example, some scholars think that just as the priest came into the holy place with blood, so Jesus must have carried his blood into the heavenly "tabernacle." Instead, Hebrews speaks of the accomplishment of Jesus's sacrifice that is appealed to in heaven (e.g., 9:21, 25–28; cf. 9:12 CSB: "Having obtained eternal redemption"). For further discussion, see the extended excursus of Hughes, *Hebrews*, 329–54; and Grindheim, *Hebrews*, 415–17, 436–37.

indicates that the entire life of the Christian is meant to be lived in worship to God. The language of sacrifice from the Old Testament is applied not just to Jesus or to events "in church" on a Sunday morning but to all life (which includes corporate worship).[17] The most well-known application of this terminology is perhaps Romans 12:1: "In view of God's mercy [through Christ's death], offer your bodies as a living sacrifice." The Christian's praises and prayers can be described in sacrifice language (Heb. 13:15; Rev. 5:8; 8:3). Evangelism can be described as a "priestly duty" (Rom. 15:16–17). Giving gifts for gospel ministry (Phil. 4:18) or sharing generously (Heb. 13:16) can be described as an offering pleasing to God. Intense dedication can also be described with sacrifice language (Phil. 2:17; 2 Tim. 4:6; Rev. 6:9). Ultimately, because of Christ's priestly ministry and ultimate sacrifice, and his gift of the Holy Spirit, all believers are both a spiritual house being built up and also priests offering spiritual sacrifices that are pleasing to God (1 Pet. 2:5, 9).

So What? Some Implications of This Theme of Sacrifice

There is much here to stir our souls. When Christ's death is understood in light of the sacrificial system of the old covenant, we can grasp even more the enormity of what his sacrificial death accomplished for us as new-covenant believers and offer our lives in gratitude and thanksgiving in response. We don't have to, nor are we able to, "atone" for our sins before a holy God. There is no need for any other sacrifice—whether from us or through church—for us to be right with God. We have no need to go through a priest or pastor today to have our prayers answered or our sins forgiven—indeed, Jesus is the only and ultimate priest we need. Read Hebrews 10:19–22 in light of 9:7–8 and draw near to God today with "confidence" ("boldness," CSB) and "full assurance." Read the quotation from Jeremiah 31:34 in Hebrews 8:12 and 10:17 and marvel at the blessing of being in a new covenant in which sin has been fully and finally dealt with through the perfect sacrifice of Christ, such that God can say, "I will remember their sins no more." In Christ we are cleansed, forgiven, and redeemed; in Christ we enjoy the blessing of God's provision and presence. Christ is the reality to which all the feasts, festivals, and sacrifices point (Col. 2:17; Heb. 10:1). Believers can confidently live a life of worship to God knowing that, in Christ, such worship is pleasing to God (Rom. 12:1; Phil. 4:18; Heb. 12:28; 13:15–16; 1 Pet. 2:5).

---

17. See Beckwith, "Sacrifice," 761. See also the summary of the theme of worship in chap. 11 of this book.

FOR FURTHER READING

Averbeck, Richard E. "Sacrifices and Offerings." In *DNTUOT*.

Beckwith, R. T. "Sacrifice." In *NDBT*.

Longman, Tremper, III. *Immanuel in Our Place: Seeing Christ in Israel's Worship*. P&R, 2001.

Morales, L. Michael. *Who Shall Ascend the Mountain of the Lord? A Biblical Theology of the Book of Leviticus*. InterVarsity, 2015.

Yarbrough, Robert W. "Atonement." In *NDBT*.

TO DIG DEEPER

- What are "penal substitution" and "propitiation," and how do they relate to both the Old Testament sacrifices and the New Testament teaching about Jesus's death? See Jeffery et al., *Pierced for Our Transgressions*.
- How does Jesus's death relate to the wider theme of the kingdom of God in the New Testament and other theories of the atonement? See Treat, *Crucified King*.
- How can Jesus be both priest and king? See Emadi, *Royal Priest*; see also Schrock, *Royal Priesthood and the Glory of God*.

7

Kingship

In Genesis 3:15 God promises a descendant who will deliver a fatal blow to the serpent. We know from the New Testament, of course, that Jesus is that promised deliverer, but how does the storyline of the Bible get from Genesis to Jesus as our king who defeats our archenemy? As we have progressed along the storyline, we have highlighted major themes that help us understand God's saving plan—God's promises (covenant), God's deliverance (exodus), God's presence (tabernacle), God's demands (law), and God's provision (sacrifice). As we saw in chapter 3, on covenants, the promises given to Abraham became focused on the promises to David and his line in 2 Samuel 7. But how did the institution of kingship arise? Even with the institution of kingship at the high point of Israel's history, it soon became clear that David and then Solomon couldn't ultimately represent God's righteous rule. Then it seems as though just after the institution was established, it all unraveled as Israel divided and eventually went into exile. How does the establishment and unraveling of kingship help us put our Bible together, and how does kingship enrich our understanding of God's saving purposes through Christ? To answer these questions, we need to first trace the rise of kingship in Israel's *history*. This will help us grasp the significance of Israel's hope expressed by the *prophets* and marvel at the *fulfillment* of God's promise in and through Jesus.

The Preparation for Kingship in Israel's History

Genesis Through Deuteronomy

The opening chapter of the Bible shows that God is king over his creation and that he rules by his word, declaring, "Let there be . . ." and then

"There was . . ." Ultimately, God is king over Israel.[1] Yet there are also hints that God's rule will be mediated through earthly kings. Humanity is made in God's image to "rule over" creation (Gen. 1:26–28; cf. 1 Kings 4:24; Ps. 72:8). Adam is to guard the garden (Gen. 2:15), and his "seed" will crush the serpent's head (3:15). Later, God promises that kings will descend from Abraham (17:6; cf. 17:16; 35:11) and that royalty will come from Judah's line (49:10; cf. Num. 24:17, 19).

More specifically, Deuteronomy 17:14–20 anticipates the time when Israel will be in the land and will request a king. The key feature of this passage is that, although the request will be for a king "like all the nations around us" (17:14), the king must still be one whom God chooses. The anticipated request, therefore, should still express submission to God's will. This is the reason for the instructions for the king to write, read, and adhere to the law—he is not to be a law unto himself, nor an imitator of the kings of the nations, nor above the law. He is to be under God's rule and must operate under the Mosaic law. The role of a mediator for the people of Israel develops in the roles of Moses (and priests) and then Joshua. Following Joshua (as a "second Moses"), the role of a mediator in the relationship between God and his people is then accentuated when we come to Judges. This book is the last major precursor for the institution of kingship in Israel's history.

Judges

Throughout the book of Judges, the state of the nation is mirrored in the kind of judge or deliverer who rules them, anticipating the need for a righteous ruler. The basic structure of the book is as follows:[2]

1. 1:1–2:5; 2:6–3:6—a double introduction
2. 3:7–16:31—a main central section called the "cycles section"
3. 17:1–18:31; 19:1–21:25—a double conclusion

This simple outline is significant for understanding the book. The central section is well known for the cycles (see fig. 7.1).

---

1. God's covenant with Israel at Sinai is expressed in terms that resemble treaties between kings and their subjects (see Waltke, *Old Testament Theology*, 409–11; Tully, *Reading the Prophets*, 13, 24–25). The ark of the covenant also represents God's rule among his people as he is "enthroned between the cherubim" (1 Sam. 4:4; 2 Sam. 6:2; Ps. 80:1; Isa. 37:16).

2. For the following discussion I have been most helped by Younger, *Judges, Ruth*, 38–55.

Figure 7.1

As figure 7.1 indicates, this cycle repeats. The role of the judge is described in Judges 2:16–17 as a deliverer or savior. However, the cycles are only one part of the story of Israel's sinfulness. The way the story is told accentuates a major moral decline in the judges that reflects the moral decline of the people. Figure 7.2 reflects this decline, listing the major judges in the sequence in which they appear in the narrative. The vertical line markers with names below refer to "minor" judges, for whom only a verse or two describes their involvement. The diagram shows that an increasing amount of narrative space is given to the description of each judge (Barak is associated with Deborah, and Abimelech is associated with his father, Gideon). This increasing amount of space parallels the decreasing level of morality in the nation. Thus, we start with the smallest account (3:7–11) about the best judge (Othniel) and end with the longest account (13:1–16:31) describing the worst judge (Samson). Even the sections dedicated to the minor judges increase as the book goes on, from one minor judge to three. By the time we get to Samson, the cycle has fallen apart—there is no "rest," the people don't call out to Yahweh, and Samson even dies in captivity.

This deterioration in Israel is also reflected in the contrasting double introduction and double conclusion. Whereas the introduction highlights Israel's challenges with foreign wars and foreign idols, the double conclusion shows Israel's horrific problems with internal wars and idolatry. This dramatically reveals that Israel's ultimate problem is not external but internal. So, the entire concluding section is dominated by a repeated refrain:[3]

> 17:6 "In those days there was no king in Israel; all the people did what was right in their own eyes."
>
> 18:1 "In those days there was no king in Israel."
>
> 19:1 "In those days, . . . there was no king in Israel."
>
> 21:25 "In those days there was no king in Israel; all the people did what was right in their own eyes."

Judges 8:23 affirms that it is the Lord who is supposed to rule over Israel (though this statement from Gideon doesn't mean Gideon affirmed all that it meant!). So, within the book of Judges this conclusion reinforces the spiritual bankruptcy that faces Israel. It is partly true that there was no physical king, but more importantly, there was no "spiritual king," no spiritual authority.[4] Instead of doing "what was right in their own eyes" or doing "evil in the eyes of the LORD" (Judg. 2:11), Israel was supposed to do what was "right in the eyes of the LORD" (or "in the Lord's sight"; e.g., Deut. 6:17–18; 12:28). So, although the book of Judges and this concluding refrain prepare us for the next stage in salvation history—the introduction of kingship (anticipated in Genesis–Deuteronomy)—at the same time, they show that Israel needs not just any king but a righteous king who will lead them in righteousness. Ultimately, they need a king who will enable them to worship Yahweh.

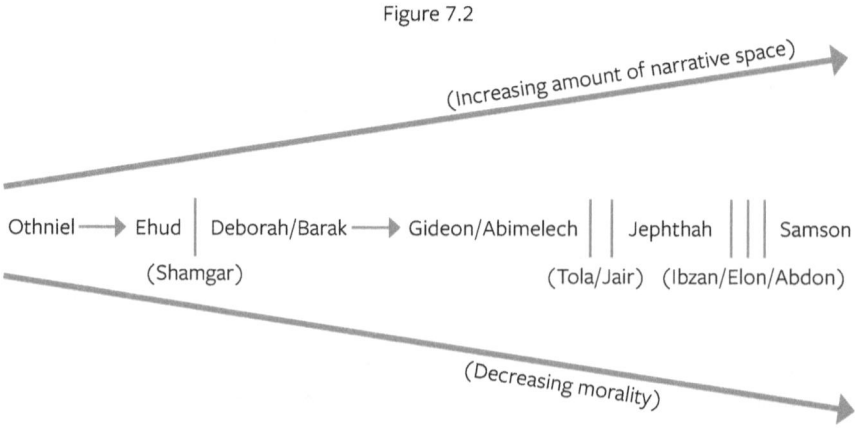

Figure 7.2

---

3. The wording of these verses is from the NRSV.
4. Younger, *Judges, Ruth*, 39.

Kingship in Israel's History

Genesis to Judges increasingly shows that God's kingship over Israel will be mediated through a ruler. Judges concludes, however, with the need for a righteous king. When we turn the page, so to speak, to 1 Samuel, the people ask for a king. Will this advance God's saving purposes through Israel?

A Rejection of God?

At first glance it appears as though the request for a king in 1 Samuel 8 is not God's will for Israel. The Lord even says to Samuel in verse 7, "It is not you they have rejected, but they have rejected me as their king." Does this mean that kingship was not part of God's plan for Israel? If so, how does that fit with all the precursors mentioned above? As is often the case, the context of Israel's request helps us here. The issue is the kind of kingship they want and the reasons for their request. In 8:5 their request is for a king "to lead us, such as all the other nations have." This is reiterated at the end of the account when they insist to Samuel, "We want a king over us. Then we will be like all the other nations" (8:19–20). But what is the problem with that? Even Deuteronomy 17:14 says this will be the context for their request. The problem is that whereas Deuteronomy 17 places kingship under God's rule, the Israelites in 1 Samuel 8 are going to be like the nations in treating their king like a god. They are seeking safety and security in having a king like the nations rather than in their covenant-keeping God. So, as the Lord says, they are forsaking him and "serving other gods" (8:8).

David

Following the appointment of King Saul as the kind of king the *people* want, Samuel is called on to anoint the king that *God* wants—King David (1 Sam. 13:14). In God's providence the institution of kingship will now display God's pattern for the redemption of the world more fully than ever before. This is the context in which the famous encounter between David and Goliath in 1 Samuel 17 should be understood. In 1 Samuel 16 David is anointed as king. Then in 1 Samuel 17 Goliath comes against Israel as the enemy of God's people. David, therefore, is the anointed king who defeats the enemy of God's people, bringing deliverance to Israel. In the grand storyline of the Bible, David's defeat of Goliath pictures the defeat of our archenemy by the ultimate King, Jesus (see Gen. 3:15; 1 John 3:8). Eventually David becomes king over all Israel, and the entire nation is united under his rule; he conquers Jerusalem and returns the ark of the covenant—a symbol of God's kingship and covenant—to Israel (see 2 Sam. 1–10; 1 Chron. 12:38–40).

God not only appoints David as ruler over his people but also makes amazing promises to David in 2 Samuel 7.[5] Just as Israel is called God's son in Exodus 4:22–23, so the descendant of David will be called God's son (2 Sam. 7:14). This sonship language is also picked up in Psalm 2:7 with reference to the enthronement of the Davidic king. Thus, the representative theme developing through Moses, Joshua, and Judges (mentioned above) is focused now on the role of the king as the representative for Israel. However, the infamous events of David's immorality with Bathsheba and his plot to have her husband, Uriah, murdered mean that once again these events in Israel's history anticipate something more. The model is becoming clearer, but we still look forward to the goal of God's promises. All eyes now turn to a descendant, a "son of David."

Solomon

Solomon is portrayed as *the* son of David, the one promised to David, through whom the temple is built and the ark is brought to the temple. Yet it soon becomes clear that, contrary to the specifications for a king in Deuteronomy 17, Solomon will focus on himself before God. Having briefly covered Judges and 1–2 Samuel, we now come to the account of Solomon's reign in 1 Kings 1–11 (see also 1 Chron. 29:22–25; 2 Chron. 9:22–26). At one level this is the high point of Israel's history. First Kings 4:20–25 provides a summary of Solomon's reign, showing that the pattern of Eden, picked up again in the promises to Abraham, is being fulfilled. God's people are numerous (1 Kings 4:20; see the promises to Abraham in Gen. 13:16; 15:5; 22:17; reiterated to Jacob in Gen. 32:12); they are enjoying the promised land (1 Kings 4:21; see Gen. 15:18; Exod. 23:31); and they are living in safety under God's rule (1 Kings 4:25; the phrase "everyone under their own vine and under their own fig tree" becomes a picture of the last days; cf. Mic. 4:4; Zech. 3:10).

First Kings 5–8 focuses on the building of the temple—the place of sacrifice and reconciliation with God, the place that represents God's presence in the midst of his people, the place that now holds the ark of the covenant—the culmination of Israel's history since the exodus (8:20–21). Yet right in the heart of this narrative, in 1 Kings 7, Solomon builds a palace for *himself*, a palace that will reveal his priorities. The narrator doesn't explicitly condemn Solomon for building a palace. Yet the last verse of 1 Kings 6 and the first

---

5. See the discussion in chap. 3 on the Davidic covenant.

verse of 1 Kings 7 (i.e., 6:38 and 7:1) suggest an implicit critique. On the one hand, Solomon's effort in spending "seven years" building the Lord's temple seems commendable. In the very next verse, however, the narrator tells us that Solomon spent "thirteen years" building his own palace—almost double the amount of time! This sounds suspiciously like a focus on self. Our suspicions seem to be confirmed when we compare the sizes of the two buildings, recorded in 6:2 and 7:2. In the NIV the measurements are given in cubits (footnotes translate this into feet or meters). The temple measurements are 60 (length), 20 (width), and 30 (height) cubits. However, the measurements for just the "Palace of the Forest of Lebanon" (because so many cedars are used) are 100 (length), 50 (width), and 30 (height) cubits. This structure, which is apparently only one of the buildings associated with Solomon's palace, is 40 cubits longer and more than double the width of the temple! No wonder it takes him more than double the amount of time to build it. In addition to a grand colonnade, a judgment hall, and his own palace residence, as the narrator points out, Solomon also builds a palace for Pharaoh's daughter (7:8; cf. 11:1, another subtle critique of Solomon's building efforts). All these structures are called Solomon's "house" (9:1, 10, 15; 10:12 ESV).

Furthermore, 1 Kings 7 is at the heart of the description of Solomon's reign in 1 Kings 1–11. Broadly speaking, the account of Solomon's reign in these chapters could be arranged as follows:[6]

1 Kings 1–2 (opposition is dealt with on Solomon's rise to the throne)

1 Kings 3 (Solomon's dream; "whatever you want," 3:5)

1 Kings 6–8 (Solomon builds a temple for God and a palace for himself)

1 Kings 9 (Solomon's dream, with a focus on warnings)

1 Kings 11:7–8 (Solomon builds temples to foreign gods)

1 Kings 11:14–43 (opposition is unable to be dealt with; internal division and final downfall)

Thus, the turning point in the account of Solomon's reign comes in 1 Kings 7, when he builds his own house and the house of the Lord. For all the many ways in which Solomon fails to live up to God's pattern for the king in Deuteronomy 17—such as his many wives from the nations surrounding Israel and his corresponding idolatry (11:1–6)—the author of

---

6. This outline is a summary and adaptation from Parker, "Repetition as a Structuring Device," 19–27. I am grateful to K. Lawson Younger for drawing my attention to the outline from this article.

1 Kings seems to identify his extravagant self-focused building as early evidence of a heart divided. What is the author trying to tell us? It seems clear that this "son of David" who reigns over a united Israel and through whom the temple is built can't be the one to bring about God's saving promises for Israel and the nations. To adapt the phrase we used in chapter 1 (from Graeme Goldsworthy), God's people may be in God's place, under the rule of God's king, even with God's presence symbolized by the temple, yet the ideal is still to come.

Kingship in Decline and Eventual Exile

The high point of Israel's history, with the institution of kingship and the building of the temple, doesn't last for long. Following Solomon, the nation of Israel splits into two kingdoms, leading eventually to the demise of both. The ten northern tribes separate, make Jeroboam their king, and center in Samaria. Solomon's son Rehoboam, therefore, is left to reign over the tribes of Judah and Benjamin in Jerusalem (1 Kings 12:20–21). Figure 7.3 summarizes visually the history of Israel from its high point with the institution of kingship, with David as king, to the exile.

Figure 7.3

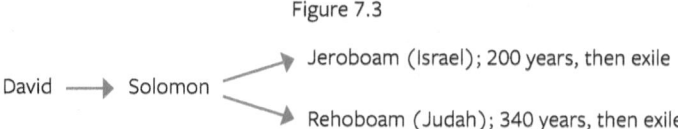

This split occurs in about 931 BC. The Northern Kingdom then has about 200 years with nineteen kings until its eventual exile to Assyria in 722 BC. Of these nineteen kings throughout this entire 200-year period, none are "good" or godly kings. Not one good king! Isn't that amazing? The Southern Kingdom lasts for about another 140 years, until its eventual exile in 586 BC—thus, about 340 years in total. It has about twenty kings in total. There are a few bright spots, with seven or eight "good" or godly kings, depending on our definition of "good." Still, the majority of the kings are wicked. One element that makes a king "good" is that he restores temple worship after the neglect and idolatry of the people and the preceding king. Table 7.1 lists the kings of the Southern Kingdom, noting if they were good or bad, and provides relevant passages for the good kings, with some qualifying descriptions of those kings.

The institution of kingship in Israel couldn't stem the slide into national judgment and exile. Indeed, it even contributed to that decline! But what about the promises to David about his line?

Table 7.1

King	Description of King	Key Scripture References
1. Rehoboam	Bad	
2. Abijah	Bad	
3. Asa	Good	1 Kings 15:8–24; 2 Chron. 14:1–16:14 (relied on Syria; died diseased, not seeking the Lord)
4. Jehoshaphat	Good	1 Kings 15:24; 22:41–51; 2 Chron. 17:1–21:1 (made alliances with Israel, including Athaliah)
5. Jehoram	Bad	
6. Ahaziah	Bad	
7. Athaliah	Bad	
8. Jehoash (Joash)	Good	2 Kings 12:1–21; 2 Chron. 24:1–27 (abandoned the Lord after Jehoiada died)
9. Amaziah	Good	2 Kings 14:1–22; 2 Chron. 24:27–25:28 (was idolatrous and defeated by Israel)
10. Uzziah	Started Good	2 Kings 15:1–7; 2 Chron. 26:1–23 (grew proud, became angry with priests, and died a leper)
11. Jotham	Good	2 Kings 15:32–38; 2 Chron. 26:21–23 (regent); 26:23–27:9 (king; didn't remove the high places, and the people still sacrificed there)
12. Ahaz	Bad	
13. Hezekiah	Good	2 Kings 16:20; 18:1–20:21; 2 Chron. 28:27–32:33 (perhaps a bitter response in 2 Kings 20:2–3; proudly showed everything to the king of Babylon and showed concern only for his own welfare)
14. Manasseh	Bad	
15. Amon	Bad	
16. Josiah	Good	2 Kings 21:26–23:30; 2 Chron. 33:25–35:27 (didn't listen to the voice of God through the Egyptian king and went to battle and died)
17. Jehoahaz	Bad	
18. Jehoiakim	Bad	
19. Jehoiachin	Bad	
20. Zedekiah	Bad	

Psalm 89

It is at this point of exile that everything looks especially bleak for God's people. In light of the promises made to David, Psalm 89 provides insight into how disastrous the exile was for God's people. It begins beautifully, highlighting the Lord's "great love," which "stands firm forever," and his "faithfulness," which is "established . . . in heaven itself" (89:1–2). The psalmist then focuses on God's covenant with David—in particular his promises to establish David's line "forever" and to make his throne "firm through all generations" (89:3–4). The psalmist continues to praise the Lord for his rule, his love, and his faithfulness. In verses 28–29 the psalmist again highlights the Lord's promises to David of a never-failing covenant and a never-ending throne. This praise for the permanence of David's line and throne in this covenant continues through to verse 37. Then everything changes. The psalmist laments, "But you have rejected, you have spurned, you have been very angry with your anointed one. You have renounced the covenant with your servant and have defiled his crown in the dust" (89:38–39). This grief continues for the rest of the psalm. "How long, Lord? Will you hide yourself forever? How long will your wrath burn like fire?" (89:46). Can you feel the angst of the psalmist? The situation is disastrous.

What does this development and institution of kingship in Israel's history tell us? The "high point" of Israel's history didn't last long, and that high point wasn't even that great when we look at the actions of David, and even of Solomon at the very point that the temple was built. The promise of kings in the line of David, mediating God's rule, sounded amazing. But the Bible is unrelenting in its description of human sin. Israel's life under the Mosaic covenant, even when administered through a king in the line and covenant of David, results in exile outside the land, just as Adam was removed from the garden. Yet the story continues to point forward. There must be more to come.

Prophetic Hopes for "Great David's Greater Son"[7]

A Shoot

As Israel's disastrous line of kings led the nation on a trajectory toward judgment and exile, the prophets looked forward to a greater David to come. Two key passages are Isaiah 11:1 and Jeremiah 23:5–7 (see also Isa. 6:13; 53:2; Jer. 33:14–22; Ezek. 17:22–24). In Isaiah 11 a "shoot" is promised from the "stump" of Jesse. Jesse, of course, was David's father. The image of a "stump" is that of a large tree that has been cut down. The tree of David's line appears to be gone, but there is a shoot—a promise of something still to come from that line. In light of the disastrous line of kings, it is fitting that this hope was for a king who would be characterized by wisdom and

---

7. These are words from the 1821 hymn by James Montgomery: "Hail to the Lord's Anointed, great David's greater Son! Hail in the time appointed, his reign on earth begun!" (https://hymnary.org/text/hail_to_the_lords_anointed).

the fear of the Lord (as we saw in chap. 5, on wisdom). Thus, "righteousness will be his belt and faithfulness the sash around his waist" (11:5). Similarly, in Jeremiah 23 the Lord promises that he will "raise up for David a righteous Branch, a King who will reign wisely and do what is just and right in the land" (23:5).

A Restoration

In light of the unrighteousness of the kings of Israel leading the nation into unrighteousness and eventual exile, it follows that the promise of a righteous king is accompanied by the promise of a restored people. A new David means a new people. One of the key passages here is Ezekiel 34. The Lord promises not only a new David but a David who will lead and feed God's people as a good shepherd: "I will place over them one shepherd, my servant David, and he will tend them; he will tend them and be their shepherd" (34:23). Ezekiel 37:24–25 looks forward to a time not only when Israel will have "one shepherd"—the Davidic king who will reign over a people of God no longer divided into two kingdoms—but also when there will be an obedient people under this king who will keep God's decrees (see also Isa. 55:3–5; Ezek. 21:26–27; Amos 9:11–12; cf. Gen. 49:10).

The Messianic Enigma (the Shoot and Root)

Yet there is something of an enigma in these promises of a king to come.[8] Let us return to the three key passages we just cited. In Isaiah 11 the Lord promises a "shoot" from the "stump" of Jesse (11:1). Yet just a few verses later the Lord says, "In that day the Root of Jesse will stand as a banner for the peoples; the nations will rally to him" (11:10). So, which is it? Is this promised king a "shoot" in the sense that he is a descendant of Jesse, or will he be "the Root of Jesse" in the sense that he is the source of Jesse? Likewise, Jeremiah 23 says this "righteous Branch" of David (23:5) will be called "the LORD Our Righteous Savior" (23:6). In Ezekiel 34:23 a new David will tend and shepherd God's people. Yet 34:11–12 says the Sovereign Lord himself will search for and look after his sheep like a shepherd. Numerous other passages either allude to (Ps. 45:6) or more directly indicate (Ps. 110:1; Isa. 9:6) a divine Messiah. It is not until the New Testament, of course, that these hints are brought together in one person. It is Jesus who enables readers of the Old Testament to see how these strands come together.

---

8. Motyer, *Look to the Rock*, 36, uses the phrase "Messianic enigma" and cites Isa. 11 and Jer. 23.

One Greater than Solomon Is Here: Kingship in the New Testament

Jesus the Son of David

The very first verse of the New Testament announces that Jesus is "the son of David" (Matt. 1:1; cf. Luke 1:32, 69; 2 Tim. 2:8), and this designation continues throughout Jesus's ministry (Matt. 21:9). But he is not just any son; he is "greater than Solomon" (12:42). Indeed, he is David's Lord as well (22:42; Luke 20:41–44). The promise of a never-ending rule on the throne of David is fulfilled, not in a continuous line but in a resurrected Lord Jesus, who defeats death and is exalted to the throne of David (Acts 2:29–31; cf. 13:32–37).

Jesus the Anointed One and Son of God

Just as the king was described as God's "anointed one" (Ps. 28:8), so Jesus is described as the ultimate "anointed one." This is the meaning of "Messiah" (from the Hebrew *mashiakh*) or "Christ" (from the Greek *christos*). So, the term "Christ" in the New Testament is essentially a title meaning that Jesus is the long-awaited "anointed one" (cf. Ps. 2:2; John 1:41; 4:25; Acts 4:25–27).[9] Likewise, just as the descendant of David would be the "son of God" upon his enthronement to rule (cf. 2 Sam. 7:14; Ps. 2:7), representing Israel's sonship to God (Exod. 4:22–23) and reflecting God's likeness as he mediates God's rule, so also Jesus is the ultimate "Son of God" enthroned to rule (Rom. 1:3–4; cf. Acts 13:33). At times, references to Jesus as the "Christ" are paralleled with the Davidic "Son of God" language, reflecting the similarity in these phrases (e.g., Matt. 26:63). Yet Jesus is also the ultimate Son of the Father, perfectly and uniquely reflecting the Father's likeness and sovereignty (Luke 1:35; John 1:18).

Jesus the Shepherd

Similarly, Jesus's description of himself as the "good shepherd" who lays down his life for the sheep, bringing in other sheep (gentiles) so God's people will be "one flock" and they will have "one shepherd" (John 10:11, 14–16), picks up on God's promises in Ezekiel (34:22–24; 37:24–25). Indeed, Jesus's description of his purpose in coming to earth "to seek and to save the lost" (Luke 19:10) uses the same language as God's promise in Ezekiel 34:12, 16, to "search for the lost" sheep.[10]

---

9. Those who belong to Christ are also described as "anointed" because they belong to the ultimate "anointed one" and have been given the Spirit (2 Cor. 1:21; 1 John 2:20).

10. Chapter 9 will identify more ways that Jesus brings together various patterns that run through Scripture.

So What? Some Implications of This Theme of Kingship

How does the pattern of Davidic kingship picture who Jesus is and what he does? To deepen our understanding of Jesus's kingship, I want to draw out three implications in this section from the patterns we noted earlier about what "good" kings were supposed to do.[11] The king was supposed to (1) fight for his people and defeat their enemies, (2) build the temple and enable or restore true worship of God, and (3) rule over his people.

First, as we noted above, God promises in Genesis 3:15 that a descendant will deliver a fatal blow to the serpent. This aspect of the king's role is immediately seen after David is anointed—he defeats the enemy of God's people, Goliath (1 Sam. 16–17). Likewise, after the Lord gives David the promises of the Davidic covenant, David defeats and subdues Israel's enemies (2 Sam. 7–8).[12] Thus, this role of Israel's king points to Jesus's accomplishment in destroying the "works of the devil" (1 John 3:8 ESV). By taking on himself the punishment we deserve at the cross, Jesus "disarmed the powers and authorities . . . , triumphing over them by the cross" (Col. 2:14–15). Satan can no longer accuse God's people, for the basis for the accusations has been removed (Rom. 8:33–34; Heb. 2:14–15). Through Jesus, believers are rescued from evil and slavery to sin (Acts 26:18; Rom. 5–6; Col. 1:13).

Second, although David would not be the one to build the temple, he supplied the furnishings for his son Solomon to build the temple (1 Chron. 18:8; 29:1–5; 2 Chron. 5:1; cf. Ezra 3:10; Zech. 6:12–13). The defining features of the "good" kings who followed David and Solomon in Judah are their restoration of temple worship or celebrations such as the Passover (e.g., Hezekiah, 2 Chron. 29–31; Josiah, 2 Kings 23; 2 Chron. 34–35) and their removal of idols (e.g., Asa, 1 Kings 15:11–12), even though (as we noted in chap. 6, on sacrifice) kings were from the line of Judah and weren't meant to be Levitical

---

11. The following is adapted from Beeke and Smalley, *Man and Christ*, 1116–17.
12. Accounts of Israel's warfare against surrounding nations also need to be read in the framework of biblical theology (e.g., Deut. 2:33–34; 7:2–5; 20:1–20; Num. 21:35; 1 Sam. 15:3). (1) These were not universal or ongoing and timeless commands to always carry out defeats of enemies like this for all people everywhere. These were limited to specific times and a specific place (i.e., related to the land and nation of Israel under the Mosaic covenant). (2) These defeats were "because of their wickedness," evidenced in practices such as child sacrifice (cf. Lev. 18:25; Deut. 9:4–6). (3) Four hundred years of warnings were given so that there was time to repent (cf. Gen. 15:13–16; Josh. 2:10–11). (4) In the context of salvation history and the Mosaic covenant, these physical or temporal judgments for idolatrous nations (including Israel) pointed forward to an eternal judgment that all who do not repent from rebellion to their Maker will receive (e.g., Luke 16; Rev. 19–20). "Land" is part of the trajectory from Eden to Jerusalem/temple to the new creation. When we understand biblical theology, we understand that we read the Bible as an account of movement from promise to fulfillment (i.e., not from bad to good or wrath to love).

priests (2 Chron. 26:16–21; cf. 8:12–16). Since Jesus is the ultimate king, his kingship is not separated from his sacrificial and priestly work, as he restores God's people to true worship. Furthermore, as we will see in the next chapter, Jesus is the ultimate fulfillment of the temple, the dwelling of God with his people (John 2:19–21). Those who belong to him worship God in truth and by the Spirit (4:23). By building the people of God, Jesus is the one who builds and gives shape to God's temple, in which he dwells by his Spirit (Acts 4:11; 1 Cor. 3:11, 16; Eph. 2:20–22; cf. Zech. 6:12–13).

Third, as king, David ruled over God's people, "doing what was just and right for all his people" (2 Sam. 8:15). This, of course, is why the king had to be characterized by righteousness and wisdom, and this also served to differentiate good kings from wicked kings, who rejected God's law and ruled harshly. Jesus now sits at the right hand of the Father as the ultimate Davidic king who rules in fulfillment of the promise for a never-ending king on the throne of David (Acts 2:30–35). As the risen and reigning Lord, he dispenses the Spirit (2:33) and enables the gospel message to spread to the nations through his people (11:21). Indeed, just as at the high point of Israel's history David and Solomon ruled over the entire land of Israel, so Jesus rules over all creation (Col. 1:15–23). It is because of this rule that he can build his church (Matt. 16:18; 28:18–20). He rules over his church by his word, as explained by his apostles (Acts 2:42), and through his "undershepherds," who are to lovingly feed, guide, protect, and lead his blood-bought flock by example and in conformity to the word of God's grace (20:28–29, 32; 1 Pet. 5:1–4).[13]

Finally, our risen Lord is truly the ultimate wise, righteous, and good king. He is "the King of kings" (1 Tim. 6:15; cf. Rev. 1:5; 15:3; 17:14; 19:16). We gladly submit to him and entrust our lives to him. And we long for the day when his reign will be seen in fullness, when death and evil are finally banished (Acts 2:35; 1 Cor. 15:50–57). But that is the subject of chapter 9!

FOR FURTHER READING

Boda, Mark J. *After God's Own Heart: The Gospel According to David*. The Gospel According to the Old Testament. P&R, 2007.

Porter, Stanley E., ed. *The Messiah in the Old and New Testaments*. Eerdmans, 2007.

Strauss, M. L. "Messiah." In *DNTUOT*.

---

13. On the application of the new covenant to the elder's leadership under God's word, see Wellum and Wellum, "Biblical and Theological Case," 70–77.

TO DIG DEEPER

- This chapter reveals again (see chap. 6) the association between kingship and priesthood (see esp. Gen. 49:10; Num. 3:10; 18:7; see also Ps. 110; Zech. 6:13; Heb. 7:11–19). The relationship between the topics of kingship and atonement could also be studied further (see Treat, *Crucified King*).
- The pattern of David's life becomes another way in which the New Testament draws on the Old Testament to describe events in the life of Jesus. Events and circumstances in David's life are seen by New Testament writers as being fulfilled in an ultimate way (e.g., the use of Pss. 69:25; 109:8 for Judas's judgment, Acts 1:20). We will explain typology in chapter 11. See the various articles in *DNTUOT* (e.g., Thompson, "Acts, Book of," 6–13).
- Discussions about the overlapping chronology of the judges, the local or regional rule of the judges, and the legitimacy of the institution of kingship can be found in commentaries on Judges and introductions to the Old Testament. See, for example, Younger, *Judges, Ruth*, 23–28, 55–61; Howard, *Introduction to the Old Testament Historical Books*, 99–123.
- What are the implications of Jesus's first and second comings for understanding his kingship as we await the fullness of his reign? See chapter 9.

8

The Prophetic Hope

Do you find the large section of books generally called "the Prophets" hard to understand?[1] If you do, you're not alone. In a survey carried out by Crossway, one infographic shows both how little the Prophets are read and also how difficult they are to understand (see fig. 8.1). In response to the question "Which section of the Bible do you read most often?" the Prophets ranked low. Correspondingly, in answer to the question "Which do you find hardest to understand?" the Prophets ranked the highest by far![2] If this is true for you, then this chapter will help.[3]

We have covered the major events and institutions in Israel's history, and in chapter 7 we arrived at the climax of God's unfolding of his plan so far with the institution of kingship. Broadly speaking, from the themes of creation and covenant to kingship, we have looked at these themes in the order in which they were introduced and revealed in Israel's history. However, in the rest of the Old Testament, we have this major body of writing—the prophetic literature. What does it contribute to God's unfolding plan, especially if we reached the high point with the institution of kingship, the building of the temple, and the reigns

---

[1]. The Hebrew Bible is basically divided up into three parts: the Torah (Genesis–Deuteronomy), the Former (Joshua–Kings) and Latter (Isaiah–Malachi) Prophets, and the Writings. This chapter focuses on the Latter Prophets, what we call the "writing prophets" or the "Major" and "Minor Prophets."

[2]. "Infographic: How Do You Read the Bible?," Crossway, accessed October 30, 2024, www.crossway.org/articles/infographic-how-do-you-read-the-bible.

[3]. I have been most helped by Robertson, *Christ of the Prophets*. So, much of this chapter is a summary of the insights gleaned from this book.

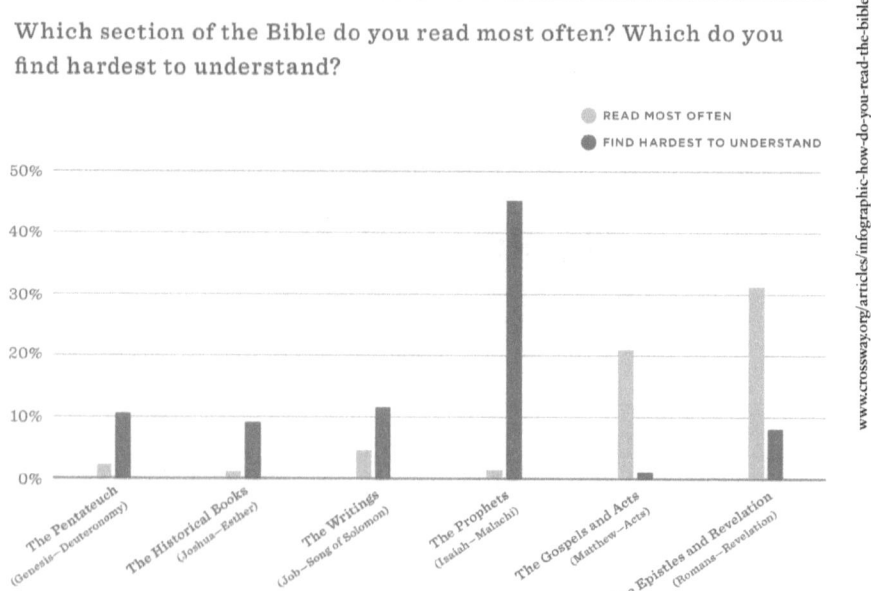

Figure 8.1

Taken from "Infographic: How Do You Read the Bible?" Used by permission of Crossway.

of David and Solomon? What led to this major development in which we move from prophets as we find them in Israel's history to these "writing prophets"?

In answering these questions, this chapter builds on the preceding chapters and draws them together. This chapter, therefore, is a major help as we seek to put our Bible together. To understand this major development, however, we need to do a little groundwork. Once we understand the role of the prophets in relation to the events in Israel's history, we'll be in a better place to grasp the importance of the writing prophets. First, however, to understand the role of the prophets in God's unfolding plan, we must go back to the origin of this institution.

Moses and the Prophetic Office

The instructions given to Moses identify him as the foundation of the prophetic office and the pattern for future prophets.[4] In Deuteronomy 18:15–16

---

4. Cf. Robertson, *Christ of the Prophets*, 25–29, 37–43.

Moses declares, "The LORD your God will raise up for you a prophet *like me* from among your own brothers. You must listen to him. For this is what you asked of the LORD your God at Horeb on the day of the assembly when you said, 'Let us not hear the voice of the LORD our God nor see this great fire anymore, or we will die'" (CSB).

Although these verses look forward to the future role of the prophets, the words "like me" indicate that Moses is already viewed as a prophet. That is, Moses functions as a mediator, communicating God's revelation, his words, to his people at Sinai (Exod. 20:18–21; Deut. 5:22–27). Thus, as Hosea says, "The LORD used a prophet to bring Israel up from Egypt, by a prophet he cared for him" (Hosea 12:13).

When the Lord repeats the promise that he will raise up prophets like Moses in Deuteronomy 18:18, he describes the role and purpose of prophets. That is, Moses provides the pattern for the long history of the prophets in Israel. Thus, the role of the prophet is the role of a gracious mediator; the prophet stands between God and the people to deliver the word of the Lord, declaring God's will. From the beginning, therefore, the key role of the prophets is to speak God's words. Thus, the Lord says, "I will put my words in his mouth. He will tell them everything I command him" (Deut. 18:18; see again in 18:19, "my words").

Unlike the offices of priest and king, therefore, the office of prophet is not passed on by natural descent. A person can be a prophet only by the direct call and commissioning of the Lord ("I will raise up" emphasizes the divine initiative; Deut. 18:18).[5] Before we get to the role of the writing prophets, let us briefly note the rise of prophets in Israel's history.

The Rise of Prophets in Israel's History

Whereas Moses provided the foundation and pattern for the role of prophets, the prophetic movement rose to prominence in a general sense with the establishment of the kingship.[6] Samuel appears "in conjunction with the establishment of Saul and David as Israel's first kings. Throughout the remainder of the history of Israel's kings, the prophets often addressed their messages particularly to

---

5. One implication of this foundational understanding of the role of the prophet is that other, unauthorized means of determining the word of the Lord are rejected, and warnings are given concerning the danger of departing from the Lord's prophet (Deut. 18:9–11, 19–22; cf. 13:1–18). See Robertson, *Christ of the Prophets*, 48–54, 91–109; Tully, *Reading the Prophets*, 58–70, 73–84. The Urim and Thummim was another means of determining God's will (Num. 27:21; 1 Sam. 14:41–42).

6. See Vos, *Biblical Theology*, 203 (cited in Robertson, *Christ of the Prophets*, 4). This section and the following one draw esp. on Robertson's helpful introduction in *Christ of the Prophets*, 4–8.

the rulers of Israel and Judah."[7] In addition to Samuel, you might be familiar with other prophets in Israel's history, like Nathan (and his confrontation with David in 2 Sam. 12) and Elijah (and his confrontation with Ahab and the prophets of Baal on Mount Carmel in 1 Kings 18) and Elisha (and the miracles associated with him in 2 Kings). We know about these prophets because of their involvement with Israel's kings in the historical books of the Bible, as they applied God's law and covenant obligations to the rulers of Israel throughout Israel's history. However, in this chapter we are seeking to understand how this vast body of literature, the writing prophets, fits into God's saving plan. How do prophets like Isaiah, Jeremiah, and Ezekiel help us put our Bible together?

The Origin of the Writing Prophets

There are clear differences between prophets such as Elijah and Elisha and prophets like Isaiah and Ezekiel, who came later. What are some of those differences? Most obviously, we don't have books named after or written by Nathan, Elijah, and Elisha, whereas we have whole books by Isaiah, Jeremiah, and Ezekiel. We find out about prophets like Elijah and Elisha in books like 1–2 Kings that describe various events and encounters in their lives, but we don't have many details about their teachings or their messages unless they relate to the specific events being described. What is distinctive about prophets like Isaiah and Jeremiah is that not only do we have books named after them, but the focus of those books is their messages, not so much the events of their lives (although there is some of that). Thus, broadly speaking, once we move beyond the ministries of Elijah and Elisha and into the eighth century BC, we enter the period of the writing prophets. That is, we have their writings! This is what makes them distinctive in the unfolding of God's saving plan. So, the question now is Why the difference? Why do we have the books and writings of Isaiah and others like him and not Elijah and others like him? What led to this development in salvation history? To understand this, we briefly need to think about the relationship between the events of salvation history and the writings of Scripture.

Events and Revelation in Salvation History

In broad terms, the general pattern of Scripture is that the great saving events in Israel's history have been recounted in God's revelation in books

---

7. Robertson, *Christ of the Prophets*, 4–5.

so that later generations of God's people will understand their significance. For example, the actual events, such as the exodus, the deliverance through the blood of the Passover lamb, and the giving of the law, could all be interpreted in a range of ways—such as political expediency, savvy leadership, and so on. Yet they are all interpreted and explained in the first five books of the Bible (the Pentateuch) as God's redemptive action, in the context of a covenant initiated by God so that God's saving action, fulfilling his promises, is revealed and recorded. The same could be said of the settlement in the land and the rise of kingship, the reigns of David and Solomon along with the building of the temple, and so on. These events could also be interpreted in a range of ways. Yet their explanation in the historical books of the Old Testament and the accompanying Psalms highlights their place in the unfolding plan of God to rule his people with kings in the line of David, fulfilling his promises.

What great developments in the movement of redemptive history led to the body of prophetic literature? If the climax of salvation history in Israel was the establishment of the monarchy, with Israel united in the promised land, with Jerusalem as its capital, and with the temple as a fixed (not temporary, tentlike) expression of God's presence with them, then what is left? What subsequent event led to the creation of such a significant corpus of written material?[8] The answer is the exile.

The Exile and the Writing Prophets

The significance of the exile in light of all that has been put in place so far is hard to overestimate. We have traced the institution of covenants, the exodus and journey into the land, the provision of the tabernacle/temple, the institution of the sacrificial system, the giving of the law, and the rise of kingship. The exile undoes everything! The people are taken from the land, the temple and sacrificial system are destroyed, and the rule of the kings comes to an end. The law was meant to guide the people on how to live in the land and how priests and sacrifices were to operate, but now they are not in the land and have no temple. Indeed, God's people are ultimately exiled to the land of the Chaldeans, where Abraham originated from. It is as if everything has come undone, and we are back to before the beginning of the outworking of God's saving promises through Israel. As seen in figure 8.2, we could represent the unfolding events along the timeline of Israel's history as building until we reach the high point of

---

8. Robertson, *Christ of the Prophets*, 5.

Israel's history with the institution of kingship. The undoing of everything in Israel's history could be represented as in figure 8.3.

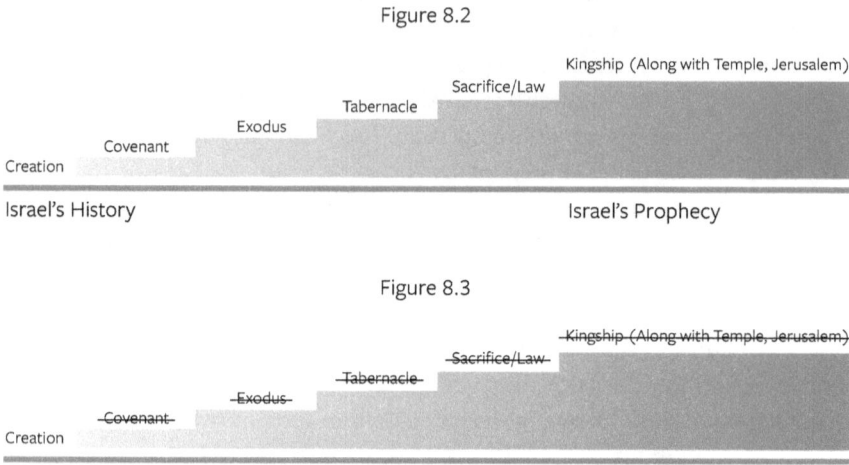

Ezekiel 7 announces the tragedy dramatically: "The end! The end has come . . . ! The end is now upon you. . . . The end has come! The end has come! . . . See, it comes!" (7:2–3, 5–7). How, then, does this dramatic event of the exile fit into God's plan of salvation if everything has come to an end? What does the future hold if God's people are now "not my people" (Hosea 1:9)? This is where the writing prophets fit into God's purposes in salvation history. Not only do these prophets proclaim the need for repentance, but their messages are also recorded, largely because of the exile. In this time of hopelessness, they are able to point to the law of God to explain why the exile is coming or why it has happened. Yet they are also able to point forward to hope beyond judgment. In committing these messages to writing, they were able to provide God's people with hope beyond the exile. If God's word about the coming judgment of exile came true, so will his word of hope, his promises of a future. What, then, is their message?

The Prophetic Application of the Law and Covenant

We will briefly survey the role of the prophets in general before returning to our main question about how they fit into the unfolding plan of God and the themes we have been surveying.[9] The prophets were essentially "covenant

---

9. For the following, see Robertson, *Christ of the Prophets*, 121–87 (Robertson uses this title on p. 143); Pate et al., *Story of Israel*, 93–96; Tully, *Reading the Prophets*, 90–109; cf. Lev. 26:33–34, 40–42.

enforcers." The Mosaic law and the covenant promises provided the prophets with the standard by which they condemned sin and promised salvation for the people. They applied the law in relation to the covenant and the bond that existed between Yahweh and his people. Thus, the prophets brought messages of both judgment and salvation, announcing that God is still king of the covenant and that the covenant sanctions still stand. We generally group the writing prophets into two groups: the Major Prophets of Isaiah, Jeremiah, and Ezekiel; and the twelve Minor Prophets ("minor" because of the size of their writings, not their importance). However, historically, they may be broadly divided into those who ministered before the exile, during the exile, and after the exile (thus they are called "preexilic," "exilic," and "postexilic," though some of the Minor Prophets, such as Joel, are difficult to date).[10]

The prophets who minister *before* the exile are characterized by warnings and promises. The eighth-century BC prophets include Amos and Hosea (for the north), and Isaiah and Micah (for the south). The seventh-century BC prophets include Nahum, Habakkuk, and Zephaniah. They warn of the judgment to come on the whole nation, as Deuteronomy warned long ago and as God warned Solomon—but there will be restoration. God himself will save his people (Zeph. 3:17). This restoration will come through a remnant—that is, a group within the nation (the survivors of judgment). "The righteous shall live by his faith" (Hab. 2:4 ESV).

The prophets who minister *during* the exile explain why it happened and look ahead. The prophets who minister in the mid-sixth century BC include Jeremiah (who spends some time in Egypt, Jer. 43:4–13) and Ezekiel and Daniel (who are both exiled to Babylon). They respond to the disaster of the exile, in which the people are scattered with no land, no Jerusalem, no temple, and no king. Thus, they emphasize God's universal sovereign rule, and they explain why this calamity has happened (judgment for sin). They also look ahead to a time when God will restore his people and a new-covenant relationship will be established, which will be more glorious than they have ever known.

Because of the return to Jerusalem, the prophets who minister *after* the exile are sometimes called "the prophets of the restoration." This period spans about 150 years (536–400 BC) and encompasses the first return and the beginning of the rebuilding (536 BC), the restart of the rebuilding (520 BC; see Haggai and Zechariah), and the second return under Ezra (458 BC) and Nehemiah

---

10. Jonah is unique in focusing on the life of the prophet (though it fits within a preexilic setting, 2 Kings 14:23–27). Nevertheless, it is an indictment on Israel, who should repent, and points to God's saving purposes for the nations.

(445 BC; see Malachi). These prophets reflect on the partial fulfillment that has not lived up to the expectations of what a return from exile would look like and thus continue to point God's people forward. It is a fulfillment of God's promises but also a "day of small things" (Zech. 4:10); there is both joy and weeping when some of them remember the former temple (Ezra 3:12–13).

The prophets call Israel to repent and warn of judgment.[11] They appeal to the law and condemn idolatry, particularly Israel's greed and false loves; they highlight Israel's neglect of the needy, orphan, widow, and stranger. They also announce judgment for the nations for their pride, idolatry, and violence; their mistreatment of God's people; and their gloating over Israel's judgment. Yet the prophets also proclaim the hope of a glorious future. What will this future be like?

The Hope of Transformation and the Place of the Prophets

Will this future just be a return to the old pattern that led to the exile?[12] Will there be yet more cycles of sin and judgment? Does the hope of Israel rest on future kings who will be no better than the kings who characterized their history, the kings who led the people into sin, idolatry, and exile, the kings who faced the condemnation of the prophets? No! The writing prophets don't point forward to a restoration to the same situation that characterized Israel before the exile. They point forward to a future hope far more glorious than Israel has ever seen. Thus, "transformation" rather than "restoration" is a better term to use. How can they describe a glorious future for God's people that is beyond their ability to comprehend? They do so by using familiar language and institutions to point forward.[13]

Broadly speaking, the prophets took the themes that we have seen being instituted in Israel's history and used them to point forward to a magnificently more glorious future than can be imagined. In our diagram showing the unfolding of these themes throughout this book, the prophets may be characterized as taking up each of the themes to point forward in hope (see fig. 8.4).

Thus, the prophets look forward to a new covenant, a new exodus, a new and perfect dwelling of God with his people in a perfect temple, a final and ultimate sacrifice, a perfect expression of God's law written on the heart of God's transformed people, a new and righteous king who will reign in righteousness and not lead his people into sin, a new Jerusalem—indeed, a new creation! This

---

11. See Robertson, *Christ of the Prophets*, 149–61, 168–73, for references.
12. For this paragraph, see Robertson, *Christ of the Prophets*, 7.
13. See the example provided in chap. 10 n. 2 on understanding the new heavens and new earth.

The Prophetic Hope 111

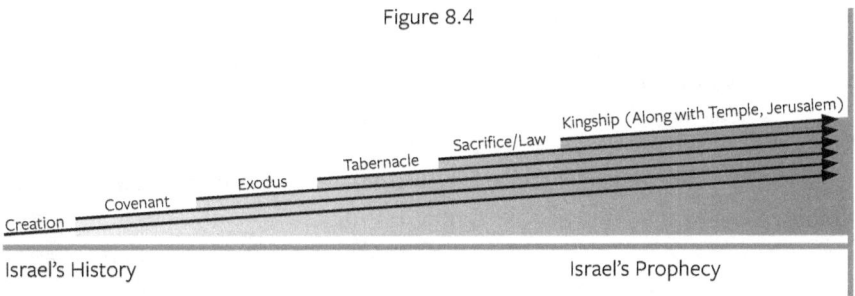

Figure 8.4

is how our Bible fits together. Ultimately, all this is brought about by Jesus. Yet the next two chapters will show that in and through Jesus this prophetic hope has arrived in some ways "already" and in some ways "not yet" in fullness.[14]

Graeme Goldsworthy's broad pattern of God's people, in God's place, and under God's rule can also be used as a way of summarizing the prophetic hope. For example, in terms of place, the prophets look ahead to a new temple in a new Jerusalem, more magnificent than has ever been seen—God's presence will be there, and a river will flow from this temple, giving life to the whole world.[15] Yet this new temple and new Jerusalem are symbolic of a new creation (cf. Isa. 11:6; Ezek. 34:25–30; 40–48; Amos 9:13–14):

> See, I will create
>   new heavens and a new earth.
> The former things will not be remembered,
>   nor will they come to mind.
> But be glad and rejoice forever
>   in what I will create,
> for I will create Jerusalem to be a delight
>   and its people a joy. (Isa. 65:17–18)

---

14. Therefore some interpreters represent the perspective of the prophets with the image of someone looking toward a mountain range. The closer mountaintops may not be distinguishable from the mountaintops in the distance. Thus, the prophets pointed ahead but without necessarily distinguishing between the timing of, say, imminent judgments and an ultimate judgment, or the first and second comings of Jesus (1 Pet. 1:11). Grindheim, *Biblical Theology*, 93. See also Tully, *Reading the Prophets*, 102–8.

15. Some expect the temple of Ezek. 40–48 to still be rebuilt in the future (including with sacrifices and priests; e.g., Ezek. 40:38–46). Yet the emphasis in Ezekiel is on this as an ideal representation of the Lord's presence with his people. Ezekiel 37:26 says this will be "forever." The river of 47:1–12 is picked up in Rev. 22 as symbolic of the eternal refreshment, restoration, life, and fruitfulness in God's presence. There are fewer details here than there were for the tabernacle or Solomon's temple. The perfect symmetry of the dimensions, however, points to God's perfect presence with his perfectly transformed people. The perfect allotment of land pictures the presence of justice and righteousness. Ultimately, the goal, as Ezek. 48:35 says, is that "the Lord is there"—that is, the glory has returned. See the "So what?" section on prophecy in chap. 9, and chap. 10, on the Holy City.

> The LORD will surely comfort Zion
>   and will look with compassion on all her ruins;
> he will make her deserts like Eden,
>   her wastelands like the garden of the LORD. (Isa. 51:3)

Likewise, when the prophets look forward to a restoration of God's rule, they look forward to an ultimate and righteous king, like David—but much better.

> For to us a child is born,
>   to us a son is given.
> . . . .
> Of the greatness of his government and peace
>   there will be no end.
> He will reign on David's throne
>   and over his kingdom,
> establishing and upholding it
>   with justice and righteousness
>   from that time on and forever. (Isa. 9:6–9)

Along with this new expression of God's rule will be a new-covenant arrangement in which God's Spirit will transform God's people, giving them a new heart, writing his law on their hearts so they will obey him (Jer. 31:33; Ezek. 36:26–27).

This means, then, that God's people will be transformed. All individuals in this new covenant will know the Lord personally, through a relationship not mediated by others. This will come about through a new exodus, a deliverance in which a remnant will return to God himself (Isa. 10:21). This transformation will come about through the Servant of the Lord, who will represent God's people and yet also restore God's people, suffering for them the punishment that they deserve (see Isa. 10:20–21; 49:1–6; 52:13–53:12; Jer. 16:14–15). Thus, this chapter draws together and integrates the themes of the preceding chapters and shows how the writing prophets help us put our Bible together. But what happened after the partial restoration we read about in the postexilic prophets Haggai, Zechariah, and Malachi?

The Silent Years

Between the end of the Old Testament and the beginning of the New Testament, there is a period that some commentators call "the silent years." This period is "silent" not because there isn't much we can learn (this is the period in which groups like the Pharisees and Sadducees arose). It is called "silent" because there were no more prophets sent by God to Israel, no more messengers declaring God's will or explaining God's actions. Some Jewish writers of the time refer to this lack of prophets:

> So they tore down the altar, and stored the stones in a convenient place on the temple hill *until a prophet should come* to tell what to do with them. (1 Macc. 4:45–46 NRSV)

> There was great distress in Israel, such as had not been since *the time that prophets ceased* to appear among them. (1 Macc. 9:27 NRSV; cf. 14:41)

> From Artaxerxes to our own time the complete history has been written, but has not been deemed worthy of equal credit with the earlier records, because of *the failure of the exact succession of the prophets*. (Josephus, *Against Apion* 1.41; italics added)

Why this silence? We reached the high point of God's unfolding plan in Israel's history with the institution of kingship and the building of the temple. Therefore, following the events and institutions already put in place in Israel's history, and following the exile and the partial return and the explanations of these events by the prophets, there were no more institutions or salvation-historical events significant for God's unfolding saving plan. As we said above, God's revelation, his words through his prophets, accompanied these events, providing explanations. God's people had all they needed to know to live for him. So, with no more salvation-historical events, there were no more prophets to explain and interpret them.[16] This makes the opening scenes of the New Testament even more significant.

Jesus: The Final Word

When we turn to the opening pages of the New Testament, we read about someone called John the Baptist. He wears unusual clothes and has an unusual diet, and he proclaims a message of repentance in the wilderness. What is he? He is a prophet! What can this mean? It means that a new saving event is on the horizon, and that saving event is bound up with a person—the Messiah, Jesus. Indeed, as Jesus says, John is the greatest of the prophets because he has the awesome privilege of pointing to . . . Jesus (Luke 7:26–28)! All the earlier prophets might have proclaimed that a servant, or a Davidic king, or a great deliverer would come. John gets to point to Jesus and say, "Here he is! It's him! He has come!" John, therefore, is greater than Isaiah, Jeremiah, or Ezekiel.

---

16. Robertson, *Christ of the Prophets*, 114.

Furthermore, Jesus himself is the ultimate prophet, the ultimate revelation or word from God.[17] He reveals and explains God's saving purposes in his own death and resurrection. He is the ultimate prophet who reveals the ultimate act of God's saving plan. Jesus is repeatedly described in terms that recall Moses, but he is greater than Moses. Sure, Moses was there when God provided manna for the people of Israel. But Jesus provides the bread of eternal life! The people wonder, therefore, if he is the prophet to come (John 6:14; 7:40). He also fulfills the role of the ultimate rejected prophet (Acts 3:22, 26).

More than this, however, Jesus is "the Word" (John 1:1). This means that he is the ultimate revelation from God. He reveals the Father perfectly because he is the beloved Son who has come from the Father's side and makes him known (1:17–18). Hebrews 1:1–2 makes explicit this comparison between Jesus and all previous ways God made himself known. If we lay out the verses clause by clause, the contrasts are seen more clearly:

In the past
>God spoke to our ancestors
>>through the prophets at many times and in various ways,

but in these last days
>he has spoken to us
>>by his Son.

By laying out these two verses in this way, we can see an overall common element: God's speech. The contrasts, however, are between two times ("the past" and "these last days"—i.e., the present period since Jesus came), two audiences ("our ancestors" and "us"), and ultimately two ways in which God has spoken. These two ways are not contradictory; they are both expressions of God's speech. They do indicate, however, a qualitative difference. The "past" (i.e., Genesis–Malachi) was characterized by a variety of ways in which God spoke, spread out over many years and in many places. Yet the contrast here implies that this was piecemeal; we might say it came in bits and pieces, "in various ways." The "Son," however, is one singular, complete, unifying, and final revelation. Furthermore, this revelation is qualitatively different—it is the revelation from none other than the Son himself! Thus, once again, Jesus is presented as the ultimate prophet in the sense that he is the ultimate revealer and revelation of God and his salvation.

Yet, remarkably, after saying that John is the greatest prophet because he has pointed to Jesus, Jesus says that every believer is greater than John

---

17. Robertson, *Christ of the Prophets*, 54–65.

The Prophetic Hope

(Luke 7:28). There is a sense, therefore, in which every believer is a prophet. Through Jesus, and with the empowering work of the Spirit, Moses's wish that "all the Lord's people were prophets" (Num. 11:29) sees fulfillment on the day of Pentecost (Acts 2:17–18; cf. Joel 2:28–29). This side of the cross and resurrection, every believer can point to Jesus and say with even greater clarity than John that this suffering, crucified, risen, and reigning Jesus is the Savior, the ultimate revelation and fulfillment of God's promised saving plan.[18]

So What? Some Implications of This Theme of Prophetic Hope

This theme reminds us again of the unity of God's Word. The prophets are connected to the earlier history of Israel by taking up the themes, events, and institutions that were introduced by God in Israel's history, and they paint a glorious future with those themes, events, and institutions, forming the basis for the content of their hope. It is hard for us to know what the age to come will be like, in which God will transform creation, defeat his enemies, remove sin, and renew his people. The language that Israel was familiar with is the language the prophets use to anticipate this hope. God's ultimate saving purposes will be like another exodus deliverance from slavery, but much better; it will be like having a perfect and permanent expression of God's presence in the temple, but much better; it will be like knowing that sin has been dealt with, but much better; it will be like being in a covenant relationship with God, but one that is unbreakable, with complete forgiveness and transformed hearts. It will be like a new creation! Understanding the role of the prophets in salvation history helps us put our Bible together. It builds our appreciation for what we have in the Lord Jesus—he is the perfect revelation of God and of God's saving purposes for us and for the nations that the prophets looked forward to. What a privilege to live this side of the cross and to know that God fulfilled his promises to dwell among his people and to rescue them, to know that he will keep his promise to bring that salvation to its ultimate fulfillment in the new creation, and to point others to the one who reveals and fulfills God's saving purposes for rebellious humanity.

---

18. See Thompson, *Acts of the Risen Lord Jesus*, 132–33.

FOR FURTHER READING

Dempster, Stephen G. "Prophetic Books." In *NDBT*.

Gentry, Peter J. *How to Read and Understand the Biblical Prophets*. Crossway, 2017.

Robertson, O. Palmer. *The Christ of the Prophets*. P&R, 2004. (See also the abridged ed., 2008.)

Tully, Eric J. "Prophet." In *DNTUOT*.

Tully, Eric J. *Reading the Prophets as Christian Scripture: A Literary, Canonical, and Theological Introduction*. Reading Christian Scripture. Baker Academic, 2022.

Williams, Michael J. *The Prophet and His Message: Reading Old Testament Prophecy Today*. P&R, 2003.

TO DIG DEEPER

- How do we interpret Old Testament prophecy now that Jesus, the ultimate prophet and revelation from God, has come? See chapter 9.
- How do we interpret the symbolism and imagery of the prophets? See Bandy and Merkle, *Understanding Prophecy*.
- How do we unpack the specific messages of individual prophetic books? See Robertson, *Christ of the Prophets*, 201–406; Tully, *Reading the Prophets*, 149–387.

9

The Kingdom of God

"Now" and "Not Yet"

In the last chapter we saw that the prophets look forward to a glorious future. Picking up on the events and institutions of Israel's *history*, the *prophets* point toward a greater and new covenant, a greater exodus deliverance, the perfect expression of God's dwelling place, the law written on transformed hearts, a servant who bears sins for the people, and a righteous king who will rule the people and defeat their enemies. In other words, they look forward to the *fulfillment* of the saving rule of God, ultimately in the new heavens and the new earth. Yet when we get to the New Testament, even though Jesus has come, clearly we haven't reached the ultimate transformation of the world. We still suffer the effects of sin and evil in this world. In what way does Jesus bring fulfillment to the patterns of Israel's history that the prophets hope to see in a glorious future? This distinction between what has *already* come and what has *not yet* come is a crucial aspect of understanding how we put our Bible together (and a crucial feature of Christian living). Although we have implied this along the way in each chapter, the arrival of Jesus and specifically his teaching clearly articulates this crucial distinction.

Since we've moved from the Old Testament to the New Testament in each chapter, we have covered many of the themes and their fulfillments in the New Testament already. This chapter will, therefore, briefly review some of what we have covered to show how Jesus brings fulfillments to Old Testament hopes and promises. Following this summary, this chapter will focus on a key feature of Jesus's teaching that will help us better understand the relationship between Old Testament hopes and New Testament fulfillment—Jesus's teaching on the mystery of the "now and not yet" of the kingdom. Finally, we will point to the pervasiveness of this distinction between the "now" and the "not yet" in the New Testament and the implications of this framework for understanding the New Testament, for interpreting Old Testament prophecy, and for Christian living.[1]

Jesus and the Hopes for God's People, Place, and Rule

The broad pattern for God's saving purposes that we noted in chapters 2 and 8 (borrowed from Graeme Goldsworthy) is that of God's people enjoying God's presence in God's place and under God's rule. In the New Testament these threads come together in one person—Jesus.

Jesus and the True People of God

In many ways, Jesus is described as the embodiment of Israel who represents Israel as God's people, and in some places in Scripture he even seems to recapitulate Israel's history. He is the ultimate "seed" (descendant) of Abraham, through whom blessing comes to the world (Gal. 3:16, 19)—a term that we've noted refers to Abraham's descendants in the people of Israel. He is the "true vine" (John 15:1) who bears good fruit. The language of "true" vine means not that Jesus is contrasted with a "false" vine but that he is the ultimate vine, the vine par excellence! This "vine" terminology alludes to passages such as Isaiah 5, which describes Israel as the vineyard that does not bring forth fruit.

In the accounts of Jesus's temptations (Matt. 4:1–11; Luke 4:1–13) Jesus is tempted just like Adam and just like Israel in the wilderness. It is instructive to note that Jesus's quotations in reply to Satan all come from Deuteronomy (6:13, 16; 8:3). The context of Deuteronomy 8 includes references to Israel's forty years in the wilderness and God testing them as a Father with his son.[2] In fact, it is possible that the early chapters of Matthew portray Jesus as embodying Israel, reenacting Israel's history at their foundational event of the

---

1. I will be using the phrase "now and not yet" interchangeably with the phrase "already and not yet."
2. In Matt. 3:17 Jesus is described as the Son with whom the Father is "well pleased." This alludes to the perfect "servant" of Isa. 42:1. This "servant" will represent Israel as well as restore Israel by himself being a "covenant" (cf. Isa. 42:6; 49:3, 5–6). Thus, the essential bond between God and his people depends on the bond between God the Father and this "Son," who will be the perfect servant.

exodus. Note the cluster of references to Egypt (Matt. 2:13–15), the Jordan River (3:1–17), and the wilderness and testing (4:1–11). These locations recall the exodus. In this context, note also that Jesus gives the Sermon on the Mount as a new Moses giving a new law (5:1–7:29).

Matthew 2:15 says that Jesus's return to the land of Israel from Egypt fulfills Hosea 11:1 ("Out of Egypt I called my son").[3] At first glance this seems to be a misreading of Hosea 11:1, since that text looks back to Israel's exodus from Egypt; it is not a prophecy of a future departure from Egypt of God's "son." How is a description of Israel's exodus a prophecy about Jesus? Two factors need to be understood. First, the "son" language. The reason Pharaoh had to let the people of Israel go is because Israel was the Lord's son (Exod. 4:22–23). The Davidic king in 2 Samuel 7, as the representative of Israel, is then also called God's son. (Jeremiah 31:9 also anticipates a new exodus in the return from exile because Israel is God's son.) So, Jesus, as the Davidic king and the embodiment of Israel, is the ultimate "Son"; he represents Israel. Second, Hosea 11:1 refers to Israel's exodus from Egypt as a demonstration of God's love that also points forward to a time when in God's compassion Israel will return to him "from Egypt" (11:10–11). This text sees the exodus as the pattern for Israel's future deliverance (as we unpacked in chap. 4). Thus, Matthew indicates that Jesus's return to the land of Israel "fulfilled" this text in the sense that Jesus is the ultimate embodiment of Israel and God's grace to Israel.

Luke's Gospel places Jesus's genealogy between Jesus's baptism as God's Son (3:22) and Jesus's testing by Satan in the wilderness as God's Son (4:3, 9). Luke's genealogy ends with Jesus as the "son of Adam," who is also the "son of God" (3:38). In other words, Luke picks up on the ancient idea of a son reflecting the likeness of the father and shows that Jesus is the ultimate Adam, the ultimate representative of God's rule (Gen. 1:26–27; 5:1–3). As the obedient son who does not succumb to Satan's temptation, Jesus is the head of a new humanity.

Likewise, in Romans 5 and 1 Corinthians 15 Paul contrasts Jesus with Adam—in particular, Paul contrasts the "first Adam" and the results of his sin with Jesus as the "last Adam" and the results of his righteousness. Therefore, those in Christ are God's new humanity. Jesus fulfills God's hopes for humanity. He is the faithful Israelite, the true, faithful covenant partner. Now the "true Israel" or the "true people of God" are defined not by race or physical descent but by their relationship to Jesus (cf. Gal. 3:26–29; Phil. 3:3). This does not mean that God has rejected Israel (Rom. 11).[4] It means that God's people now, Jew and gentile, are defined by their relationship to Jesus.

3. For the following, see Carson, "Matthew," 118–20.
4. See our discussion of Rom. 9–11 in chap. 11.

Jesus and the Place of God's Presence

In chapters 2, 4, and 8, we noted the development of the theme of "the place" of God's presence from Eden to the tabernacle, to the temple, and then to the hopes for the new temple (Isa. 11:9; 65:17–25; Ezek. 37:24–28; 48:35). This theme is especially developed in John's Gospel. The tabernacle as the dwelling of God with his people is alluded to in John 1:14. Jesus "made his dwelling," or "tabernacled," among us (along with other allusions to Exod. 34 with references to his glory, full of grace and truth). Likewise, in John 2:19–21 Jesus is said to be the temple, and John 4:21–24 says that worship now takes place not through the temple but through the Spirit, whom Jesus gives, and truth—that is, the ultimate revelation now given in Jesus, who is the truth. So, if we want to meet with God, we must go not to a building, a city, or a mountain but to Jesus. Incredibly, because believers belong to Jesus, they have become part of the temple that he is building, a dwelling of God's Spirit (1 Cor. 3:16; Eph. 2:21–22; 1 Pet. 2:5).

Jesus and the Rule of God

Jesus is the ultimate anointed one. He is the ultimate judge and deliverer (the one who bears God's Spirit in his fullness and the one on whom the Spirit remains; John 1:32; 3:34–35); the ultimate king (Luke 1:27, 31–33; Acts 2:29–31); the ultimate lawgiver (Matt. 5–7); and the ultimate prophet, the one who reveals God's character and will (John 1:1–3; Heb. 1:1–3). Thus, believers, through Jesus and his gift of the Spirit, are those who know the Lord, who are anointed, and who point to Jesus, the revealer and fulfillment of God's will (1 John 2:20, 27).

In the broad structure of promise and fulfillment, therefore, the promise of God's plan to restore his creation is ultimately fulfilled in a whole variety of ways in and through Christ. He is the second Adam, the ultimate faithful Israelite, obedient Son, and true servant—that is, he is the embodiment of the obedient covenant partner. Yet, since Jesus is the ultimate ruler, judge, and king, his rule is also what the Old Testament law and prophets were pointing forward to—that is, not only is he the ultimate covenant partner, but he is also the Lord of the covenant. As the fullness of God in bodily form (Col. 2:9), he is the ultimate revelation of God's presence and character, tabernacling among us—the Eden/temple/place we must go to in order to meet God.

Jesus, the one who is the fullness of God and his revelation, enables us to understand what the Old Testament is pointing to. However, obviously everything the Old Testament points to for the new creation has not come to pass. This is why Jesus's teaching on the nature and timing of the kingdom is so important. This teaching filters through the whole of the New Testament. The rest of this chapter, therefore, will unpack this mystery.

Jesus's Teaching on the Now and Not Yet of the Kingdom

As many people know, Jesus often spoke about the kingdom of God. This is the framework we gave at the beginning of this book for understanding how the whole Bible fits together—the kingdom promised and the kingdom fulfilled. As we noted in chapter 1, in the Old Testament the phrase "kingdom of God" can sometimes refer more generally to God's sovereignty over all (Ps. 103:19). In this sense everyone is in God's kingdom, or under God's sovereign rule, whether they realize it or not. However, there was also an expectation for a great reversal when good would triumph, evil would be defeated, and God's rule would come crashing in on all the enemies of God's people, as the following verses indicate:

> For the LORD Almighty will reign
>   on Mount Zion and in Jerusalem,
>   and before its elders—with great glory. (Isa. 24:23)

> In the time of those kings, the God of heaven will set up a kingdom that will never be destroyed. (Dan. 2:44)

> The LORD will be king over the whole earth. On that day there will be one LORD, and his name the only name. (Zech. 14:9)

In this sense there was a broad expectation for *this age* to be followed by a glorious *age to come*, an age of God's unrivaled rule. A common way of picturing this is figure 9.1 (a diagram that we will develop further below).

Figure 9.1

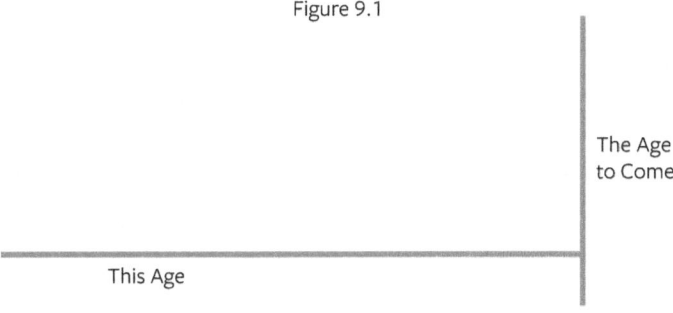

Jesus and the Future Kingdom of God

This future aspect of the arrival of God's rule in fullness is also a feature of Jesus's teaching (e.g., Luke 22:16, 18). He speaks of a future judgment when "the King" will say to those on his right, "Come . . . take your inheritance, the kingdom prepared for you" (Matt. 25:34). Jesus adds that the righteous will then go to "eternal life" (25:46). A similar interchange of language between "enter[ing] the kingdom of God" and inheriting future "eternal life" (or "life of the age to come") is found in Jesus's exchange with the rich young ruler (Matt. 19:16–30; Mark 10:23). However, in one sense, this aspect of Jesus's teaching was not controversial. What was controversial was what he said about the presence of the kingdom.

Jesus and the Present Kingdom of God

The distinctive aspect of Jesus's teaching on the kingdom is that it has arrived already, in advance of the last day. Jesus says in Matthew 12:28 (also Luke 11:20), "The kingdom of God has come upon you." The verb "has come" refers to the actual presence of the kingdom, not merely its proximity. Because some translations of Luke 17:21 read, "The kingdom of God is within you" (KJV, NIV footnote), some Bible readers have misunderstood Jesus to be teaching that the kingdom is more of an internal, "spiritual" reality. However, in this context Jesus is speaking to the Pharisees, and the word used here for "within" (*entos*), when followed by the plural pronoun "you" (i.e., "y'all" [for some US readers] or "you's" [for some Australian readers]), more likely means "among." So, what Jesus says here is that the kingdom of God is "in your midst" (as most translations now have). Jesus does not say to the Pharisees, therefore, that the kingdom is "in" them; he says that the kingdom is present "among" them, because the King is among them! Furthermore, Jesus does not say just that God's kingdom will one day come in fullness. He says that in *him* the kingdom of God is present now; in *him* God's plans of restoration for the world are accomplished. Therefore, this is a reference not just to God's overall sovereign rule, nor merely to the hope of a future saving rule of God, but to something that must be entered now (Matt. 21:31; 23:13); it is a gift that must be received by trusting in Jesus (Mark 10:15; Luke 12:32; 18:16–17).

Since this present aspect of the kingdom was controversial, much of Jesus's teaching concerning the kingdom explained this "already" but "not yet" presence of the kingdom. Many commentators use the phrase "inaugurated eschatology" to explain this aspect of Jesus's teaching. Let's unpack this a little. The theological word "eschatology" refers to events promised for the end or the last days. The word "inaugurated" means that something has begun or been introduced. What this combination, "inaugurated eschatology," means, therefore, is that the kingdom (God's saving rule) that will be seen in its fullness at *the end* in the age to come has been *inaugurated*, or introduced, already, in advance. That is, Jesus says that the promises for God's final saving rule that are part of the scriptural hope for "the end" have come *already* because he has come, but this kingdom that he brings has also *not yet* come in its fullness. I like George Ladd's phrase for this: "the presence of the future."[5] A shorthand way of saying this is the "already and not yet" of the kingdom. This arrival already of the age to come, in Jesus's ministry, gives a preview of this glorious future. Jesus's exorcisms show the ultimate overthrow of Satan, and Jesus's miracles of healing point forward to the removal of death and the renewal and transformation of creation (e.g., Luke 8:26–39; 11:20; 13:10–20).

So, to adapt figure 9.1, what Jesus taught may be described with figure 9.2. The arrow stretching from the age to come to the cross is meant to convey the idea that the future has been brought into the present through Jesus. Jesus brings the blessings of the age to come into this age.

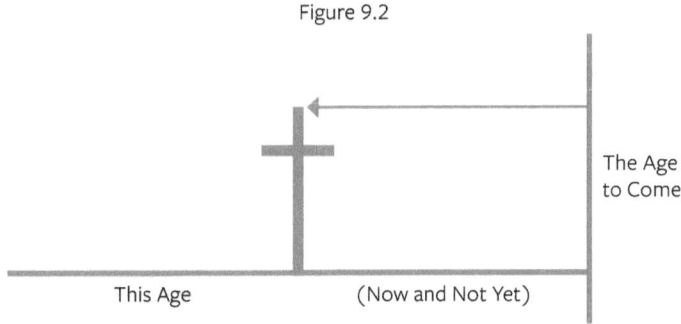

Figure 9.2

This simple framework has enormous implications for our understanding of the whole of the New Testament, for how we put our Bible together, and for our understanding of the Christian life. We will come to these implications later in this chapter. But first, how did Jesus explain this significant development in salvation history?

Parables and the Mystery of the Kingdom

If the Old Testament looks forward to a future reign of God in which evil and enemies are destroyed, but Jesus announces that the kingdom has come already without these features of the final kingdom, then how can he

5. Ladd, *Presence of the Future*.

say that the kingdom has arrived? What does Jesus say the kingdom is like? Jesus's teaching on the "already and not yet" kingdom is especially seen in his parables, particularly his teaching on the mystery of the kingdom in Matthew 13 (see also Mark 4).[6] The central idea of these parables is that the kingdom of God (as the rule of God in its fullness), which will appear at the end of the age, has already come into human history in advance in the person of Jesus. There is both fulfillment within history and completion at the end of history. Jesus explains this idea of the presence of the anticipated kingdom without the accompanying final removal of evil as "the mystery of the kingdom" (Mark 4:11 NASB). The word "mystery" refers to something that was previously hidden but is now revealed in Jesus's teaching and ministry. To see how Jesus explains this, let's briefly walk through the parables of Matthew 13.

The Four Soils (Matt. 13:3–9, 18–23)

The parable of the soils shows the variety of responses to the good news of the kingdom. Even though the kingdom has come, evil is not eradicated, not all who respond initially are genuine, and there is still trouble and persecution. Nevertheless, the kingdom must be received. Some do respond and bear fruit. But mixed responses and continued suffering do not negate the arrival of the kingdom in Jesus's ministry.

The Weeds (Matt. 13:24–30, 36–43)

The parable of the weeds shows that even though the kingdom has come, the final judgment is still to come. The field is the world, and believers and unbelievers coexist in the world. The world is not removed, and believers must continue to live in the world. "Both grow together until the harvest" (Matt. 13:30). Just because the final separation and judgment haven't come yet, that doesn't mean the kingdom hasn't come.

The Mustard Seed (Matt. 13:31–32)

The mustard seed is small. The point is that even though the kingdom has arrived in a small and seemingly insignificant way, this does not mean that the kingdom hasn't come or that it won't eventually prevail. The contrast between the seed and the tree highlights the contrast between the inauguration of the kingdom and the final kingdom in fullness. Don't be fooled by the apparent smallness of the kingdom.

---

6. The following discussion and summary of the parables in Matt. 13 summarize Ladd, *Theology of the New Testament*, 89–97.

The Yeast (Matt. 13:33)

The parable of the yeast makes a point similar to that of the parable of the mustard seed. Although the kingdom seems almost imperceptible, that doesn't mean the kingdom hasn't come. Again, the inauguration of the kingdom may be small, and even hard to detect, but one day it will be all-pervasive. Thus, the emphasis in this parable may also be that one day the kingdom will be unrivaled. The rule of the kingdom will one day be seen in its fullness.

The Treasure and the Pearl (Matt. 13:44–46)

The parables of the treasure and the pearl highlight the infinite value of the kingdom. Even though the kingdom has come into this world in a small and apparently insignificant way, this does not mean that the kingdom is of no value. The significance of the kingdom could easily be overlooked. Yet Jesus's kingdom is supremely valuable and precious and must be sought and valued above all else.

The Net (Matt. 13:47–50)

Like the parable of the weeds, the parable of the net addresses the question of the arrival of the kingdom without the expected judgment of evil. The kingdom has indeed arrived. Yet the final judgment of the wicked will most assuredly also take place. Until then, it is possible for appearances to be deceiving (e.g., Judas). Just because the kingdom has not brought the final judgment in advance does not mean there is no judgment to come.

The God of the Kingdom

Further assurance of the arrival of God's kingdom for Jesus's disciples comes from the phrase "kingdom of God" itself (and the equivalent phrase "kingdom of heaven"). This phrase reminds us that this is God's kingdom! That is, it belongs to him, it is subject to him, and it is the outworking of his purposes in keeping with his character. Some authors have highlighted this aspect in their paraphrases of this phrase: R. T. France paraphrases it as "God in saving action." G. Beasley-Murray paraphrases it as "God's saving sovereignty."[7] The various verbs or action words associated with the phrase in the passages in table 9.1 highlight the kingdom as the outworking of God's purposes.[8]

---

7. France, *Divine Government*, 13, 15; Beasley-Murray, *Jesus and the Kingdom of God*, 74, 125, 339.
8. Ladd, *Theology of the New Testament*, 101–2.

Table 9.1

"Kingdom of God" Passages	Verbs/Action Referring to the Kingdom
Matthew 3:2; 4:17; Mark 1:15	The kingdom can draw near
Matthew 6:10; 12:28; Luke 17:20	The kingdom comes/arrives
Luke 19:11	The kingdom appears
Matthew 21:43; Luke 12:32	God gives the kingdom to people, or he can take it away
Matthew 5:20; 7:21; Mark 9:47; 10:23	People can enter the kingdom
Mark 10:15; Luke 18:17	People receive the kingdom
Matthew 25:34	People inherit the kingdom
Matthew 5:3	People possess the kingdom
Matthew 23:13; Luke 10:11	People can refuse to receive or enter the kingdom
Luke 23:51	People can look for the kingdom or pray for it and seek it
Matthew 5:19; 8:11; Luke 13:29	People may be in the kingdom
Matthew 10:7; Luke 10:9	People can preach the kingdom

In these passages the kingdom is not destroyed, established, or brought into being by people. The kingdom is God's. As George Ladd observes, "The Kingdom is the outworking of the divine will; it is the act of God himself. It is [of course] related to human beings and can work in and through them; but it never becomes subject to them. It remains God's Kingdom."[9] God is the one who brings the kingdom. We, as his people through Christ, enter it, receive it, and proclaim it, but we don't "grow it." It is not subject to us. In this sense the church is "the community of the kingdom."[10]

Jesus's disciples can take much encouragement from his teaching on the now and not yet of the kingdom. God's work will be accomplished in God's way. There are divided responses, there is continued persecution, and evil is still present in the world, yet God's saving rule through Jesus's life, death, and resurrection has truly arrived and is being made known in the world and received as people trust in him. Jesus's ministry, however, provides a preview of this glorious future.

So What? Some Implications of the Now and Not Yet of the Kingdom

If we combine the theme of the last chapter (that the prophets look forward to a glorious future, a new creation, covenant, exodus, law, sacrifice, and king) and the theme of this chapter (that Jesus announces he is the fulfillment of

---

9. Ladd, *Theology of the New Testament*, 102.
10. Ladd, *Theology of the New Testament*, 109.

these hopes and the one inaugurating God's saving rule), then we can begin to see the significance of this theme of inaugurated eschatology (the now and not yet of God's saving plan). We will note three significant implications here.

1. New Testament Theology

Inaugurated eschatology (the now and not yet) is pervasive in the New Testament. We will briefly summarize some big topics that each could require their own book. Each of these topics is better understood through this teaching of inaugurated eschatology. These topics, while not identical with the phrase "kingdom of God," are all aspects of this saving rule of God.[11] Let's start with "justification." This is a legal word that refers to a verdict in which one is declared righteous. Strictly speaking, it should be reserved for the end, when we will appear before God to receive the King's verdict of either acquittal or condemnation at the final judgment. However, in Romans 5:1 Paul says, "We *have been* justified through faith," and in 5:9, "We *have now been* justified by his blood" (see also 1 Cor. 6:11). In other words, amazingly, this verdict has already been rendered for those who belong to Jesus by faith.

We have focused on the way the Gospels of Matthew, Mark, and Luke refer to both the presence of the kingdom in Jesus and the future fullness of the kingdom of God. This same framework is used in John's Gospel with reference to "eternal life." On the one hand, this is a way of speaking of the life of the age to come (Isa. 26:19; Dan. 12:1–2). In John 6:39–40 Jesus says those who have been given to him from the Father will be raised up "at the last day" and shall have "eternal life." On the other hand, John also emphasizes that those who believe in Jesus have this eternal life already! Jesus declares, "Whoever hears my word and believes him who sent me *has* eternal life and will not be judged but *has crossed over from death to life*" (John 5:24).

This framework of now and not yet is also key to understanding Paul's teaching about the Holy Spirit. In keeping with the promises of the prophetic hope, the Holy Spirit is called the "promised Holy Spirit" (Eph. 1:13; cf. Acts 2:33, 38–39; Gal. 3:14). Thus, in salvation-historical terms Paul can contrast the law of the Mosaic covenant with the Spirit of the new covenant (2 Cor. 3:6–8; cf. Rom. 7:6; Gal. 5:18). Yet Paul also speaks of the Spirit with the language of inaugurated eschatology (or, as Ladd puts it, "the presence of the future"). Paul describes the Spirit as a "deposit" (or "down payment," 2 Cor. 1:22; 5:5; Eph. 1:14). A deposit, of course, is an initial payment, guaranteeing

---

11. E.g., the life of the kingdom (Matt. 25:34, 46), the Spirit poured out as Jesus reigns (Acts 1:3–5), the "reign" of grace (Rom. 5:21).

a full and complete future payment. A deposit is a part of more to come. It is inherently future looking, a foretaste of the full amount. This is why the NIV translates the Greek phrase "the deposit of the Spirit" (to render a more word-for-word translation) in 2 Corinthians 1:22 and 5:5 as "a deposit, guaranteeing what is to come" (see Eph. 1:14). With the phrase "guaranteeing what is to come," the NIV communicates the future orientation inherent in the term "deposit." This is similar to Paul's "firstfruits" language (Rom. 8:23). Picked up from Old Testament harvest terminology, the firstfruits are the first indicators of the full harvest yet to come. There is a greater and fuller experience of God's presence to come!

Paul also speaks of the resurrection in this way. Jesus's resurrection is the firstfruits in the sense that it is the first of the general resurrection that will occur at the end of time. Jesus's resurrection is also the guarantee of the resurrection to eternal life for all those who belong to him (1 Cor. 15:20, 23). Because Jesus is the "last Adam" (1 Cor. 15:45; cf. 15:22), all those who belong to him are part of the new humanity. Jesus's resurrection, therefore, signals his headship over a new humanity (Col. 1:18). Thus, the "now and not yet" framework also applies to Jesus's resurrection. Jesus's resurrection has already brought into this age the life of the age to come, in advance, for all those who belong to him. In the book of Acts, the risen Lord Jesus, as the "first to rise from the dead" (in the sense of a full and final resurrection, not just a "resuscitation" like with Lazarus or Eutychus, John 11; Acts 20), is the embodiment of the "hope of Israel" for the final resurrection (e.g., Acts 24:15, 21; 26:6–8, 22–23).[12] Because believers belong to the risen Lord Jesus, their resurrection is inseparably tied to his. So we look forward to the new creation that his miracles and resurrection point toward.

The Christian life can also be understood within this framework. Romans 5:12–21 is especially important for understanding what Paul says about the Christian life in Romans 6–8. In 5:12–21 Paul makes several contrasts between Adam and Christ and the effects of each man's actions. He builds on these contrasts throughout Romans 6–8. (Below, I will briefly explain the significance of the circles and arrow in fig. 9.3.)

These contrasts are the basis for Paul's argument that the one who belongs to Christ has experienced what some commentators call a "realm transfer."[13] The believer is no longer under the rule of sin, death, and condemnation

---

12. Thompson, *Acts of the Risen Lord Jesus*, 71–88.
13. I am influenced by Doug Moo's many works on Romans here. See Moo, *Theology of Paul*, 34–35, 218, in Zondervan's Biblical Theology of the New Testament series. Moo's volume is appropriately subtitled *The Gift of the New Realm in Christ*.

Figure 9.3

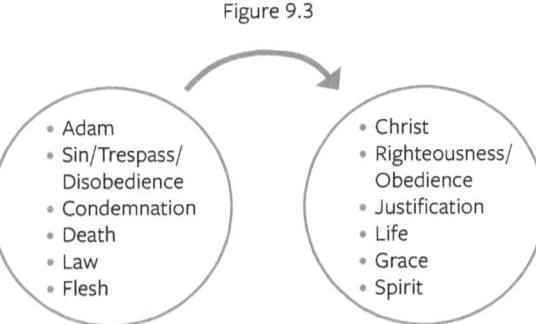

because of Adam and our association with him. Nor are we still helpless in the weakness and sinfulness of our flesh, with the law incapable of delivering us. No, by God's grace, through Christ, we have been "transferred" out of that realm and into the realm in which grace reigns (Rom. 5:21). No longer under condemnation and death, we have justification and life. No longer helpless in the weakness and sinfulness of our flesh, we who belong to Christ have the Spirit and life (7:6; 8:9). Thus, we have "crossed over" from death to life, from condemnation to justification—already! Yet, of course, we still sin. Paul still commands believers not to "let sin reign" (6:12) and to "put to death the misdeeds of the body" (8:13). We still have bodies that are "subject to death" (8:10). In other words, although a significant change has come to the believer in Jesus, there is a "not yet" aspect to all this. We are new people, yet we still feel the pull of the old (Col. 3:1–11).

2. Old Testament Prophecy

This framework illustrates a way of reading the Bible that prioritizes God's later revelation in Christ in order to better understand what the Old Testament points forward to, without changing what the Old Testament anticipates. One specific example of this relates to the prophecy of a grand temple in Ezekiel that we touched on in chapter 8, on the prophetic hope.[14] Some interpreters who read the Bible only forward from the Old Testament to the New may get to the New Testament, so to speak, expecting a focus on a restored Israel, with a much greater and permanent temple as Ezekiel describes (overlooking for now that Ezekiel more likely speaks in ideal terms of a perfect dwelling of God with his people).[15] In this view,

---

14. See also n. 15 in chap. 8.
15. E.g., Pentecost, *Things to Come*, 512–31; Saucy, *Case for Progressive Dispensationalism*, 31, 89, 165, 232, 290, 295. See also Bock ("Progressive Dispensationalism," 124–26), and

since these things didn't happen with the arrival of Jesus, they must be postponed until a later time (a future millennium—more on that in the next chapter). This might be visualized as in figure 9.4.

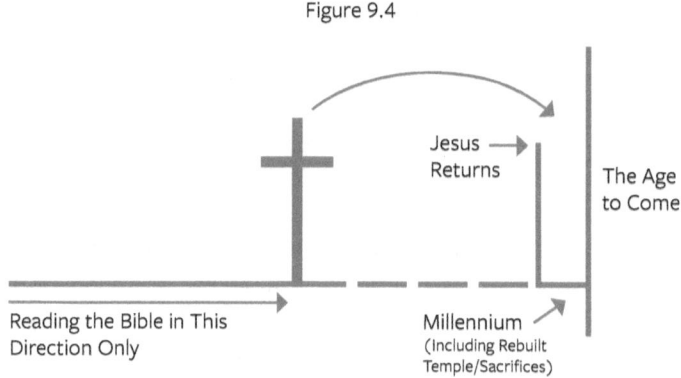

Figure 9.4

This focus on a future temple (and sacrificial system) overlooks what is said about Jesus in the New Testament. He is the ultimate meeting place between God and humanity and the fulfillment and goal of the temple and sacrificial system. He is the object of our worship, and he enables true worship. He now builds his temple, his people, among whom God dwells by his Spirit. To go back to the temple is to go backward in salvation history. There was a trajectory from Eden to the tabernacle to Solomon's temple to Ezekiel's ideal and permanent temple. Now that Jesus has come, we can look back and better see what this trajectory was pointing toward (our discussion of Rev. 21–22 in the next chapter will add to this).

Likewise, Joel 2 looks forward to the Lord pouring out his Spirit on Israel, and Jeremiah 31 looks forward to a new covenant with the people of Israel. Yet because of Jesus, the embodiment of Israel and the one who restores Israel, Acts 2 says Joel's promise of the Spirit is fulfilled for those who belong to Jesus, and Hebrews 8 says Jeremiah's promise of the new covenant is fulfilled for those who belong to Jesus.[16] As we noted above, Paul regularly insists that his proclamation of the risen Lord Jesus as the embodiment of the hope of

---

Snoeberger ("Traditional Dispensationalism," 244–45) in Parker and Lucas, *Covenantal and Dispensational Theologies*. Since Ezekiel's vision of a glorious temple includes a sacrificial system, there is also some discussion in this view about how sacrifices might operate in this future temple.

16. The apostles' question about Jesus's plans to restore Israel (Acts 1:6) is answered by Jesus with reference to their reception of the promised Spirit and their witness of Jesus (fulfilling Isa. 32:15; 43:10–12; 49:5–6) in Jerusalem, Judea and Samaria (i.e., Israel), and to the gentiles (Acts 1:8). Peter, therefore, proclaims the fulfillment of God's promise for "all Israel" (2:36; cf. 2:14,

Israel is what Moses and the prophets said (Acts 24:14–15; 26:22–23). This is what Jesus himself says—that the Scriptures are about him and that they point forward to his death and resurrection, *and also* to the spread of the good news to the nations (Luke 24:44–47; cf. Acts 3:24). In summary, since Jesus is the goal of the Scriptures, Jesus (and his apostles) enables us to better understand what those Scriptures point toward.

3. Balancing Expectations in Christian Life and Ministry

Finally, this "now and not yet" framework of the New Testament also helps us with our expectations for the Christian life and for Christian ministry. We "already" have forgiveness of sins, justification, the gift and presence of the Spirit, and new and everlasting life.[17] But we must not forget the "not yet" aspects of God's saving rule. That is, we must not overlook, downplay, or forget that this life is still characterized by suffering, sickness, and death. We do not yet have our resurrection bodies. There is still more to come! Downplaying the "not yet" aspect of God's saving rule may be evident when people overemphasize miracles, health, and wealth, or the transformation of the nations.[18] This may also be evident when people are always impressed with the outwardly spectacular, the big event, perhaps forgetting what Jesus said in the parable of the sower (Matt. 13) about the nature of the kingdom in this age.

An opposite possibility is overemphasizing the nature of the opposition the gospel faces in this world or the extent of suffering, thereby neglecting or downplaying God's continued work to spread the gospel through the reign of the Lord Jesus by his Spirit-empowered people. This neglect of what we "already" have may then lead us to miss all the assurances in the New Testament of God's gracious purposes being worked out in our lives to conform us to the likeness of the Lord Jesus.

In summary, in this overlap of the ages we have much to be thankful for. In Christ, we have the greater revelation of God's saving purposes, the assurance of sins forgiven, the blessings of a new heart and a new-covenant relationship with God by his Spirit, and the assurance of security in Christ for the future judgment (Rom. 5–8). Yet we still groan in our weakness (Rom. 8:26) and long for the fullness of the kingdom, knowing that "we must go through many hardships" to enter the kingdom in fullness (Acts 14:22). It is to the final goal, therefore, that we turn for our second-to-last chapter.

22, 29). Thus, Jesus does not exclude Israel from God's saving rule. See on Rom. 11 in our next chapter. Cf. Thompson, *Acts of the Risen Lord Jesus*, 103–11.

17. As we noted above, this framework is commonly called "inaugurated eschatology."
18. This could be called "overrealized eschatology" or "triumphalism."

FOR FURTHER READING

Ladd, George Eldon. *Crucial Questions About the Kingdom of God*. Eerdmans, 1952.

Ladd, George Eldon. *A Theology of the New Testament*. Rev. ed. Eerdmans, 1994. (See esp. 54–117.)

Morgan, Christopher W., and Robert A. Peterson, eds. *The Kingdom of God*. Crossway, 2012.

VanDrunen, David. *Living in God's Two Kingdoms: A Biblical Vision for Christianity and Culture*. Crossway, 2010.

TO DIG DEEPER

- How does this framework of "already and not yet" affect our understanding of the mission of the church in this era? A good book to get oriented to this discussion is DeYoung and Gilbert, *What Is the Mission of the Church?*
- How does this framework relate to Luke's account of the early church and the spread of the gospel in the book of Acts? See Thompson, *Acts of the Risen Lord Jesus*.
- What does the New Testament's focus on fulfillment mean for our understanding of God's purposes for Israel between the "now" and the "not yet"? Romans 9–11 is especially important here. See Compton and Naselli, *Three Views on Israel and the Church*; Parker and Lucas, *Covenantal and Dispensational Theologies* (and the brief summary at the end of the next chapter).
- Once again, this framework highlights the importance of thinking through the ways that the New Testament authors use the Old Testament. See the books listed at the end of chapter 1.

10

The Holy City

Complete Transformation at Last

With this chapter we have reached the end—the end of the Bible as well as the end goal of God's saving plans (and almost the end of this book). Throughout this book we have seen that, following the expulsion of Adam and Eve from God's presence in Eden, God has been fulfilling his purposes to bring about the glorious eternal transformation and renewal of his people so that they may enjoy his presence. In the last chapter we noted how the various strands that run through the Bible come together in Jesus. However, a crucial part of Jesus's teaching is that the fullness of the kingdom is yet to come. Since we have regularly made this connection throughout this book, we will first briefly review the main elements of this future hope that we have covered. The focus of this chapter, however, is on what we can learn about the end goal from Revelation 21–22, after John announces the arrival of the new heavens and the new earth. John's focus here helps keep us focused on God's ultimate goal throughout the patterns of Israel's *history*, the hopes of Israel's *prophets*, and the *fulfillment* in and through Jesus. We will conclude the chapter with a summary of two matters that Christians disagree about concerning events associated with the end: the millennium and the future of Israel. We touch on them at this point because these discussions often make a big difference to how we put our Bible together. First, let's briefly summarize the anticipation of the goal of the final transformation in the material we've covered.

Anticipation of a New Creation

In chapters 2 (creation/rebellion), 3 (covenant), and 4 (exodus/tabernacle) we saw that Israel's history provides hints of Eden-like blessing in Israel's land. Although Adam's disobedience results in expulsion from God's presence in Eden, the creation language of the tabernacle and temple provides glimpses or hints of "little Edens" along the way—symbolizing access to God's presence. Israel's Mosaic covenant shows the way of obedience in the land and Eden-like blessing (Lev. 26:1–13). At the high point of Israel's history, Solomon's kingship and temple point to Eden-like blessing in the land (1 Kings 4:20–28). Exile from the land means exile from the blessing of God's presence (2 Kings 17:18–20).

In these same chapters, and especially in chapter 8 (on the prophetic hope), we saw that Israel's prophecy looks forward to a "new heavens and a new earth" (Isa. 65:17; cf. 11:6–9; 27:6; 65:25; 66:22). The prophets point to a return to God (10:21). There will be harmony in the new creation, God's wrath will be removed (12:1), and God's people will be restored and given obedient hearts; they will be transformed and enjoy the blessing of God's presence (Ezek. 40–48).

In the last chapter we saw that the New Testament is permeated with what many commentators call "inaugurated eschatology" (because of Jesus's teaching on the presence of God's saving purposes already, in anticipation of the future fullness of those purposes). The transformation that is reserved for the age to come has, in many ways, already begun. Jesus's resurrection, in particular, brings into this age something reserved only for "the end" (i.e., the end-time resurrection of the dead). Those who belong to Jesus enjoy already the verdict "declared righteous," the gift of the life of the age to come (eternal life), and the presence of the Spirit (guaranteeing what is to come). The New Testament uses "new creation" language to describe this reality enjoyed by believers. "If anyone is in Christ," Paul says, "the new creation has come" (2 Cor. 5:17). Believers belong to the new creation because they belong to Christ. Likewise, Paul says, "Neither circumcision nor uncircumcision means anything; what counts is the new creation" (Gal. 6:15). Similar "new creation" language is implied in John 1 and Colossians 1, where Jesus is the Lord and Creator of both the old and the new creation. Colossians 1 especially highlights Jesus's resurrection as the sign that he is the "beginning" and "head" of his new humanity so that "in everything he might have the supremacy" (1:18). Thus, from Genesis, through hints in Israel's history, hopes in Israel's prophets, and fulfillment through Christ, God's saving plan anticipates a new creation. However, one question that I have omitted so far is What is this new creation? Let's discuss this briefly before we get to Revelation 21–22.

The New Creation: Restoration, or Dissolution and Replacement?

One of the questions that we haven't covered yet is whether the Bible points to a restoration of the current creation or whether the new creation is something that is entirely new and replaces the old one, which is destroyed and done away with. We could use the language of "discontinuity" (no connection with this creation) or "continuity" (this current creation restored) to highlight the question. Some passages in the Bible appear to point one way, and some passages appear to point a different way. Two representative passages are Romans 8:18–25 and 2 Peter 3:10–13.

Romans 8:18–25 looks like restoration is in view (i.e., continuity). It is this current creation, which is groaning, that is "waiting" to be "liberated from its bondage to decay" (8:19, 21). Second Peter 3:10–13, however, sounds more like a total destruction of the old is in view (i.e., discontinuity). The words "disappear" and "destroy" appear frequently (3:10, 11, 12). We should note, however, that the language of "destruction" in 2 Peter refers to a total change from what was there before rather than total annihilation. The flood is used as a comparison in the preceding context (3:6–7): "The world of that time was deluged and destroyed" (3:6). The destruction of the flood led not to nonexistence but to a total change and removal of the old. Even in English we might use the word "destroyed" for an overwhelming defeat of a sports team or more seriously for the effects of a storm on a town. When we use the word in these ways, we mean something more like "unrecognizable from what it was before" rather than "no longer in physical existence at all." A removal of the old seems evident in the reference in 2 Peter 3:7 to the "day of judgment and destruction of *the ungodly*" (not nonexistence but judgment). The "new heaven" and "new earth" that we look forward to is "where righteousness dwells" (3:13).[1]

Nevertheless, this emphasis on fire and the disappearance and destruction of the elements, together with passages such as Hebrews 1:10–12 and Luke 21:33, leads me to be cautious about the amount of certainty we can have about how much continuity to expect. Certainly, the emphasis in 2 Peter is on purification and transformation. Yet there also seems to be an emphasis on a total change—to the extent that the new creation could be very different from what we know or currently experience. Romans 8 reminds us that

---

1. Jesus's resurrection body was both similar (i.e., the body that went into the tomb was the body that came out of the tomb) and yet dissimilar to his previous bodily existence (it was transformed and seemingly able to appear with his disciples in a locked room). In 1 Cor. 15:35–38 Paul compares a seed to a plant to illustrate the nature of our own resurrection bodies. In that illustration there is continuity, but a significant transformation!

there will be continuity as well. I think our speculation about what the new creation will be like needs to be tempered with a level of uncertainty, since it is beyond our capacity to grasp at this point. It is enough to say that there will be continuity and discontinuity with the current creation, but the new creation will be much more glorious than we can imagine.[2]

Let us now zero in on the one passage that tells us the most about the new creation, Revelation 21. We will do this because, with a range of images from the Old Testament, especially Isaiah and Ezekiel, this passage focuses our attention on what the goal of God's saving plan has been all along—the dwelling of God with his people, and the people of God enjoying his presence forever. This illustrates the theme of this book, that the Old Testament patterns in Israel's history and prophecy help us understand the New Testament and that the fuller revelation in the New Testament completes the picture, showing us what the goal was all along.

The Holy City, the Bride: Revelation 21:1–22:5

A New Home for the Bride (Rev. 21:1–8)[3]

The opening eight verses of Revelation 21 are tied to the previous verses by showing us the outcome for those who are in the Lamb's book of life. The primary purpose of 21:1–8, however, is to prepare us for the description of

---

2. An illustration I heard from Don Carson about our comprehension of eternity is that it is like trying to explain what electricity is like to those who have never experienced it, such as to a remote tribe.

> You will say, in their language, "I've come to tell you about something. . . . Well, you don't have a word for it. Let's call it electricity. Electricity is like a powerful spirit that runs . . . along vines. . . . In fact, what we do is we loop these vines from tree to tree . . . and then we pump in this electricity at one end in this hard thing like a vine, and at the other end, it loops through the trees until it comes to our mud hut. It comes through our thatched roof, and up inside our thatched roof, we have little round things that we make. The electricity goes in there and goes around and around so fast that it makes a little light, like a small sun or something, so you can stay up late at night."

The illustration goes on to explain how electricity helps boil water, and so on. At this point Carson notes that he has said nothing about AC or DC or computers and so on. All this is unfamiliar to them, not because of any lack of intelligence but because of a lack of exposure to electricity. The explanation uses what they do know, such as vines, trees, and sun, to explain what they have never experienced. The same applies to our grasp of what eternity will be like. I also think that the same applies to reading the Old Testament prophets. They spoke of a glorious future of God's eternal presence with language Israel was familiar with, such as a temple with perfect dimensions! See Carson, "Revelation—Part 7."

3. This heading and the following summary of this passage are taken from Johnson, *Triumph of the Lamb*, 301–31.

The Holy City

the bride in the following verses, where the focus is on the dwelling of God with his people (terms and images introduced in 21:1–8 will be developed further in 21:9–22:5).

"A New Heaven and a New Earth" (Rev. 21:1)

The opening words in Revelation 21:1 reflect the hopes of Isaiah 65:17–25 (cf. 66:22). The reference to "a new heaven and a new earth" and the passing away of "the first heaven and the first earth" with no more sea sounds like the language of destruction in 2 Peter that we mentioned above. However, Revelation 21:4 unpacks what it is that has passed away—death, pain, and the "old order of things." The absence of the sea is symbolic of the absence of evil and hostile forces that would threaten the peace and security of the new home (see Rev. 13:1). It is symbolic of the permanent removal of all challenges to God's order.

Announcing the Bride (Rev. 21:2)

In Revelation 21:2 we're told that John sees "the Holy City, the new Jerusalem" (cf. Isa. 52:1; 65:19). This will be important when we come to the next section. This "Holy City," however, is "prepared as a bride." This announcement of the bride in verse 2 anticipates her entrance in the next section (21:9). The placement of this announcement here emphasizes that the new heaven and new earth is the perfect home for her.[4]

Fulfillment at Last! (Rev. 21:3–4)

Verses 3–4 explain what John has just seen: "Look! God's dwelling place is now among the people, and he will dwell with them. They will be his people, and God himself will be with them and be their God" (see Ezek. 37:27). This has been the goal all along! This is the culmination of the covenant formula that has been running throughout Scripture (see the discussion in chap. 3, on covenants). The aim all along has been for God's people to enjoy his presence. Verse 4 beautifully portrays the result: "*He* will wipe every tear from their eyes." God's presence is what brings ultimate eternal comfort and joy. He is the reason why there will be no more mourning or crying or pain. Death has been defeated—finally and completely—and he has done away with all things associated with death (cf. Isa. 25:8; 65:19–20). Again, this proclamation of God's presence is the key to understanding the following section (21:9–22:5).

---

4. Johnson, *Triumph of the Lamb*, 304: "The perfect home—is for her sake."

The Sovereign Lord (Rev. 21:5-6)

The announcement that God is "the Alpha and the Omega, the Beginning and the End" (because *alpha* is the first letter of the Greek alphabet, and *omega* is the last letter; Rev. 21:6) emphasizes God's sovereign control over history and the outworking of his purposes. The idea is that if he's both the beginning and the end, then he's also in control of everything in between. In this context, the emphasis is on God accomplishing his saving purposes—we have reached the culmination of God's purposes (cf. Isa. 42:9; 43:18–19).

The Recipients (Rev. 21:7-8)

Finally, before John turns to the vision, he contrasts two groups of people who face eternity—those who receive "water without cost" (Rev. 21:6), who know the covenant Lord, and those who are unbelieving and idolatrous. One group receives life; the other faces the second (eternal) death—the ultimate and eternal judgment of separation from God's good presence.

The Bride (Rev. 21:9–22:5)

In Revelation 21:9 the angel says to John, "Come, I will show you the bride, the wife of the Lamb."[5] Who is the bride? "The bride" is a reference to the people of God—those who belong to Christ. We expect, therefore, to see a group of people. In 21:10, however, the angel shows John "the Holy City, Jerusalem" (see Ezek. 40:2, 5). Wait, what? What does this mean? Remember, this same combination was given in Revelation 21:2. This means that the following description of "the Holy City, the new Jerusalem" is actually a description of . . . the bride! The following dimensions and imagery, therefore, describe various aspects of God's people—us. Let us now unpack the symbolic language that describes the bride.

Beauty (Rev. 21:11, 18-21)

The dazzling light and shining brilliance of costly, "clear as crystal" jasper (Rev. 21:11) emphasize beauty. Verses 18–21 describe precious stones that could allude to a number of things in the Old Testament, such as Eden's beauty (Gen. 2:12; Ezek. 28:12–19), the high priest's breastplate (Exod. 28:15–21; 39:8–14), or the precious value of Jerusalem (Isa. 54:11–12). The beauty and costly nature of these stones symbolize the spiritual quality of purity and the

---

5. This section on Rev. 21:9–22:5 summarizes the arguments of Johnson, *Triumph of the Lamb*, 308–24; and Gundry, "New Jerusalem" (who is cited by Johnson).

infinite value of the people of God. God's people have been transformed into the likeness of the glorious Son—pure and holy, no longer stained with sin.

Complete (Rev. 21:12–14, 24)

The reference to the twelve tribes of Israel and the twelve apostles (in Rev. 21:14), along with the repeated references to "twelve," emphasizes that this is the whole redeemed covenant people of God (cf. Isa. 60:3–5; Ezek. 48:31)—God's old- and new-covenant people are together. This is seen also in the reference to nations in verse 24. God's people are complete; none of God's people are missing.

Safe and Secure (Rev. 21:12, 15–17, 25)

In Revelation 21:12 John says that this city has a "great, high wall." In verses 15–17 John then provides the dimensions for the wall (cf. Ezek. 41:13; 42:16–20; 45:1–3). This truly is a "great" wall! In 21:16 John says that the wall is 12,000 stadia long. The NIV provides a footnote to clarify that this is about 1,400 miles, or about 2,200 kilometers, long. For Australian readers, that makes the wall roughly the length of a drive from Sydney to Townsville. For US readers, the wall is about a drive from San Diego to Kansas City.[6] The idea is that this is a long wall. The height of the wall is the same. So, this wall extends 1,400 miles / 2,200 kilometers into the sky. In 21:17 John tells us the thickness of the wall—144 cubits, which is about 200 feet or 65 meters. This is a little less than the width of a rugby field (and a little more than the width of an American football field). That is a very thick wall!

What do these figures mean? Remember that John has told us he is describing "the bride, the wife of the Lamb," who is "the Holy City, Jerusalem." Therefore, just as the number twelve in the preceding verses was symbolic of the complete nature of God's people, so these dimensions are not giving us the actual dimensions of a very high or very long or very thick wall—they are communicating safety and security. Unlike elsewhere in Revelation, God's people finally find rest and peace and are no longer threatened by the enemies of God. However, in verse 25 it looks like someone has accidentally left the gates open (Isa. 60:11). Why have such high and impenetrable walls if the gates are left open? This is again symbolic language, communicating safety ("for there will be no night," referring to when the gates of a city would normally be shut for security reasons).

---

6. British readers would need to complete a return trip from the lowest point of England to the top of Scotland!

In the Presence of God (Rev. 21:16, 22–23)

Let's return to the measurements in verse 16. John states that the city is a square. Then he adds that the measurement 12,000 stadia (again, the number twelve is symbolic) is the same for the length, width, and height. That's a cube. Where else in the Bible do we encounter a cube? In the holy of holies (Exod. 26:15–25; 1 Kings 6:20; 2 Chron. 3:8–9; Ezek. 41:4). Remember what John is describing here. He is describing the bride. What does this mean, then? The bride experiences the presence of God. This is why John later says that there is no "temple in the city, because the Lord God Almighty and the Lamb are its temple" (Rev. 21:22). This is a way of saying that finally God's people experience the joy of God's presence eternally (Isa. 60:19–20; Ezek. 48:35). Remember the introduction to this section? After the Holy City, prepared as a bride beautifully dressed, comes down, the loud voice from the throne says, "Look! God's dwelling place is now among the people, and he will dwell with them" (Rev. 21:3).

If we were to measure out the dimensions that John provides, the scale of the city might reflect figure 10.1. However, it is important to read Revelation 21:2 and 21:9–10 together so we recognize that John is describing the transformed bride in the presence of God, secured by Christ, the Lamb (Rev. 5:1–14).

Figure 10.1

Courtesy of TourOfHeaven.com

https://tourofheaven.com/eternal-heaven/new-jerusalem/size-of-new-jerusalem

Abundant Provision for the Bride (Rev. 22:1–5)

The focus here is on "the abundant life, refreshment, and nourishment that the Lord will provide for his people."[7] The image of life-giving water from

---

7. Johnson, *Triumph of the Lamb*, 319–20.

"the throne of God and of the Lamb" (Rev. 22:1, 3) picks up the promises of the prophets, especially Ezekiel, regarding the work of the Spirit, who cleanses and brings life (Gen. 2:9–10; Isa. 44:3; Ezek. 36:25–27; 37:9–10, 14; 47:1–12). The fruit and healing leaves highlight a contrast with Eden (Rev. 22:2; cf. Zech. 14:8, 11). Thus, Revelation 22:3 emphasizes that there will no longer be any curse—again, looking back to Eden (reflecting the wording of 21:4: "There will no longer be any death," NASB). The water, fruit, and leaves are therefore symbolic of complete and satisfying life in God's presence. The reference to the presence of the "throne of God and of the Lamb" without any need for the sun again emphasizes the presence of God (Isa. 60:19–20). With the removal of the threat of death and Satan, as we noted in chapter 2, the consummation is better than Eden. With no sin or guilt, believers will "see his face" (Rev. 22:4), and with resurrection bodies no longer subject to death, believers will finally enjoy his presence forever!

In Summary: God's People Enjoying God's Presence

Just when we might expect to find a detailed description of what the new creation will look like, Revelation 21–22 focuses instead on the goal of all Scripture—that God's people enjoy God's presence. The whole description here is not meant to fascinate us with gold streets, long walls, and specific jewels.[8] Nor do we find a detailed description of how much continuity or discontinuity there is with the old creation, except for the discontinuity of death and the grief and pain associated with death. The focus of this concluding description in the last two chapters of the Bible is the redeemed and transformed people of God—the bride of the Lamb. Everlasting joy is finally theirs, as he is the one who is dwelling "with them" and who wipes away "every tear" with the assurance that there will be "'no more death' or mourning or crying or pain, for the old order of things has passed away" (21:3–4).

Before we conclude this chapter, there are two matters that Christians disagree on that many relate to events close to "the end" (i.e., the study of

---

8. The symbolism in Revelation is esp. obvious in the first chapter. John's description of Jesus is clearly symbolic in 1:12–16. The references to Jesus's golden sash, white hair, blazing eyes, bronze feet, and his holding seven stars, with a double-edged sword coming out of his mouth, point to Jesus's priestly, royal, and divine power, and the power of his word. He clearly does not have a literal double-edged sword coming out of his mouth. This is one reason why the best-selling stories of people coming back from heaven with (contradictory) descriptions of what heaven and Jesus supposedly look like are unreliable at best. The "descriptions" are often put together from wrongly interpreted images from this kind of (apocalyptic) literature (and they contradict, e.g., Luke 16:31; John 3:13; 2 Cor. 12:4).

eschatology) but before the new creation. We will touch on them here because they relate to how we put our Bible together and how Old Testament expectations relate to New Testament fulfillment, sometimes resulting in quite different approaches to the continuity and discontinuity across the Testaments and the outworking of God's saving plan. These are the nature of the millennium and the future of Israel.

What About the Millennium?

In Revelation 20:1–7 a "thousand years" is referred to six times (i.e., a "millennium"). Although in recent years this has not been as heated a topic among Bible-believing Christians as it was in previous decades, some may wonder if what I said in the last two chapters (and in chap. 8, on the prophetic hope) affects one's millennial view. Basically, there are four views about where to put the millennium in relation to Jesus's return, and they are identified with prefixes: "a-," "pre-," and "post-" (with an additional "pre-" view).

1. The *amillennial* view has the prefix "a-" because this view argues that Revelation 20 does not speak of a future millennium but presents again the picture throughout Revelation of Jesus's current reign during the church age between Jesus's first and second coming. Satan was "bound" at the cross so that the gospel would go to the nations, believers "reign" spiritually with Jesus in heaven, and "a thousand years" is symbolic of this church age. This view can be represented with basically the same figure we introduced in chapter 9 (on the now and not yet of the kingdom, fig. 9.2; as we noted there, the arrow pointing toward the cross signifies the idea that Jesus brings into this age the life and blessing of the age to come; see fig. 10.2).

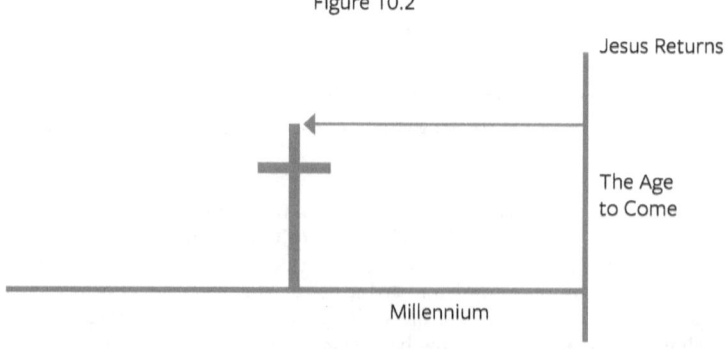

Figure 10.2

2. The *postmillennial* view argues that there will be a "millennium" of increasing prosperity and Christian influence in the world. Christ will return

after this time of increased blessing—thus, "post" or "after" a millennium of blessing. As with the amillennial position, the "thousand years" are symbolic of this age. But the millennium is characterized by the increasing success of the gospel among the nations so that large numbers across the world become Christians and influence society and government (see also chap. 5, on law). The line going upward in figure 10.3 reflects the increasing influence of Christianity on society. This seems unlikely in view of the message of Acts that the period between the first and second comings of Jesus will be characterized by the spread of the gospel being met by acceptance as well as rejection and persecution (reflecting the parable of the sower). This view potentially falls into the trap of triumphalism that we mentioned at the end of the last chapter.

Figure 10.3

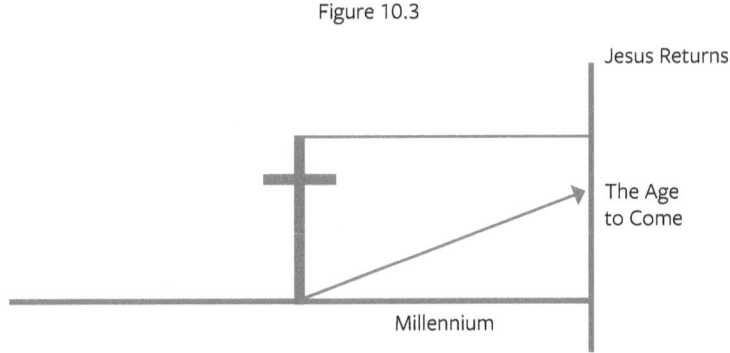

3. The *historic premillennial* view argues that the account of Jesus's return in Revelation 19 before the account of a "millennium" in 20:1–7 means that Jesus returns before (thus, "pre-") the millennium. This view argues that the phrases "and I saw" in 19:11, 19; 20:1, 4, 11; and 21:1 are sequential (while recognizing the presence of recapitulation and intensification in Rev. 6–19). The references to "seized," "bound," "[thrown] into the Abyss," "locked," and "sealed" are all totally restrictive and contrary to descriptions of Satan's current activity elsewhere in the New Testament (e.g., 2 Cor. 4:4; Eph. 2:2; 1 Pet. 5:8; 1 John 5:19). The binding so that Satan is kept "from deceiving the nations anymore until the thousand years were ended" (Rev. 20:3) is contrary to descriptions of Satan's current deceiving activity elsewhere in Revelation (e.g., 12:9; 13:14; 19:20). Finally, "came to life" (20:4) most likely refers to physical resurrection (as is the usual meaning for the word) rather than "spiritual life," since all agree that "the rest of the dead" (20:5) refers to a physical resurrection. This view does not necessarily interpret "a thousand years" as literal. It could be symbolic for a period of time. However,

it is likely a long period of time, since it is contrasted with a "short time" in 20:3.[9] The historic premillennial view was held by the early church, but it is essentially the same as the amillennial view in terms of how the rest of Scripture is interpreted. In this sense, figure 10.4 is again similar to the figure we introduced in chapter 9 (the now and not yet of the kingdom), except for the line representing Christ's return before the millennium. Some premillennialists see hints in passages such as Isaiah 65:20 for a millennium ("the one who dies at a hundred will be thought a mere child"). However, passages like this are better understood as symbolic and poetic descriptions of a glorious future rather than specifying millennial conditions (as, e.g., the temple in Ezek. 40–48).

Figure 10.4

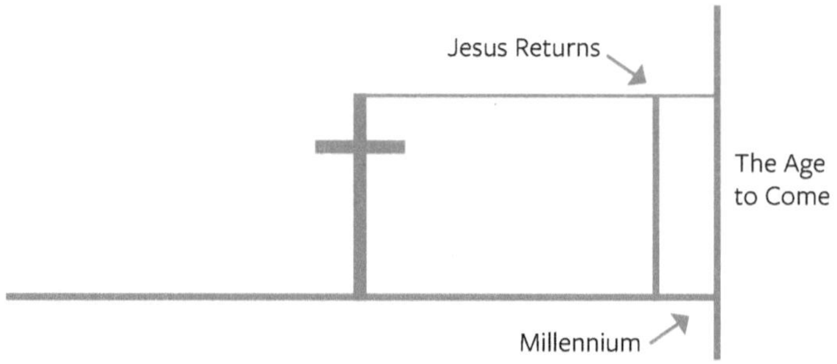

4. Finally, there is a variation on the premillennial position—the *dispensational premillennial* view. This view, like the preceding view, interprets Revelation 20 (the millennium) as coming after Revelation 19 (Jesus's return) and before Revelation 21 (the new heavens and new earth). The main difference is that it places into the millennium prophecies for national Israel that are interpreted as including a central role for Israel and a rebuilt temple (often including the reinstitution of the sacrificial system; see fig. 10.5). (See the reflections at the end of chapter 9, fig. 9.4, and the resources listed for further study.)

There are variations within each view, but all four views hold to a visible return of the Lord Jesus. My own view is that historic premillennialism makes the best sense of Revelation 20 (as you can tell by the amount of space I dedicated to it above!).

---

9. Carson, "Revelation—Part 24."

The Holy City

Figure 10.5

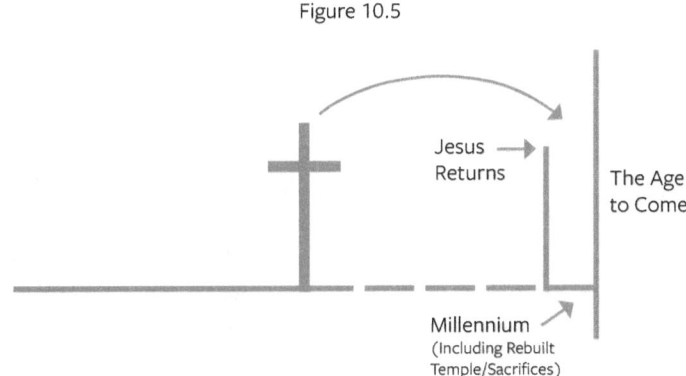

What About Israel?

In chapter 9 (on the now and not yet of the kingdom) we saw that the New Testament emphasizes that Jesus is the one who embodies the Old Testament hopes for Israel. Jesus is the "seed" of Abraham, the "true vine," the "Servant of the Lord" who represents Israel. The people of God, therefore, are defined by their relationship to Jesus. Those who belong to Jesus are the true children of Abraham (Gal. 3:29); those who believe are the ones who are of the faith of Abraham (Rom. 4:16; Gal. 3:7); those who remain trusting in Jesus are those who belong to the true vine (John 15:1–4). What, then, of the people of Israel? Paul raises this question in Romans 9. If the gospel is promised in the Old Testament Scriptures, what has happened to the people who initially received those promises? Have they been rejected? If they have been rejected, what does that say about God's trustworthiness and the wonderful assurances from God's promises that Paul extols in Romans 8? Paul addresses this question in Romans 9–11, concluding that "all Israel will be saved" (Rom. 11:26). There are three main views among Bible-believing Christians about this reference to Israel.[10] The first is the least likely, leaving us with two that are surprisingly similar.

The least likely view is that "Israel" in Romans 11:26 is just a way of referring to spiritual Israel—that is, anyone who believes in Jesus, including gentiles.[11] The reason this is most unlikely is that this is not the way the term "Israel" is used in Romans 11, it does not answer the question raised by Paul about whether God has rejected Israel (11:1, 11), and the preceding phrase

---

10. There is another view that Israel will be saved without believing in Jesus, but this contradicts the emphasis in Romans on the need for faith in Jesus (Rom. 3:22, 28; 4:5; 11:20, 23).

11. N. T. Wright holds this view. See Wright, *Climax of the Covenant*, 246–51.

speaks of "Israel" as having received a partial hardening (11:25). There is no evidence in this context that Paul shifts meaning within the same sentence.

This brings us to two views that both interpret Paul as referring to ethnic Israel.

1. One view argues that Romans 9–11 refers to ethnic Israel and that Israel's salvation (11:26) is a reference to the ongoing conversion of some Israelites throughout church history, with Paul as exhibit A. This view says that Paul essentially restates what he says in Romans 9 and 11:1–10 that a remnant of Israelites will continue to be saved, just as there was a remnant in Elijah's day.

2. The other view argues that Romans 9–11 refers to ethnic Israel and that Israel's salvation refers to a future conversion of a large number of Israelites (likely close to Jesus's return; see 11:26). Support for this view is found in the different question that is raised in Romans 11:11, compared to 11:1. In 11:1 Paul asks and then answers whether Israel's rejection is total. Paul's answer is no, Israel's hardening is partial; a remnant is still being saved (with Paul as exhibit A). In 11:11, however, Paul asks if this current (partial) rejection is permanent. Again, Paul's answer is no. Then Paul develops his answer with a sequence: Israel's (partial) rejection → gentile acceptance → Israel's (full) acceptance.

Paul states that Israel's current (partial) rejection has meant that the gospel has gone to gentiles, but then he contrasts their current state (transgression, loss, rejection, broken off) with another state (inclusion, full inclusion, grafted back in). This contrast culminates in 11:25–26 as a contrast between their current partial hardening and their salvation. In this context their "salvation" is different from the current state of hardening and must therefore be future. "All Israel" in this view refers to a large number of Israelites who are alive at the time (not necessarily every single individual Israelite).

Of these last two views, view 2 makes the most sense to me of Paul's argument in Romans 9–11. This view is also not bound to any of the millennial views we summarized above (representatives of each of the millennial views have held to a future large-scale conversion of Israel based on Rom. 11). What is common to both of these views, however, is that in neither case is Israel replaced or rejected without any future in God's saving purposes. The spread of the gospel to "all nations" means that God's people are made up of both Jews and gentiles who belong to Jesus, the "seed" of Abraham, the "true vine." Paul makes clear in these chapters, therefore, that God's saving plan is not the subtraction of Israel but the addition of gentiles.[12] All Christians, therefore, ought to have the yearning of Paul for the Jewish people to come to know the

---

12. Moo, *Romans*, 756.

Messiah, who is the son of Abraham, the son of David, the embodiment of the true Israel (9:1–5). God, in his grace, has included gentiles in the promises. God, in his grace, has also not rejected Israel from his promises—they, too, will be saved (11:26).

So What? Some Implications of This Theme of the Final Transformation

This completes our look at how to put our Bible together. The goal of this chapter has been to primarily treat matters associated with the end goal of God's saving purposes, including matters that Christians disagree about concerning events associated with that end goal and how the New Testament shapes our interpretation of Old Testament expectations. Our primary concern, however, is to remember John's focus in Revelation 21–22. The final goal is one in which through Christ God's people are finally transformed, able to enjoy God's presence forever, without fear, in complete safety and security. We as believers continue to face the effects of sin in this world, both our own sin and the sin of others. Thus, we struggle with emotional as well as physical weakness, not to mention our ongoing spiritual weaknesses and temptations. We experience life's joys, the delight that comes with family and friends, the beauty of God's creation, the assurances of what we already have in Christ (forgiveness of sins, the gift of the Spirit, the outworking of God's saving plan, communion with God), and the encouragements from God's people. Yet still, tears, mourning, crying, pain, and ultimately death come to us all. Thus, the prospect held out by those magnificent words of the loud voice from the throne fills us with hope and glad expectation. The pictures and patterns and promises of the whole Bible are finally realized in full when we as God's transformed people through Christ's death and resurrection get to enjoy his presence forever.

> Look! God's dwelling place is now among the people, and he will dwell with them. They will be his people, and God himself will be with them and be their God. "He will wipe every tear from their eyes. There will be no more death" or mourning or crying or pain, for the old order of things has passed away. (Rev. 21:3–4; cf. Isa. 25:8)

The unity of Scripture in pointing to this ultimate goal, from beginning to end, provides us with assurance in God's promises, strengthens our trust in God's purposes, increases our thankfulness for Christ's saving work, and reinforces our gratitude for the Spirit's power in enabling us to trust in Christ and to persevere. Because of this we are filled with joy and hope even now. In anticipation of that day, by the Spirit's help, we sing,

> To him who sits on the throne and to the Lamb
> be praise and honor and glory and power,
> for ever and ever! (Rev. 5:13)

FOR FURTHER READING

Beale, G. K. "The Final Vision of the Apocalypse and Its Implications for a Biblical Theology of the Temple." In *Heaven on Earth: The Temple in Biblical Theology*, edited by T. D. Alexander and Simon Gathercole. Paternoster, 2004.

Gundry, Robert H. "The New Jerusalem: People as Place, Not Place for People." *Novum Testamentum* 29 (1987): 254–64.

Johnson, Dennis E. *Triumph of the Lamb: A Commentary on Revelation*. P&R, 2001.

Ladd, George Eldon. *Crucial Questions About the Kingdom of God*. Eerdmans, 1952.

Lewis, Daniel J. *Three Crucial Questions About the Last Days*. Eerdmans, 1998.

TO DIG DEEPER

- There are countless books on the millennium in Revelation 20 and Israel in Romans 9–11. An accessible way into these discussions can be found in the following two books: Clouse, *Meaning of the Millennium* (there are more-recent books on millennial views, but George Ladd's chapter in this volume is closest to the view I presented above); and Compton and Naselli, *Three Views on Israel and the Church*. Discussion about the place and future of Israel in Romans 9–11 features in each of the four views represented in Parker and Lucas, *Covenantal and Dispensational Theologies*.
- A neglected theme to ponder is what Christians throughout church history have called the "beatific vision." On the basis of texts such as Psalm 42:2; Matthew 5:8; and 1 John 3:2, Christians have looked forward to our ultimate joy—seeing God. One helpful way into this discussion is Michael Allen's chapter in Wittmer, *Four Views on Heaven*. More comprehensively, see Parkison, *To Gaze upon God*.

11

Putting Your Bible Together

Patterns and Principles

After reaching heaven in the last chapter, what could possibly be left to cover? In this chapter we will take a step back and provide pointers for further study. We will briefly reflect on how a handful of other themes might be approached in light of the framework we have followed throughout this book and then focus on broader questions of method—specifically, How do we move from the Old to the New Testament? We will point to some pitfalls to watch out for and some tools to employ in making this move.

The Overall Structure of This Book

First, a reminder: We began this book by setting out an overall structure of promise and fulfillment that we would follow. The overall structure, in keeping with Jesus's introduction to his public ministry, was one of God's kingdom (or saving rule) promised and then inaugurated with the arrival of Jesus. Matthew 1 and Acts 7 and 13 provide a broad outline of Israel's history that culminates with the institution of kingship, followed by the prophets and the exile. Thus, we traced major events and institutions in Israel's *history* from creation to kingship, then showed how these themes were picked up by the *prophets* as part of their proclamation of God's future glorious salvation in an age to come, and finally brought these themes to their culmination through *Jesus*. We began with the visual representation shown in figure 1.7 (repeated here):

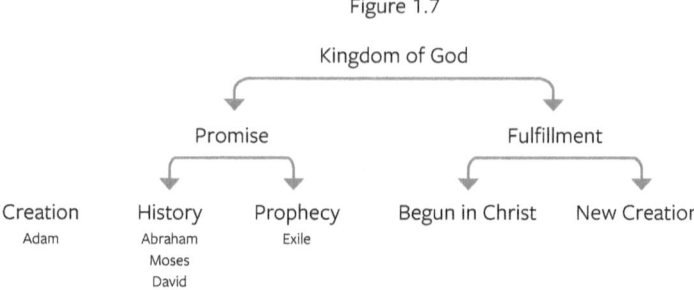

Figure 1.7

We suggested that the themes of creation/rebellion, covenant, exodus/tabernacle, law, sacrifice, kingship, and prophecy were not themes that were randomly chosen but themes that the Bible itself raises to prominence. The Bible emphasizes these themes as indispensable to understanding God's saving plan through salvation history. How would we go about tracing other themes not mentioned here? We could begin by following the same broad outline and connecting each theme to the major themes that we have covered. Let's try a few.

Approaching Other Themes Through Biblical Theology

How does biblical theology (what we have been doing in this book) approach themes such as worship, prayer, the nature of God's people, and worldview?

Worship

How would we develop a *biblical theology of worship*—that is, an understanding of how the theme of worship develops throughout the Bible?[1] We might start with what is said in Israel's *history*, then what the *prophets* point forward to, and then what the *New Testament* says about the fulfillment of these hopes in *Jesus*. In the garden, Adam and Eve are to "serve" God and enjoy his presence as they obey his instructions. Following their rebellion, judgment means exclusion from God's presence. Then in Israel's history there is an emphasis on God's instructions. God's people are to approach him on his terms, in the way he provides (through the sacrificial system), at the place he designates (altars, tabernacle, temple), and at times specified by him (days, festivals, the three pilgrim feasts—Passover, Weeks, Tabernacles). The place is identified as the place of God's presence or glory or name (1 Kings 8:29–30).

---

1. See Carson, "Worship Under the Word"; Peterson, *Engaging with God*; Scobie, *Ways of Our God*, 567–612.

The Psalms speak of confession, adoration, praise, and lament, both at the temple and individually.

Old Testament prophecy looks ahead to a new, ideal temple of the Lord's permanent presence (Ezek. 40–48), and a time when Sabbaths and festivals will be kept (Isa. 33:20; 66:23) and everything will be "holy to the Lord" (see Zech. 14:20–21). This will take place through cleansed hearts, with offerings pleasing to the Lord, including from the gentiles and even Egypt (Isa. 19:19–22; 56; Zeph. 3:10; Mal. 3:4). The prophets also show that the sacrificial system is focused on not just the operation of sacrifices. Repentance, not mere reliance on the temple system, is expected (Isa. 1:11–17; Jer. 7).

In the New Testament, descriptions of God's dwelling place are fulfilled in an ultimate way in Jesus (John 1:14; 2:19; Col. 2:9), so that true worshipers are those who know Jesus, the truth and the one who grants the Spirit—enabling them to "worship the Father in the Spirit and in truth" (John 4:23). John's Gospel emphasizes that Jesus is the fulfillment of all the feasts and festivals, and Hebrews says much the same, focusing especially on the Day of Atonement. Because of the gift of the Spirit, the local body of believers in Christ, rather than a building, is called God's temple (1 Cor. 3:16–17; Eph. 2:21–22). Special days and festivals are no longer indicated as the specific times for worship (Rom. 14:5–6; Gal. 4:10; Col. 2:16–17). In light of Jesus's resurrection, believers meet on the "first day of the week," and this seems to be behind its designation as "the Lord's day" (see Luke 24:1; Acts 20:7; 1 Cor. 16:2; Rev. 1:10).

For the believer, the language of "sacrifice" is applied to all of life (Rom. 12:1–2; 15:16; Phil. 4:18; Heb. 13:16; 1 Pet. 2:5). Worship is for all of life (1 Cor. 10:31), but this, of course, includes times when believers gather together. "Corporate worship" includes corporate praise, adoration, attentive hearing of God's Word, and regular celebration of the Lord's Supper, under the leadership of qualified elders. Instructions for new-covenant gatherings can be found in 1 Corinthians, Ephesians, Colossians, 1 Timothy, and elsewhere in the New Testament. In the new covenant, corporate worship still makes use of the Psalms as well as songs and hymns extolling God's grace in Christ (Col. 3:16). New-covenant worshipers recognize that Christ and his sacrifice, not the song leader, enable believers to know God's presence, and they aim for intelligible edification as well as adoration and gratitude to God for all they have in Christ (Col. 3:16). In summary, we might say that worship across the Bible is God centered, has always been shaped by his word, and requires genuine response to his word, yet it is determined differently in the new covenant. Thus, this theme links with and integrates a number of the themes we have covered in this book—covenant, exodus/tabernacle, law, and sacrifice.

Prayer

How would you develop a *biblical theology of prayer*?[2] Sometimes when a country is going through difficult times, like a drought, or obvious rejection of God, you might hear 2 Chronicles 7:14 quoted by well-meaning Christians ("If my people . . . will humble themselves and pray . . . , then I will . . . heal their land"). How would biblical theology help us apply passages such as this?

We could start with the creation account, recognizing our dependence on our Creator. At the beginning of Israel's history we meet Abraham and learn about prayer that is based on God's promises and his faithfulness to his covenant (Gen. 18; 24). Throughout Israel's history we see how God's people cry out and how God acts on his promises, and we see the development of Moses, judges, kings, and priests as mediators, culminating at the high point of Israel's history with the dedication of the temple (1 Kings 8) and the Psalms and Wisdom literature associated with Israel's kings. Israel's prophets look forward to a restored people in a "new covenant" who will all "know the Lord" (Jer. 31:34). This will be a time when God's people call on his name and he will answer prayer (Isa. 58:9; 65:24; Jer. 29:12–13; Zeph. 3:9, 14–20). In the New Testament, Jesus is the perfect mediator as well as the perfect revelation from God. He is the ultimate "Word" from God and to God. Amazingly, believers are "in Christ" and therefore also have perfect access to the Father, able to cry out as loved children, like the Son, "Abba, Father" (Gal. 4:6; see Heb. 4:16; 10:19–22).

A biblical theology of prayer, therefore, takes into consideration the covenant theme we traced in chapter 3. Believers pray on the basis of the confidence they have in Christ and on the basis of the promises they have in the new covenant. We ask, "What covenant is in view?" when we encounter prayers in the Old Testament. Thus, we don't misapply prayers such as 2 Chronicles 7:14 to every nation and every land—recognizing instead the context of the Mosaic covenant for this prayer. Yet we can see the trajectory of this prayer, and others in the Old Testament, toward the assurances found in passages such as 1 John 1:9 and the outworking of God's sovereign purposes to conform believers to the likeness of the Lord Jesus (cf. John 14:14; Rom. 8:26, 28–30). It is also important to take into consideration the implications of Jesus's teaching on the now and not yet of God's saving rule as we pray and "not give up" while waiting for Jesus's return (Luke 18:1, 8). Thus, we draw on the themes of covenant, law, sacrifice, and the now and not yet of the kingdom.

---

2. Cf. Clowney, "Biblical Theology of Prayer," 136–73.

The Nature of God's People

Who are God's people today? We might begin a *biblical theology of the people of God* in the garden, noting the pattern of trust in God's word, obedience to his rule, and enjoyment of his presence. With Abraham, we see the development of God's revelation in promises and the need to trust in those promises. As the biblical story moves to Moses and the nation of Israel, we see God's people as those in a covenant relationship with him, also in obedience to his will for the enjoyment of his presence. At the high point of Israel's history, David and the institution of kingship show God's people enjoying God's rule through his king. Yet throughout Israel's history there is a difference between those who belong to God in the nation of Israel in the Mosaic covenant and those (few) who trust him and follow his word (as evidenced in the handful of "good" kings or in references to the "remnant"). The disobedience of the nation culminates in their exile from God's presence, as Adam and Eve were exiled from the garden. Thus, the prophets look forward to a new covenant of forgiven and obedient people through a servant who will represent Israel, restore Israel, and include gentiles (Isa. 49; Jer. 31).

The New Testament reveals Christ to be the true locus of God's obedient people as the one who overcomes Satan's temptations and perfectly obeys God's will. By God's grace, God's new-covenant people are those who belong to Christ—both Jew and gentile. God's people are those who know him and enjoy his presence, through trust in his word and his promises to grant the Spirit and to forgive through Christ. In God's unexpected grace, this people at this time is mainly made up of gentiles—those who were far from the covenants. Yet, in his unexpected grace, God still has gracious plans to extend mercy to save many Jews. Thus, we draw on the themes of creation/rebellion, covenant, the prophetic hope, and fulfillment in Jesus.

Worldview

For the above themes, and many others, we can observe a trajectory as a theme develops across God's unfolding plan. Yet biblical theology can also bring a unique contribution to an overall consideration of a topic. What contribution would biblical theology make toward constructing a *biblical worldview*? If we begin with a very broad and basic definition that a "worldview" is how we view the world around us—such as the nature of humanity, what happens after death, how we know right and wrong, the meaning of human history—how would biblical theology inform this topic?[3] We could

---

3. These elements are some of the topics James Sire notes in *Universe Next Door*, 9.

initially note that the overarching plan of redemption shows us the value of humanity and creation as well as humanity's accountability to God.

However, there is an even more basic contribution that biblical theology can make. The foundational feature of biblical theology is a focus on the sequence or unfolding of salvation history (see again chap. 1). Among other things, this teaches us that "history is linear, a meaningful sequence of events leading to the fulfillment of God's purposes for humanity."[4] This means that history is going somewhere; there is a goal, an end. This also means that there is a judgment, that choices have consequences, and that there is divine providence over history. Biblical theology, therefore, helps contrast a Christian view of the world with a view that thinks history is cyclical, repeatable, or an illusion. Events are not as confusing, chaotic, or meaningless as they appear. Sin has affected all humanity and the world we live in. Yet we have seen repeatedly throughout this book that God's purposes are worked out in the world, through Christ, for his people to know him and enjoy his presence (Rev. 21:3).

Methodology in Developing Themes

As we wrap up our discussion of the main themes that help us put our Bible together, now is a good time to clarify some of the key aspects of how we trace a theme or build up our understanding of a topic that develops across the Bible. What are the potential pitfalls of tracing themes, doing word studies, and assessing patterns?

Biblical and Systematic Theology

In chapter 1 we outlined the distinctives of biblical and systematic theology. When it comes to building up a picture of what the Bible teaches on any given topic, both approaches have their strengths, but in isolation both approaches also have potential weaknesses. Thus, approaching a topic like "worship" from a systematic theology framework without sensitivity to biblical theology may take into consideration what the Bible says about God and what the Bible says about humanity, so that we might say that worship involves the recognition of God's greatness and the need for humanity to acknowledge and submit to God's holy rule.[5] However, if the developments across the Bible's storyline

---

4. Sire, *Universe Next Door*, 31. The following sentences draw on Sire's summary of the implications of this point on 31–32. See also Carson, *Christ and Culture Revisited*.

5. For this discussion about biblical and systematic theology for a theology of worship, see Carson, "Worship Under the Word," 16–18.

that biblical theology takes into consideration are overlooked, then the biblical evidence could potentially be flattened. Differences and developments may be overlooked. So, one may pick and choose various details about worship and apply them directly to contemporary church life. We might note that choirs were used in temple worship and argue that this means choirs should be used in church today. Or we might note that leaders were called "priests" in the Old Testament, so ministers should be called "priests" today. Thus, when done without an awareness of the developments across salvation history, a topic study of a theme may flatten the evidence.

At the same time, an approach to summarizing a topic from only a biblical theology framework that does not also take into consideration the wider integration of the theme also has potential weaknesses. This approach, as we have seen, helps us pay more attention to the differences and developments across the storyline, such as the move from the Mosaic covenant to the new covenant. One potential weakness of thinking that biblical theology is all we need, however, is that we may end up being purely descriptive about the topic without making any claims about the difference the topic makes to current Christian living or church life. For example, for the topic of "worship," we might trace the fulfillment of the sacrificial system in Christ and then not have anything constructive to say about what that has to do with how believers approach God when they gather together today. Or preachers may end every sermon with "and my third point is: . . . Jesus," marveling at the cross-references and connections drawn across the Testaments without any application or "So what?"

Word Studies

Another potential pitfall we face as we seek to trace a theme through the Bible involves the way in which we might study a word to understand a theme. There are some common dangers of word studies, as helpful as these studies are.[6] One common pitfall is what some scholars call the "word-concept fallacy." This is where we think of a word, look up all the uses of that word, and then think that we know all there is to know about an issue or topic (i.e., that concept). However, there are at least four complications with this approach. (1) It reduces a concept to just the occurrences of that word (the concept is likely bigger than just the meaning or uses of a particular word). (2) It neglects other terms that are used—that is, passages or contexts where the

---

6. For some guidance, see Carson, *Exegetical Fallacies*, 27–64; Silva, *Biblical Words and Their Meaning*; Naselli, *How to Understand and Apply the New Testament*, 206–29; Merkle and Plummer, *Greek Word Studies for Everyone*.

idea is discussed even if that word doesn't occur. (3) This approach might be insensitive to the different uses of particular words by different authors (e.g., "world" in John often refers to the people who are opposed to God, whereas elsewhere it often refers to the creation or cosmos; or "call" in the Gospels may mean something like "invitation" [see Matt. 22:14], whereas in Paul the word means something like "effective conviction from God" [see Rom. 8:30]).[7] (4) Even if we were to look up a specific Greek or Hebrew word used by a particular author on a particular topic, we need to remember that these words can be translated differently in different contexts. Thus, for the subject of worship, we may look up the occurrences of the Greek word *proskyneō*.[8] The word is translated as "worship" in Matthew 2:2 and 2:8 (once for the wise men and once for Herod's false claim). Yet in Matthew 18:26 the servant becomes bankrupt and faces slavery, so he "fell on his knees" before his master. The same Greek word is used, but the idea here is more like "beg" and relates more to fear than adoration or worship.

Thus, this potential problem of word studies needs to be kept in mind when studying a theme. The most important factor in looking up words is the context in which the word is used. In developing a biblical theology of a theme, however, we shouldn't restrict our understanding of what the Bible says about a topic to just the occurrences of a specific word (e.g., a biblical theology of worship based primarily on passages where the term "worship" appears).[9]

Typology Versus Allegorical Interpretation

Typology is another way in which we can trace a theme. In fact, that is largely what we have been doing in this book! Typology is based on an awareness that God has worked in a way that provides patterns, which are developed and anticipate something more. There is a type and an antitype. An antitype is something that is in place of the type (i.e., it is the reality to which the type points). The term "typology" draws from the language of the Greek word *typos* in the New Testament (not "typo," as in "typographical error"), but it is much broader than just specific references to this word (the word is used to refer to Adam as a "type" of Christ in Rom. 5:14 ESV). The patterns of typology are patterns in persons, institutions, and events. We have covered

---

7. Carson, *Exegetical Fallacies*, 63.
8. This example is used by Carson, "Worship Under the Word," 19.
9. This issue comes up in other debates as well. For example, the word "covenant" isn't used in 2 Sam. 7, or in Gen. 1–3; the word "Trinity" doesn't occur in the Bible, even though the concept is all-pervasive. These discussions illustrate the point that a concept or idea may be found where the word isn't found.

many of them in this book. *People* would include Adam, Moses, and David. *Institutions* would include kingship, the sacrificial system, and the temple. *Events* that come to mind might be creation and the exodus. These patterns in people, institutions, and events foreshadow aspects of who Christ is and what he has accomplished. Because these patterns are found in the context of God's progressive revelation (i.e., God revealing more and more across the timeline of the Bible), there is always development, escalation, and consummation from type to antitype. What the type anticipates is greater than the type itself. Jesus's deliverance is greater than the exodus from one geographical location to another. Jesus's priesthood far exceeds any priesthood encountered in the Old Testament. Jesus's kingship is far superior to David's. Thus, there is not another David, priest, exodus, or covenant to come that can surpass Jesus and what he has done.

Are there any controls on this typology? Yes! Biblical typology is constrained by the texts and contexts in which the types are found. In this regard, typology is distinguished from allegorical interpretation. Typology depends on the historical reality of the original person, event, or institution and is based on what the text itself teaches about that person, event, or institution. Thus, for there to be a greater "deliverance" from a greater "Moses" for an ultimate "salvation," there must be an original deliverance through an original Moses that this surpasses. As we have seen, the exodus became the pattern for the prophets as they looked forward to a "second exodus."

Allegorical interpretation, however, does not look for historical reality or the emphasis of the text in its context.[10] Rather, it picks out isolated details and reads double meanings into the text where there are none emphasized by the author in the context. That is, an allegorical interpretation is interested not in the actual historical persons and events but in incidental words and signs in the text, and links are made by some extratextual key (i.e., something outside the text itself).[11] For example, the first-century Jewish writer Philo refers to Abraham, Isaac, and Jacob as the three elements that Aristotle emphasized concerning what was important in education (teaching, practice,

---

10. I am distinguishing between allegorical interpretation (as an illegitimate means for determining meaning) and allegory (as a literary device, a fictional symbolic story). My thanks to Sigurd Grindheim for this clarification.

11. Some may suggest that Paul gives validity to an allegorical approach in Gal. 4:24 (ESV uses the word "allegorically"). However, in this context Paul is using the word more like we would use the word "illustrations." He says that to ignore the promise is to be like Hagar and Ishmael. Thus, he sees a pattern (picked up in his quotation of Isa. 54:1; cf. 51:2–3), and he is not doing the same as Philo with unrelated extratextual keys for interpretation (hence CSB and NIV translate the word as "figuratively," HCSB as "illustrations," NKJV as "symbolic").

nature)—something not evident in Genesis.[12] A contemporary example might be a preacher who emphasizes the redness of Rahab's cord because Jesus's blood was red, and so Rahab's deliverance points to our deliverance by the blood of Christ. There are lessons to be learned from Rahab's trust in the promises given to her, but the lessons do not depend on red being the color of blood. Allegorical interpretation, therefore, is characterized by a focus on incidental details that are interpreted through the lens of something else, apart from what can legitimately be derived from the author's intention in the emphasis of the text itself.

Moving from the Old Testament to the New Testament

In this book we have emphasized two key features of putting our Bible together: (1) an overall framework of Israel's *history*, Israel's *prophecy*, and New Testament *fulfillment*, both already and not yet, and (2) key themes that help us understand how God's saving plan unfolds. In this last section we will briefly summarize a range of ways to move from the Old Testament to the New Testament. As we have seen, biblical theology focuses on the temporal sequence in which God reveals his saving plan. Thus, we want to recognize that we can also move across the Old Testament, from one period to another (e.g., from Israel's history to the prophets), and across the New Testament (e.g., from the Gospels to the letters), and we have regularly seen how we should also move from the New to the Old Testament, so to speak, so that we can understand the New Testament better.

Nevertheless, there are unique dangers in making the move from the Old to the New Testament, so we will zero in on this broader move here. One danger is that we could move too quickly, in the sense that we ignore the original message of a passage in its Old Testament context, missing the point that the author is making in, say, Judges, or Kings, or Ezekiel in order to jump straight to Jesus. Another danger is that we may make only very predictable moves to the New Testament, missing the richness and variety of the Old Testament to say, "This points to Jesus!" Hopefully we have helped to minimize that danger by starting each theme in the context and setting in which it arises. My concern here, however, is that we do indeed move to the New Testament, taking into consideration the fuller revelation that comes with the Lord Jesus and the covenant and setting in salvation history that we are in.

---

12. See, e.g., Philo, *On Abraham* 11.52; *On Joseph* 1.1; and *On the Change of Names* 2.12; 14.52.

We will begin with three broad principles and then briefly summarize some specific pointers others suggest.

Broadly speaking, for a Bible study or Bible talk or for your own regular Bible reading, when you seek to move from the Old Testament to the New Testament, there are three general principles to keep in mind. (1) Treat the Old Testament passage in its Old Testament context first—that is, don't move straight to the New Testament without understanding the emphasis in the context of the Old Testament. (2) Don't just look at the Old Testament setting and context—that is, don't stay there. You could ask, Is my Bible study or explanation of this Old Testament text something that would be acceptable in a synagogue or mosque (i.e., perhaps just moral lessons apart from any integration into God's overarching saving plan or without reference to the difference that the rest of God's revelation makes)? (3) Keep in mind God's overarching saving purposes throughout the Bible—that is, ask, (a) What does this passage say about God and his grace and sufficiency? and (b) What does this passage say about me and my need of his grace (that comes through Christ)?[13]

There are a variety of ways to move from the Old Testament to the New Testament. My goal in the following paragraphs is not to make this overly complicated or make you afraid of making this move. My goal is to show that in light of what we have covered throughout this book, there are many ways you can do this. We will summarize the recommendations of three authors as examples. These are suggestive only and not comprehensive. Only brief explanations are provided, as the rest of the book has illustrated these broad categories.

First, one way to move from the Old Testament to the New is to think in terms of four main paths:[14]

1. "Follow the plan" (e.g., look for the way the passage or theme fits into the broad pattern of promise and fulfillment, such as the promise of the new covenant).
2. "Expose the problem" (e.g., identify the sin or need for a better leader, such as in the books of Judges and Kings, and show how Jesus is better).
3. "Focus on the action" (e.g., ask what God is doing through his agent and point to the faithfulness of God, such as the contrast between God and the gods of Egypt).

---

13. See Chapell, *Christ-Centered Preaching*.
14. This is based on Gary Millar's presentation "How to Preach Christ from the O.T. in a Way That Does Justice to the Text," provided at the May 2005 Sydney Missionary and Bible College preaching conference, "Preaching the Old Testament: The Why and How."

4. "Explain the category" (e.g., titles such as Messiah, Son of God, or Son of Man or feasts such as the Passover; in the David and Goliath story explain the category of the anointed king opposing the enemy of God's people).

Second, Sidney Greidanus, in his book *Preaching Christ from the Old Testament*, lists a series of ways to move to the New Testament.[15] Many of these overlap with what we have been doing throughout this book.

1. "The way of redemptive-historical progression" (this approach places a passage in the context of when the revelation was given in God's unfolding plan [from creation to Israel, to Christ, to church, to new creation] and sees it in light of what came before and in light of the completion in God's rule over a new creation).
2. "The way of promise-fulfillment" (this approach emphasizes the language of fulfillment in the New Testament; e.g., the word "fulfilled" occurs in Matthew thirteen times; the promise of the Spirit in Joel 2 is fulfilled in Acts 2).
3. "The way of typology" (as noted above, this approach notes patterns that foreshadow Christ's work in persons, events, and institutions, recognizing development, escalation, and consummation).
4. "The way of analogy" (this approach finds parallels that highlight continuity; e.g., the Lord is my shepherd in Ps. 23; we can express lament as the psalmists do).
5. "The way of longitudinal themes" (this approach traces themes such as law, covenant, redemption, sacrifice, holiness).
6. "The way of New Testament references" (this approach asks, "Is this Old Testament passage quoted in the New Testament?"; e.g., Hosea 11:1 in Matt. 2:15).
7. "The way of contrast" (this approach emphasizes discontinuity; e.g., circumcision versus transformed hearts in the New Testament; Sabbath versus rest in Christ in Hebrews).

Third, Don Carson notes a variety of ways in which there is continuity across the two Testaments.[16] The first three repeat what we have already said, so I won't elaborate on them any further. The next three are also reasonably clear, but I will add a brief explanation for each.

15. Greidanus, *Preaching Christ*, 203–77.
16. Carson, "Mystery and Fulfillment," 398–412.

Putting Your Bible Together

1. "Verbal predictions and event-fulfillments" (e.g., Acts 2).
2. "Typological fulfillment" (e.g., the types we mentioned above).
3. "A temporal (i.e., salvation-historical) reading of the Old Testament" (e.g., recognizing the movement from Abraham to law to Jesus as Paul does in Gal. 3).
4. "Common, more-or-less unchanged beliefs" (e.g., in Rom. 1 there is continuity in the recognition that there is only one God, who is the Creator of all, that God's wrath is revealed against all who reverse the created order or elevate it above God, and that idolatry is judged).
5. "Moral application of Old Testament narrative" (e.g., in 1 Cor. 10:1–13, Paul uses the example of the immorality of the Israelites as a moral warning; likewise, in 2 Cor. 11:3 Paul uses the example of Eve's deception to show the common experience of temptation).
6. "Common legal/ethical prescriptions" (e.g., marriage in the New Testament is based on Gen. 2; the need to keep God's commandments / Christ's law is shown in 1 Cor. 7:19).

In summary, with any given Bible passage, after prayer, we could begin by asking the following simplified questions:[17]

1. What does this passage mean in the context of this chapter, sequence of chapters, and book? What is the aim of this passage? How does it contribute to the overall aim of this section?
2. What stage of salvation history is this passage in?
3. What covenant is in operation at this stage of salvation history?
4. What elements of similarity or dissimilarity are there between this passage and the new covenant in Christ?
5. Does this passage relate to one or more of the major themes that run through the Bible? Is there development of this theme through Israel's history, Israel's prophets, and Christ's "now and not yet" kingdom?
6. What does this passage tell me about God, his provision, and my need of his grace in Christ?
7. Are there links that I can make across the Testaments based on some of the suggestions listed above (e.g., the need for a better judge/king, the consistent action and character of God, a later quotation of the passage)?

17. See Lawrence, *Biblical Theology*, for an accessible practical guide.

Conclusion

Ultimately our goal is to be careful and faithful readers and interpreters of God's Word. The Bible is a big book, and this *Basic Guide to Biblical Theology* can only introduce some ways of putting our Bible together and provide pointers to some of the many resources that expand on each of the themes introduced here. Our goal is to be attentive to the context and place in the timeline of each passage we read. By recognizing an overall structure to the unfolding saving plan of God and the main themes that help explain it, we are better able to put our Bible together. By God's grace and the empowering work of his Spirit, this will hopefully enable us to reflect more of Christ's character, point others to Christ, and bring honor and glory to Christ.

FOR FURTHER READING

Chase, Mitchell L. *40 Questions About Typology and Allegory*. Kregel Academic, 2020.

Hamilton, James M. *Typology—Understanding the Bible's Promise-Shaped Patterns: How Old Testament Expectations Are Fulfilled in Christ*. Zondervan Academic, 2022.

Lawrence, Michael. *Biblical Theology in the Life of the Church: A Guide for Ministry*. Crossway, 2010.

Poythress, Vern S. *Biblical Typology: How the Old Testament Points to Christ, His Church, and the Consummation*. Crossway, 2024.

TO DIG DEEPER

- How do we add depth to the themes of this book, trace other themes in biblical theology, or interpret individual Bible books or an author's corpus of books (e.g., Paul's letters) in light of biblical theology? In addition to the dictionaries mentioned in chapter 1 (*DNTUOT*, *NDBT*), the following biblical theology series provide rich resources:
    - The Gospel According to the Old Testament (P&R)
    - Short Studies in Biblical Theology (Crossway)
    - Essential Studies in Biblical Theology (InterVarsity)
    - New Studies in Biblical Theology (InterVarsity)
    - Biblical Theology of the New Testament (Zondervan)

BIBLIOGRAPHY

Abernethy, Andrew T., and Gregory Goswell. *God's Messiah in the Old Testament: Expectations of a Coming King.* Baker Academic, 2020.

Alexander, T. Desmond, Brian S. Rosner, D. A. Carson, and Graeme Goldsworthy, eds. *New Dictionary of Biblical Theology.* InterVarsity, 2000.

Anderson, Gary A. "Sacrifice and Sacrificial Offerings: Old Testament." In vol. 5 of *The Anchor Yale Bible Dictionary*, edited by David Noel Freedman. Doubleday, 1992.

Averbeck, Richard E. *The Old Testament Law for the Life of the Church: Reading the Torah in the Light of Christ.* IVP Academic, 2022.

Averbeck, Richard E. "Sacrifices and Offerings." In *DNTUOT*.

Bandy, Alan S., and Benjamin L. Merkle. *Understanding Prophecy: A Biblical-Theological Approach.* Kregel, 2015.

Barker, William S., and W. Robert Godfrey, eds. *Theonomy: A Reformed Critique.* Academie Books, 1990.

Beale, G. K. "The Final Vision of the Apocalypse and Its Implications for a Biblical Theology of the Temple." In *Heaven on Earth: The Temple in Biblical Theology*, edited by T. D. Alexander and Simon Gathercole. Paternoster, 2004.

Beale, G. K. *The Temple and the Church's Mission: A Biblical Theology of the Dwelling Place of God.* NSBT 15. InterVarsity, 2004.

Beale, G. K., and D. A. Carson, eds. *Commentary on the New Testament Use of the Old Testament.* Baker Academic, 2007.

Beale, G. K., D. A. Carson, Benjamin L. Gladd, and Andrew David Naselli, eds. *Dictionary of the New Testament Use of the Old Testament.* Baker Academic, 2023.

Beasley-Murray, G. R. *Jesus and the Kingdom of God.* Eerdmans, 1986.

Beckwith, R. T. "Sacrifice." In *NDBT*.

Beeke, Joel R., and Paul M. Smalley. *Man and Christ.* Vol. 2 of *Reformed Systematic Theology.* Crossway, 2020.

Belcher, Richard P. *The Fulfillment of the Promises of God: An Exploration of Covenant Theology*. Mentor, 2020.

Block, Daniel I. *Covenant: The Framework of God's Grand Plan of Redemption*. Baker Academic, 2021.

Boda, Mark J. *After God's Own Heart: The Gospel According to David*. The Gospel According to the Old Testament. P&R, 2007.

Carson, D. A. "Apostolic Hermeneutics: Present-Day Imitation." In *DNTUOT*.

Carson, D. A. *Christ and Culture Revisited*. Eerdmans, 2008.

Carson, D. A. *Collected Writings on Scripture*. Crossway, 2010.

Carson, D. A. *Exegetical Fallacies*. 2nd ed. Baker Academic, 1996.

Carson, D. A. *The Gagging of God: Christianity Confronts Pluralism*. Zondervan Academic, 1996.

Carson, D. A. *Jesus the Son of God: A Christological Title Often Overlooked, Sometimes Misunderstood, and Currently Disputed*. Crossway, 2012.

Carson, D. A. "Matthew." In *Matthew and Mark*, vol. 9 of *The Expositor's Bible Commentary*, edited by Tremper Longman III and David E. Garland. Rev. ed. Zondervan, 2010.

Carson, D. A. "Mystery and Fulfillment: Toward a More Comprehensive Paradigm of Paul's Understanding of the Old and New." In *The Paradoxes of Paul*, vol. 2 of *Justification and Variegated Nomism*, edited by D. A. Carson, Peter T. O'Brien, and Mark A. Seifrid. Baker Academic, 2004.

Carson, D. A. "New Covenant Theology and Biblical Theology." In *God's Glory Revealed in Christ: Essays on Biblical Theology in Honor of Thomas R. Schreiner*, edited by Denny Burk, James M. Hamilton Jr., and Brian Vickers. B&H Academic, 2019.

Carson, D. A. "Revelation—Part 7 (Revelation 4:1–4)." In *D. A. Carson Sermon Library*. Faithlife, 2016.

Carson, D. A. "Revelation—Part 24 (Revelation 19–20:6)." In *D. A. Carson Sermon Library*. Faithlife, 2016.

Carson, D. A. "Worship Under the Word." In *Worship by the Book*, edited by D. A. Carson. Zondervan, 2002.

Chapell, Bryan. *Christ-Centered Preaching: Redeeming the Expository Sermon*. 3rd ed. Baker Academic, 2018.

Chase, Mitchell L. *40 Questions About Typology and Allegory*. Kregel Academic, 2020.

Clouse, Robert G., ed. *The Meaning of the Millennium: Four Views*. IVP Academic, 1977.

Clowney, Edmund P. "A Biblical Theology of Prayer." In *Teach Us to Pray: Prayer in the Bible and the World*, edited by D. A. Carson. Baker, 1990.

Compton, Jared, and Andrew David Naselli, eds. *Three Views on Israel and the Church: Perspectives on Romans 9–11*. Kregel, 2019.

Dempster, Stephen G. "Prophetic Books." In *NDBT*.

DeRouchie, Jason S. *Delighting in the Old Testament: Through Christ and For Christ.* Crossway, 2024.

DeRouchie, Jason S. *How to Understand and Apply the Old Testament: Twelve Steps from Exegesis to Theology.* P&R, 2017.

DeRouchie, Jason S. *What the Old Testament Authors Really Cared About: A Survey of Jesus' Bible.* Kregel, 2013.

DeRouchie, Jason S., Oren R. Martin, and Andrew David Naselli. *40 Questions About Biblical Theology.* Kregel, 2020.

DeYoung, Kevin, and Greg Gilbert. *What Is the Mission of the Church? Making Sense of Social Justice, Shalom, and the Great Commission.* Crossway, 2011.

Dumbrell, William J. *Covenant and Creation: A Theology of the Old Testament Covenants.* Paternoster, 1984.

Emadi, Matthew H. *The Royal Priest: Psalm 110 in Biblical Theology.* NSBT 60. IVP Academic, 2022.

Feinberg, John S., ed. *Continuity and Discontinuity: Perspectives on the Relationship Between the Old and New Testaments.* Crossway, 1988.

Fesko, J. V. *Adam and the Covenant of Works.* Mentor, 2021.

Fesko, J. V. *Last Things First: Unlocking Genesis 1–3 with the Christ of Eschatology.* Mentor, 2007.

France, R. T. *Divine Government: God's Kingship in the Gospel of Mark.* SPCK, 1990.

Gentry, Peter J. *How to Read and Understand the Biblical Prophets.* Crossway, 2017.

Gentry, Peter J., and Stephen J. Wellum. *God's Kingdom Through God's Covenants: A Concise Biblical Theology.* Crossway, 2015.

Gentry, Peter J., and Stephen J. Wellum. *Kingdom Through Covenant: A Biblical-Theological Understanding of the Covenants.* 2nd ed. Crossway, 2018.

Goldsworthy, Graeme. *According to Plan: The Unfolding Revelation of God in the Bible; An Introductory Biblical Theology.* InterVarsity, 1991.

Goldsworthy, Graeme. *Christ-Centered Biblical Theology: Hermeneutical Foundations and Principles.* Apollos, 2012.

Goldsworthy, Graeme. *Gospel and Kingdom: A Christian Interpretation of the Old Testament.* Paternoster, 1981.

Goldsworthy, Graeme. *Preaching the Whole Bible as Christian Scripture.* Eerdmans, 2000.

Greidanus, Sidney. *Preaching Christ from the Old Testament: A Contemporary Hermeneutical Method.* Eerdmans, 1999.

Grindheim, Sigurd. *Introducing Biblical Theology.* Bloomsbury, 2013.

Grindheim, Sigurd. *The Letter to the Hebrews.* Pillar New Testament Commentary. Eerdmans, 2023.

Grudem, Wayne. "Perseverance of the Saints: A Case Study from Hebrews 6:4–6 and the Other Warning Passages in Hebrews." In vol. 1 of *The Grace of God and the*

Bondage of the Will, edited by Thomas R. Schreiner and Bruce A. Ware. Baker, 1995.

Gundry, Robert H. "The New Jerusalem: People as Place, Not Place for People." *Novum Testamentum* 29 (1987): 254–64.

Guthrie, Nancy. *Even Better than Eden: Nine Ways the Bible's Story Changes Everything About Your Story*. Crossway, 2018.

Hamilton, James M. *Typology—Understanding the Bible's Promise-Shaped Patterns: How Old Testament Expectations Are Fulfilled in Christ*. Zondervan Academic, 2022.

Howard, David M., Jr. *An Introduction to the Old Testament Historical Books*. Moody, 1993.

Hughes, Philip Edgcumbe. *A Commentary on the Epistle to the Hebrews*. Eerdmans, 1977.

Jeffery, Steve, Michael Ovey, and Andrew Sach. *Pierced for Our Transgressions: Rediscovering the Glory of Penal Substitution*. Inter-Varsity, 2007.

Johnson, Dennis E. *Triumph of the Lamb: A Commentary on Revelation*. P&R, 2001.

Josephus. *The Life; Against Apion*. Translated by H. St. J. Thackeray. Loeb Classical Library 186. Harvard University Press, 1926.

Kaiser, Walter C. "The Blessing of David: A Charter for Humanity." In *The Law and the Prophets*, edited by John Skilton. Presbyterian and Reformed, 1974.

Kaiser, Walter C. "Wisdom Theology and the Centre of Old Testament Theology." *Evangelical Quarterly* 50 (1978): 132–46.

Kidner, Derek. *Proverbs: An Introduction and Commentary*. InterVarsity, 1964.

Klink, Edward W., III, and Darian R. Lockett. *Understanding Biblical Theology: A Comparison of Theory and Practice*. Zondervan Academic, 2012.

Köstenberger, Andreas J., and Gregory Goswell. *Biblical Theology: A Canonical, Thematic, and Ethical Approach*. Crossway, 2023.

Ladd, George Eldon. *Crucial Questions About the Kingdom of God*. Eerdmans, 1952.

Ladd, George Eldon. *The Presence of the Future: The Eschatology of Biblical Realism*. Eerdmans, 1974.

Ladd, George Eldon. *A Theology of the New Testament*. Rev. ed. Eerdmans, 1994.

Lawrence, Michael. *Biblical Theology in the Life of the Church: A Guide for Ministry*. Crossway, 2010.

Lewis, Daniel J. *Three Crucial Questions About the Last Days*. Eerdmans, 1998.

Longman, Tremper, III. *The Fear of the Lord Is Wisdom: A Theological Introduction to Wisdom in Israel*. Baker Academic, 2017.

Longman, Tremper, III. *Immanuel in Our Place: Seeing Christ in Israel's Worship*. The Gospel According to the Old Testament. P&R, 2001.

McComisky, Thomas E. *The Covenants of Promise: A Theology of the Old Testament Covenants.* Baker, 1985.

Merkle, Benjamin L., and Robert L. Plummer. *Greek Word Studies for Everyone: An Easy Guide to Serious Study of the Bible.* B&H Academic, 2025.

Moo, Douglas J. *The Letter to the Romans.* 2nd ed. New International Commentary on the New Testament. Eerdmans, 2018.

Moo, Douglas J. *A Theology of Paul and His Letters: The Gift of the New Realm in Christ.* Biblical Theology of the New Testament. Zondervan Academic, 2021.

Morales, L. Michael. *Who Shall Ascend the Mountain of the Lord? A Biblical Theology of the Book of Leviticus.* InterVarsity, 2015.

Morgan, Christopher W., and Robert A. Peterson, eds. *The Kingdom of God.* Crossway, 2012.

Motyer, Alec. *Look to the Rock: An Old Testament Background to Our Understanding of Christ.* Inter-Varsity, 1996.

Naselli, Andrew David. *How to Understand and Apply the New Testament: Twelve Steps from Exegesis to Theology.* P&R, 2017.

Naselli, Andrew David. "What Is the Spectrum of Major Views on Political Theology? A Proposed Taxonomy of Seven Views on Religion and Government." Christ Over All, November 10, 2023. https://christoverall.com/article/longform/what-is-the-spectrum-of-major-views-on-political-theology-a-proposed-taxonomy-of-seven-views-on-religion-and-government.

Parker, Brent E., and Richard J. Lucas, eds. *Covenantal and Dispensational Theologies: Four Views on the Continuity of Scripture.* IVP Academic, 2022.

Parker, Kim Ian. "Repetition as a Structuring Device in 1 Kings 1–11." *Journal for the Study of the Old Testament* 42 (1988): 19–27.

Parkison, Samuel G. *To Gaze upon God: The Beatific Vision in Doctrine, Tradition, and Practice.* IVP Academic, 2024.

Pate, C. Marvin, J. Scott Duvall, J. Daniel Hays, E. Randolph Richards, W. Dennis Tucker Jr., and Preben Vang. *The Story of Israel: A Biblical Theology.* IVP Academic, 2004.

Pentecost, J. Dwight. *Things to Come: A Study in Biblical Eschatology.* Zondervan, 1964.

Peterson, David. *Engaging with God: A Biblical Theology of Worship.* InterVarsity, 1992.

Piotrowski, N. G. "Exodus, The." In *DNTUOT*.

Piper, John. *Counted Righteous in Christ: Should We Abandon the Imputation of Christ's Righteousness?* Crossway, 2002.

Porter, Stanley E., ed. *The Messiah in the Old and New Testaments.* Eerdmans, 2007.

Poythress, Vern S. *Biblical Typology: How the Old Testament Points to Christ, His Church, and the Consummation.* Crossway, 2024.

Poythress, Vern S. *The Shadow of Christ in the Law of Moses.* Presbyterian and Reformed, 1991.

Roberts, Vaughan. *God's Big Picture: Tracing the Storyline of the Bible*. Inter-Varsity, 2003.

Robertson, O. Palmer. *The Christ of the Covenants*. Presbyterian and Reformed, 1980.

Robertson, O. Palmer. *The Christ of the Prophets*. P&R, 2004.

Robertson, O. Palmer. *The Christ of Wisdom: A Redemptive-Historical Exploration of the Wisdom Books of the Old Testament*. P&R, 2017.

Rosner, Brian S. *Paul and the Law: Keeping the Commandments of God*. NSBT 31. InterVarsity, 2013.

Saucy, Robert L. *The Case for Progressive Dispensationalism: The Interface Between Dispensational and Non-Dispensational Theology*. Zondervan, 1993.

Schreiner, Thomas R. *Covenant and God's Purpose for the World*. Crossway, 2017.

Schreiner, Thomas R. *40 Questions About Christians and Biblical Law*. Kregel, 2010.

Schrock, David S. *The Royal Priesthood and the Glory of God*. Short Studies in Biblical Theology. Crossway, 2022.

Schultz, Richard L. "Unity or Diversity in Wisdom Theology? A Canonical and Covenantal Perspective." *Tyndale Bulletin* 48 (1997): 271–306.

Scobie, Charles H. H. *The Ways of Our God: An Approach to Biblical Theology*. Eerdmans, 2003.

Silva, Moisés. *Biblical Words and Their Meaning: An Introduction to Lexical Semantics*. Rev. and exp. ed. Zondervan, 1994.

Sire, James W. *The Universe Next Door: A Basic Worldview Catalog*. 6th ed. IVP Academic, 2020.

Strauss, M. L. "Messiah." In *DNTUOT*.

Strickland, W. G., ed. *Five Views on Law and Gospel*. Zondervan, 1993.

Strom, Mark. *The Symphony of Scripture: Making Sense of the Bible's Many Themes*. InterVarsity, 1990.

Swain, Scott R. "New Covenant Theologies." In *Covenant Theology: Biblical, Theological, and Historical Perspectives*, edited by Guy Prentiss Waters, J. Nicholas Reid, and John R. Muether. Crossway, 2020.

Tabb, Brian J., and Andrew M. King, eds. *Five Views of Christ in the Old Testament*. Zondervan Academic, 2022.

Thompson, Alan J. "Acts, Book of." In *DNTUOT*.

Thompson, Alan J. *The Acts of the Risen Lord Jesus: Luke's Account of God's Unfolding Plan*. NSBT 27. InterVarsity, 2011.

Thompson, Alan J. *Colossians and Philemon: An Introduction and Commentary*. Tyndale New Testament Commentaries. IVP Academic, 2022.

Treat, Jeremy R. *The Crucified King: Atonement and Kingdom in Biblical and Systematic Theology*. Zondervan, 2014.

Tully, Eric J. "Prophet." In *DNTUOT*.

Tully, Eric J. *Reading the Prophets as Christian Scripture: A Literary, Canonical, and Theological Introduction*. Reading Christian Scripture. Baker Academic, 2022.

VanDrunen, David. *Living in God's Two Kingdoms: A Biblical Vision for Christianity and Culture*. Crossway, 2010.

Vos, Geerhardus. *Biblical Theology: Old and New Testaments*. Banner of Truth Trust, 1975.

Waltke, Bruce K. "The Book of Proverbs and Old Testament Theology." *Bibliotheca Sacra* 136 (1979): 302–17.

Waltke, Bruce K. *An Old Testament Theology: An Exegetical, Canonical, and Thematic Approach*. With Charles Yu. Zondervan, 2007.

Watts, R. E. "Exodus." In *NDBT*.

Wellum, Stephen J., and Kirk Wellum. "The Biblical and Theological Case for Congregationalism." In *Baptist Foundations: Church Government for an Anti-Institutional Age*, edited by Mark Dever and Jonathan Leeman. B&H Academic, 2015.

Whitley, C. F. *The Prophetic Achievement*. Brill, 1963.

Williams, Michael D. *Far as the Curse Is Found: The Covenant Story of Redemption*. P&R, 2005.

Williams, Michael J. *The Prophet and His Message: Reading Old Testament Prophecy Today*. P&R, 2003.

Williamson, Paul R. *Sealed with an Oath: Covenant in God's Unfolding Purpose*. NSBT 23. InterVarsity, 2007.

Wittmer, Michael E., ed. *Four Views on Heaven*. Zondervan, 2022.

Wright, N. T. *The Climax of the Covenant: Christ and the Law in Pauline Theology*. Fortress, 1993.

Yarbrough, Robert W. "Atonement." In *NDBT*.

Younger, K. Lawson, Jr. *Judges, Ruth*. Rev. ed. NIV Application Commentary. Zondervan Academic, 2020.

SCRIPTURE AND ANCIENT WRITINGS INDEX

Old Testament

Genesis
1 14, 15n2, 18, 28
1–2 16
1–3 13, 17, 22, 26, 156n9
1:1 13
1:2 14
1:2–4 44
1:3–5 14
1:6–8 14, 28
1:9–10 28, 44
1:9–13 14
1:14–18 28
1:14–19 14, 15
1:20–22 28
1:20–23 14
1:23–24 19
1:24–25 28
1:24–31 14
1:26 16n4, 28
1:26–27 18, 28, 119
1:26–28 15, 16, 88
1:28 18, 28, 83
1:29–30 28
2 161
2:1–3 14, 15
2:2 15
2:2–3 15
2:8–9 16
2:9–10 141
2:10 19
2:12 48, 138
2:15 48, 78, 83, 88
2:15–17 16
2:19 28
3:1 16
3:4 16
3:8 16, 48
3:15 10n14, 17, 27, 88, 91, 99
3:21 10n14
3:24 19, 48
4–11 29
5 17
5:1–3 119
6–9 27
6:18 28
7:11 28
7:15 28
8:1–3 28
8:3–4 44
8:17–19 28
8:20–21 74, 77
8:22 28
9:1 18, 28
9:2 18, 28
9:3 28
9:6 18, 28
9:7 18, 28
9:8–11 27
9:8–17 27
9:9–17 28
9:10 28
9:12 28
9:15 28
9:16 28
9:17 28
9:21 29, 36
11 29
11:4 29
12 17, 18, 29
12:1 30
12:1–3 29
12:2 29–30, 34
12:3 29, 30
12:7 34
13:16 92
14:18 82
15 29
15:1–21 29
15:5 92
15:6 6
15:8–21 30
15:9–17 74
15:13–16 99n12
15:17 30
15:18 92
17 31
17:1 30
17:1–16 29
17:4–8 34
17:6 34, 88
17:7 26
17:7–8 34
17:16 34, 88
18 152
22:15–18 29
22:17 34, 92
22:18 30, 34
24 152
26:3–4 30
28:14 30
32:12 92
35:11 88
48:22 28n4
49:10 88, 97, 101

Exodus
1:11 49
1:14 49
2:23–25 44
2:24 31
3:12 46
4:22–23 35, 51, 92, 98, 119
5:1–21 49
6:4 31
6:5 45
6:6–8 44–45
6:7 26, 31
10:21–23 14
12 45, 74, 75
12:2 49
12:3–4 75
12:5 76, 80
12:6 49
12:12 75
12:12–13 75
12:21–28 49
12:48–49 37
13:21 30
14:20–21 19, 44
15:1–21 19, 44
15:17 20
19–24 32
19:5 26
19:6 32, 83
19:18 30
20 45
20:1–2 57
20:2 26, 45
20:2–3 57
20:11 15n2
20:18 30
20:18–21 105
22:21 49

171

22:25 59
23:14–15 49
23:31 92
24:4–8 74
24:12–31:18 46
24:12–39:31 46
25:7 48
25:8 19, 46
25:11–39 48
25:31–36 19
26:1 19
26:15–25 140
26:31 19
26:36 19
28 78
28:3 69
28:9–12 48
28:11–12 78
28:15–21 138
28:20 48
28:29–30 78
28:38 78
29:9 83
29:38–42 76n7
29:45–46 26, 46
31:3 69
31:6 69
31:12–18 68
31:13–17 32
32:4 49
32:8 49
32:11–12 81n14
32:13 30, 31
32:14 81n14
34 120
35:3 68
35:10 69
36:8–39:31 46
39:8–14 138

Leviticus

1–6 76
1–7 77
1:4 76, 77
1:9 80
1:10 80
1:13 80
1:17 80
3:6 80
4 77n9
4:35 76
6–7 77
6:1–5 77
6:1–7 77n9
6:8 77
9:7 77
9:8 77
9:8–12 77
9:8–21 77
9:12 77
9:15 77
9:15–21 77
9:16–17 77
9:18–21 77
9:22 77
10:1–2 75
10:3 75
10:6–7 75
10:17 78
11:45 49
14:20–21 77
14:31 77
15:13–15 77
15:28–30 77
16 74, 74n1, 75, 80
16:1 75, 76
16:2 81
16:5 75
16:6 75
16:9 75
16:15–17 75
16:20 75
16:21 75
16:21–22 76
16:22 75
16:24 77
16:27 80
16:30 75
16:34 75
17:11 81
18:5 70
18:25 99n12
19:20–22 77
19:33–34 49
20:3 75
20:22–26 32
21:23 20
22:17–25 76
23:42–43 49
25:42 49
25:43 49
26:1–13 57, 134
26:12 48
26:14–44 33
26:33–34 108n9
26:40–42 108n9
26:40–45 30
26:42 31
26:42–45 33

Numbers

2 46
3:7–8 48, 78
3:10 83, 101
6:24–26 78
8:25–26 48
11:29 115
13–14 6, 7
15:22–36 77n9
15:30–31 77
15:32–36 68
16 76n4
16:46 81n14
16:46–47 76n4
16:47 81n14
18:1 78
18:5–6 48
18:5–7 78
18:7 83, 101
18:32 76
21:35 99n12
24:9 31–32
24:17 88
24:19 88
25 76n4
25:10–13 76
25:11 81n14
25:13 81n14
27:21 105n5
28:2–8 76n7
28:9–10 76n7
28:11–15 76n7
28:19–25 76n7
28:26–31 76n7
29:1–6 76n7

Deuteronomy

1:8 32
2:33–34 99n12
4:6 70
4:6–8 57
4:10 70
4:31 32
5:15 49
5:22–27 105
6:1–3 70
6:6–9 70
6:13 118
6:16 118
6:17–18 90
7:2–5 99n12
7:7–9 31
8 118
8:3 118
9:4–6 99n12
10:17–19 49
11:18–21 70
12:28 90
13:1–18 105n5
15:13–15 49
16:9–12 49
17 91, 92, 93
17:14 88, 91
17:14–20 88
18:9–11 105n5
18:15–16 104–5
18:18 105
18:19 105
18:19–22 105n5
19:14 70
20:1–20 99n12
22:8 55, 67–68
23:14 48
24:18 49
24:22 49
26:5–10 49
26:19 57
27:15–26 33
27:17 70
27:26 80
28:15–68 33
28:45 33
29:13 31
29:19–21 77n9
31:29 33

Joshua

2:10–11 99n12
18–19 21
24:12 28n4
24:19–20 33

Judges

1:1–2:5 88
2:6–3:6 88
2:11 90
2:16–17 89
3:7–11 89
3:7–16:31 88
8:23 90
13:1–16:31 89
17:1–18:31 88
17:6 90
18:1 90
19:1 90
19:1–21:25 88
19:30 49
21:25 90

Ruth

2:12 37

1 Samuel

2:4 28n4
2:12 37
4:4 88n1
8 91
8:5 91
8:7 91
8:8 91
8:19–20 91
13:14 91
14:41–42 105n5
15:3 99n12
15:22–23 79
16 91
16–17 99
16–1 Kings 11 9
17 91

2 Samuel

1–10 92
6:2 88n1
6:17–18 83
7 25, 34, 87, 92, 119, 156n9
7–8 99
7:5 34
7:9 34
7:10 34
7:11 34
7:11–17 33
7:12 34
7:12–16 34

7:14 26, 34, 35, 92, 98
7:19 34
7:29 34
8:15 100
12 106

1 Kings

1–2 93
1–11 92, 93
3 93
3:5 93
3:12 70
3:28 70
4:20 92
4:20–25 92
4:20–28 134
4:21 92
4:24 88
4:25 92
4:32 70
4:34 70
5–8 92
5:7 70
6–8 93
6:1 48
6:2 93
6:20 140
6:20–22 48
6:29 19
6:29–35 48
6:38 92–93
7 92, 93
7:1 92–93
7:2 93
7:8 93
7:19–20 19
7:22 19
7:23 19
7:42 19
8 70, 152
8:20–21 92
8:21 48
8:29–30 150
8:63 83
9 93
9:1 93
9:10 93
9:15 93
9:15–19 49
10:12 93
11:1 93
11:1–6 93
11:7–8 93
11:14–43 93
12:8–11 49
12:15 49
12:20–21 94
12:28–33 49
12:31 83
13:33–34 83
15:8–24 95
15:11–12 99
15:24 95
18 106
22:41–51 95

2 Kings

12:1–21 95
13:23 29, 30, 33
14:1–22 95
14:23–27 109n10
15:1–7 95
15:32–38 95
16:20 95
17 36, 57
17:7–8 57
17:7–23 49
17:13 57
17:15 33
17:15–16 58
17:18 19
17:18–20 134
17:20 19, 58
17:32 83
18:1–20:21 95
18:12 33
20:2–3 95
21:26–23:30 95
22:13 78
22:17 78
23 99
23:26 78, 81n14
24:4 81n14
24:20 81n14

1 Chronicles

12:38–40 92
16:1–2 83
16:15–16 29
17:10–14 33
18:8 99
23:32 48
29:1–5 99
29:2 48
29:22–25 92

2 Chronicles

3:8–9 140
5:1 99
7:14 152
8:12–16 100
9:22–26 92
11:14–15 83
13:9 83
14:1–16:14 95
17:1–21:1 95
21:7 34
23:6 83
24:1–27 95
24:18 78
24:27–25:28 95
26:1–23 95
26:16–18 83
26:16–21 100
26:21–23 95
26:23–27:9 95
28:27–32:33 95
29–31 99
29:7–8 77
29:8 78
29:27 83
33:25–35:27 95
34–35 99
34:25 78
36:16 78

Ezra

3:10 99
3:12–13 110

Job

1:1 70
1:5 70, 77
1:8 70
12:13 69
28 69
28:28 70
38–41 22n10
42:7–8 70

Psalms

1 69
2 35
2:2 98
2:7 92, 98
8 22n10
19 22n10
19:7 70
23 160
28:8 98
37 69
37:30–31 70
42:2 148
44:13–14 57
45:6 97
49 69
69:25 101
72:8 19, 88
72:8–11 34
72:17 34
74:13–14 19, 44
78:31 81n14
78:38 81n14
78:53–54 44
80:1 47, 88n1
85 76n4
85:2–3 76n4
89 95–96
89:1–2 95
89:3–4 34, 96
89:23 34
89:26 34
89:28 34
89:28–29 96
89:34 34
89:37 96
89:38–39 96
89:46 96
95 6, 7
103:19 9, 121
105:8–9 29
105:8–11 31
105:42–45 31
109:8 101
110 82, 83, 101
110:1 97
112 69
132:11–18 34

Proverbs

1:1 70
1:7 70
2:6 70
2:21–22 70
3:7 70
3:9–10 70
3:19–20 69
4:4 70
4:10 70
6:21–23 70
8:15–16 70
8:22 70
8:22–31 69
9:10 70
10:1 70
10:30 70
15:8 70
16:6 70
21:27 70
22:8 70

Ecclesiastes

1:1 70
1:12 70
5:1–7 70
12:13 70

Isaiah

1:11–14 79
1:11–17 151
5 118
6:13 96
9:6 97
9:6–9 112
10:11 134
10:20–21 112
10:21 112
11 19, 96, 97, 97n8
11:1 96, 97
11:1–2 70
11:5 97
11:6 111
11:6–9 134
11:9 19, 120
11:10 97
11:16 50
12:1 134
19:19–22 151

19:56 151
24:23 8, 121
25:6–9 8
25:8 137, 147
26:19 127
27:6 134
32:15 130n16
33:20 151
35:1–10 19
37:16 88n1
40 22n10
40–55 50n11
40–66 36
40:3 51
42:1 118n2
42:6 36, 39, 80, 118n2
42:9 138
43:10–12 130n16
43:18–19 138
44:3 141
44:24–28 50n11
49 153
49:1–6 112
49:3 80, 118n2
49:5–6 80, 118n2, 130n16
49:6 36
49:8 39
51:2–3 157n11
51:3 19, 112
51:10–11 50
52:1 137
52:13–53:12 112
53 80
53:2 96
53:4–12 80
53:5 80
53:5–6 80
53:9 80
53:10 80
53:11–12 80
54:1 157n11
54:9 28
54:10 80
54:11–12 138
55:3 38, 80
55:3–5 36, 97
58:9 152

60:3–5 139
60:11 139
60:19–20 140, 141
61:8 38
65:17 19, 20, 134
65:17–18 111
65:17–19 19
65:17–25 120, 137
65:19 137
65:19–20 137
65:20 144
65:24 152
65:25 19, 134
66:22 19, 20, 134, 137
66:23 151

Jeremiah

2:8 37, 37n16
4:1–2 32
4:22 37
5:31 37n16
7 33, 151
7:21–23 79
8:8–9 70
11:2–5 31
11:7–8 78
13:13 37n16
14:10 37
14:14–15 37n16
16:14–15 50, 112
17:21–27 68
23 97, 97n8
23:5 70, 97
23:5–7 96
23:6 97
23:7–8 50
23:9–31 37n16
24:9 57
25:4–7 78
26:8–16 37n16
29:12–13 152
30–33 36
30:22 26
31 41, 130, 153
31:9 119
31:31–34 36

31:32 38, 58, 79
31:32–33 58
31:33 26, 36, 58, 112
31:33–34 36
31:34 37, 41, 79, 84, 152
32:30–33 78
32:32 37n16
32:38 26
32:39–40 36, 58
32:40 38
33:8 37, 75n2, 79n11
33:9 36
33:14–22 96
33:20 28
33:25 28
34:18 30
43:4–13 109
50:5 38
50:20 37
51:51 20

Lamentations

3:42 81n14
3:43 81n14

Ezekiel

5:11 75n2
5:14–15 57
7 108
7:2–3 108
7:5–7 108
7:24 20
8:1–10:22 75n2
16:60 38
16:63 37
17:22–24 96
20:4–10 75
20:7 45
20:12 32
20:20 32
21:26–27 97
22:4–5 57
23:10 57
24:13 75n2
28:12–19 138
28:13–14 20
28:14 20, 48
28:16 20, 48

28:18 20
31:33 36
34 36, 97
34:11–12 97
34:12 98
34:16 98
34:22–24 98
34:23 97
34:25–30 111
34:30 26
36–37 36
36:17–18 75n2
36:25–27 141
36:26 36, 41
36:26–27 58, 112
36:27–28 36
36:28 26
36:33 37
36:35 19
36:36 36
37:9–10 141
37:14 36, 58, 141
37:23 26
37:24–25 97, 98
37:24–27 36
37:24–28 120
37:26 38, 111n15
37:27 26, 137
37:28 36
40–48 111, 111n15, 134, 144, 151
40:2 138
40:5 138
40:6 19, 48
40:38–46 111n15
41:4 140
41:13 139
41:17–20 48
42:16–20 139
43:12 20
44:14 48
45:1–3 139
45:21–24 50
47:1–12 19, 111n15, 141
48:31 139
48:35 111n15, 120, 140

Daniel

2:44 8, 121
12:1–2 127

Hosea

1:9 108
1:10–2:1 50n11
2:14 50n11
6:6 79
6:7 42
11:1 50n11, 51, 119, 160
11:10–11 50n11, 119
12:13 105

Joel

2 130, 160
2:28–29 115

Amos

5:21–27 79
9:11–12 97
9:13–14 111

Micah

4:4 92
6:6–7 76
7:14–20 31
7:18 76n4
7:20 31

Habakkuk

2:4 109

Zephaniah

3:9 152
3:10 151
3:14–20 152
3:17 109

Zechariah

3:10 92
4:10 110
6:9–15 83
6:12–13 99, 100
6:13 101
9:10 19

Scripture and Ancient Writings Index

14:8 141
14:9 8, 121
14:11 141
14:20–21 151

Malachi
3:4 151

New Testament

Matthew
1 149
1:1 39, 98
1:1–16 9
1:1–17 9
1:17 9, 39
1:22 63
2:2 156
2:8 156
2:13–15 51, 119
2:15 63, 119, 160
2:17 63
2:23 63
3:1–17 51, 119
3:2 126
3:9 39
3:17 118n2
4:1–11 51, 118, 119
4:14 63
4:17 126
5–7 120
5:1–7:29 51, 119
5:3 126
5:5 21
5:8 148
5:17 39, 62–63
5:19 126
5:20 126
5:22 63
5:28 63
5:32 63
5:33–37 63
5:34 63
5:39 63
5:44 63
6:10 126
7:12 66
7:21 126
7:24 71
7:28–29 63
8:11 126
10:7 126
11:13 8, 33n8, 39, 63
11:28 68
12:28 122, 126
12:42 98
13 124, 124n6, 131
13:3–9 124
13:18–23 124
13:24–30 124
13:30 124
13:31–32 124
13:33 125
13:36–43 124
13:44–46 125
13:47–50 125
13:54 71
16:18 100
18:26 156
19:4 15n2
19:16–30 122
21:9 98
21:31 122
21:43 126
22:14 156
22:37–40 66
22:42 98
23:13 122, 126
25:34 122, 126, 127n11
25:46 122, 127n11
26 51, 80
26:63 98
28:18–20 100

Mark
1:1–3 51
1:15 8, 126
3:28–30 77n9
4 124
4:11 124
9:47 126
10:15 122, 126
10:23 122, 126

Luke
1:27 120
1:31–33 120
1:32 98
1:32–33 39
1:35 98
1:55 39
1:69 98
1:69–70 39
1:72–73 39
2:40 71
2:52 70
3:22 119
3:38 119
4:1–13 118
4:3 119
4:9 119
7:26–28 113
7:28 114–15
7:35 71
8:26–39 123
9:31 51
10:9 126
10:11 126
11:20 122, 123
11:31 71
11:50 15n2
12:32 122, 126
13:10–20 123
13:29 126
16 99n12
16:16 39
16:31 141n8
17:20 126
17:21 122
18:1 152
18:8 152
18:16–17 122
18:17 8, 126
19:10 98
19:11 126
20:41–44 98
21:15 71
21:33 135
22 51, 80
22:16 122
22:18 122
22:20 40, 41
23:51 126
24:1 151
24:44–47 131

John
1 134
1:1 114
1:1–3 120
1:14 51, 120, 151
1:16–17 8, 33n8
1:17–18 114
1:18 98
1:32 120
1:41 98
2:19 51, 151
2:19–21 100, 120
2:42 100
3:3 41
3:13 141n8
3:34–35 120
4:11 100
4:20–24 51
4:21–24 120
4:23 100, 151
4:25 98
4:53 41
5:24 127
5:46 39
6:14 114
6:39–40 127
7:40 114
8:29 39
8:44 17
10:11 98
10:14–16 98
11 128
13:34 52
14:14 152
15:1 118
15:1–4 145
17:3 40
20:28–29 100
20:32 100

Acts
1:3–5 127n11
1:6 130n16
1:8 130n16
1:20 101
2 130, 160, 161
2:14 130n16
2:17–18 115
2:22 131n16
2:29 131n16
2:29–31 98, 120
2:29–35 39
2:30–35 100
2:33 41, 100, 127
2:35 100
2:36 130n16
2:38–39 41, 127
2:41 41
3:22 114
3:24 131
3:25–26 39
3:26 114
4:25–27 98
7 9, 149
7:2 9
7:2–53 9
7:43 9
7:45–47 9
8 41
11:14 41
11:21 100
13 9, 149
13:1 61n4
13:16–41 9
13:17 9
13:22 9
13:32–37 98
13:33 98
14:17 22n10
14:22 131
15 41
16:15 41
16:31–34 41
16:32 41
16:34 41
17 18
18:8 41
20 128
20:7 151
24:14–15 131
24:15 128
24:21 128
26:6–8 128
26:18 99
26:22–23 128, 131

Romans
1 161
1:2–3 8

1:3–4 98
1:18 81
1:20 15n2
1:21 22n10
1:23–25 22n10
1:25 22n10
1:32 81n14
2:5 81
2:29 41
3 81
3:9 6
3:19 33
3:20 6
3:21 8, 33n8
3:22 145n10
3:22–26 66n6
3:24 51
3:24–25 81
3:25 39, 51, 81, 81n14
3:28 145n10
3:31 66n6
4 6, 41
4:3 6
4:5 145n10
4:9–12 6
4:10 6
4:13–14 21
4:16 145
4:22 6
5 22, 119
5–6 99
5–8 131
5:1 127
5:8 81
5:9 81, 127
5:9–10 81n14
5:12–21 20, 128
5:14 156
5:17 59
5:19 39, 59, 72
5:20 32, 33
5:21 127n11, 129
6–8 128
6:12 129
7:6 127, 129
7:7 32
8 135, 145
8:3 80
8:3–4 39, 72
8:4 59

8:9 129
8:10 129
8:13 129
8:17–19 21
8:18–25 135
8:19 135
8:21 135
8:23 128
8:26 131, 152
8:28–30 152
8:30 156
8:33–34 99
9 145, 146
9–11 119, 132, 145–47, 148
9:1–5 146–47
9:6–8 39
10:4 39, 64
11 119, 131n16, 145, 146
11:1 145, 146
11:1–10 146
11:11 145, 146
11:20 145n10
11:23 145n10
11:25 146
11:25–26 146
11:26 145, 146, 147
12:1 52, 84
12:1–2 151
13:8–10 68
13:9 65
13:10 65
14:5 68
14:5–6 68, 151
15:4 66
15:16 151
15:16–17 84
16:20 17
16:25–26 8

1 Corinthians

1:16 41
1:24 70
2:6–7 71
3:11 100
3:16 100, 120
3:16–17 151
3:21–22 22n10
5:7 51, 80

6:11 127
7:19 161
9:20 64
9:20–21 63–64
9:21 64
10:1–13 161
10:11 66
10:31 151
11:25 40
13:1–13 66
13:6 66
13:12 38
15 21, 119
15:20 128
15:22 128
15:23 128
15:35–38 135n1
15:45 20, 128
15:47 20
15:50–57 100
16:2 151
16:15 41

2 Corinthians

1:20 39
1:21 98n9
1:22 38, 127, 128
3:6 40
3:6–8 127
4:4 143
5:5 38, 127, 128
5:17 20, 134
5:20–21 39, 80
5:21 59
11:3 161
12:4 141n8

Galatians

2 41
3 64, 161
3:7 39, 41, 145
3:8 39
3:10 6, 80
3:13 39
3:14 39, 127
3:16 21, 39, 118
3:17 32
3:17–19 6, 8
3:18 21

3:19 6, 32, 33, 39, 64, 65, 118
3:24 8, 39, 64, 65
3:24–25 65
3:25 64, 65
3:26–29 41, 119
3:29 21, 39, 145
4:4 39
4:4–5 64
4:6 152
4:10 151
4:21–31 39
4:24 157n11
5:14 65
5:18 127
6:15 20, 134

Ephesians

1:13 127
1:14 38, 127, 128
2:2 143
2:12–13 39
2:20–22 100
2:21–22 120, 151
3:10 71
4:25–5:2 65
4:32 52
5:1–2 80
5:2 65
5:25 52

Philippians

2:8 59
2:17 84
3:3 41, 119
3:9 59
4:18 84, 151

Colossians

1 134
1:9 71
1:13 17, 99
1:15–23 100
1:16 22
1:18 20, 128, 134

1:28 71
2:3 70
2:9 120, 151
2:11–12 41
2:14–15 99
2:15 17
2:16 68
2:16–17 68, 151
2:17 68, 84
2:23 71
3:1–11 129
3:16 71, 151
4:5 71

1 Timothy

4:3–4 22n10
6:15 100
6:17 22n10

2 Timothy

2:8 98
3:15 71
4:6 84

Hebrews

1:1–2 114
1:1–3 120
1:10–12 135
2:14 17
2:14–15 99
2:17 82
3–4 6, 68
3:5 39
3:14 41
4 7
4:3 68
4:6–10 6
4:7 6, 7
4:8 7
4:9–10 68
4:14–5:10 82
4:15 39
4:16 152
5:3 82
6:18–19 82
7:11 82
7:11–19 101
7:12 39, 82
7:13–14 83
7:14 83

7:19 82
7:22 40, 82
7:23–27 82
7:26 39
8 130
8:1–6 82
8:6 40, 82
8:6–13 40
8:11 37
8:12 82, 84
9–10 82
9:5 81
9:7 82
9:7–8 82, 84
9:9–10 82n15
9:11–14 82
9:12 40, 83n16
9:13–14 82n15
9:15 40, 76n6, 82, 82n15
9:21 83n16
9:23–28 82
9:25–28 83n16
10:1 84
10:1–3 33, 82
10:11 82
10:11–14 76n6
10:16–17 41
10:16–18 82
10:17 82, 84
10:19–22 84, 152
10:19–23 82
10:26 77n9
11:40 76n6
12:24 40, 82
12:28 84
13:12 80
13:15 84
13:15–16 84
13:16 84, 151

James

1:5 71
2:8 66

1 Peter

1:1 61n4
1:10–12 8
1:11 111n14
1:18 51
1:19 51, 80
2:5 84, 120, 151
2:9 84
2:22 59
5:1–4 100
5:8 143

2 Peter

3:6 135
3:6–7 135
3:7 135
3:10 135
3:10–13 135
3:11 135
3:12 135
3:13 21, 135

1 John

1:9 152
2:19 41
2:20 40, 98n9, 120
2:27 40, 120
3:2 148
3:5 59
3:8 17, 91, 99
5:19 143

Revelation

1:5 100
1:10 151
1:12–16 141n8
4:11 22n10
5:1–14 140
5:8 84
5:13 148
6–19 143
6:9 84
8:3 84
12:9 17, 143
13:1 137
13:14 143
15:3 100
17:14 100
19 143, 144
19–20 99n12
19:11 143
19:16 100
19:19 143
19:20 143
20 142, 144, 148
20:1 143
20:1–7 142–44
20:3 143, 144
20:4 143
20:5 143
20:11 143
21 136, 144
21–22 11, 21, 51, 130, 133, 134, 141, 147
21:1 13, 21, 137, 143
21:1–8 136, 137
21:1–22:5 136
21:2 137, 138, 140
21:3 21, 27, 140, 154
21:3–4 137, 141, 147
21:4 137, 141
21:5–6 138
21:6 138
21:7–8 138
21:9 137, 138
21:9–10 140
21:9–22:5 137, 138, 138n5
21:10 20, 138
21:11 138
21:12 139
21:12–14 139
21:14 139
21:15–17 139
21:16 139, 140
21:17 139
21:18–21 138
21:22 140
21:22–23 140
21:24 139
21:25 139
22 111n15
22:1 141
22:1–2 19
22:1–5 140
22:2 21, 141
22:3 21, 141
22:4 21, 141

Other Ancient Sources

1 Maccabees

4:45–46 113
9:27 113
14:41 113

Josephus

Against Apion

1.41 113

Philo

On Abraham

11.52 158n12

On the Change of Names

2.12 158n12
14.52 158n12

On Joseph

1.1 158n12

SUBJECT INDEX

Abraham, 6, 17, 29–31, 33, 34, 39, 44, 87, 88
Adam
  and Christ, 20, 22, 118–19, 128–29, 156
  covenant with, 16, 27n3, 42
  and Eden, 16, 18, 27
  and Israel, 49, 58, 71, 78, 96
  judgment of, 17, 78
  and kingship, 15–16, 27, 28, 88
  and Noah, 27–28
  and priestly service, 16, 48, 78, 83
  See also Noah
amillennial view, 142
assurance, 41–42, 82, 84, 108, 131, 141, 147

Beale, G. K., 23, 47n6, 53
Bible
  as God's revelation, 3–4
  overall structure of, 7–10, 120, 149–50
  as progressive revelation, 2–4, 8–10, 129–30, 157, 159
  promise and fulfillment in, 8–10, 26, 38, 39, 50–51, 62, 80, 99n12, 100, 120
  revelation and history, 106–7
  unity, 3–4, 41, 115, 147
biblical theology
  and allegorical interpretation, 157–58
  definition, 2
  different approaches to, 2n1, 12
  and God's sovereignty, 3, 138, 154
  and God's word, 3–4
  historical sequence examples, 6–7
  and Old Testament interpretation, 10–11, 52, 53, 66–68, 73, 82–83, 113–14, 115, 117–20, 122–24, 129–31, 136n2, 147, 158–61
  relationship to exegesis, 4–5, 161

  relationship to systematic theology, 5, 154–55
  and tracing themes, 150–58
  and typology, 156–58
  and wisdom, 69–71
  and word studies, 155–56
blessing, 18, 28, 29–31, 34, 35, 56, 77–78, 118

Carson, D. A., 4n4, 4n5, 6n7, 35n12, 119n3, 136n2, 144n9, 154n5, 156n8, 160–61
circumcision, 6, 20, 31, 40–41, 134, 160
cleansing, 75, 75n2, 77, 79n11, 82, 82n15, 84, 139, 151
covenant
  Abrahamic, 29–31, 33, 34, 36, 39, 44, 92, 118, 145
  and Adam, 16, 20, 27, 42
  and baptism, 40–41, 42
  and creation, 13–16, 27–28
  Davidic, 33–35, 39, 92, 96
  definition, 25
  formula, 26–27, 45, 137
  and kingdom, 25–26, 55
  Mosaic, 31–33, 36, 37–38, 39, 55–58, 64–65, 69–70, 82, 109
  new, 36–38, 39, 40–41, 58, 71, 79, 82, 112, 130, 151, 152
  Noahic, 27–29, 36, 39, 42
creation, 1, 10, 10n14, 55–56
  and Eden, 18–19, 28, 44
  and the exodus, 44
  and Genesis, 13–15
  and God, 13–15, 87–88
  and humanity, 15–17, 87
  and Jesus, 20–21, 22, 88, 100, 120, 123, 128
  and the nations, 17–18. *See also* nations
  and Noah, 18, 27–29, 42

and wisdom, 69
See also Adam; Eden; exodus; new creation

David, 9, 70, 87, 91–92, 96–97, 99–100, 101
death, 17, 20, 77, 123, 126, 129, 131, 137, 141, 147
   and atonement, 81, 85
   and judgment, 75, 81n14, 138
   and life, 20, 98, 127, 128–29, 138
   and new covenant, 39, 84, 127–29
   and resurrection, 20, 21, 22, 39, 98, 100, 147. See also Jesus: death and resurrection of; resurrection
   and sacrifice, 51, 60, 73, 76, 77n8, 80, 81, 82, 84
   and salvation, 51, 52, 59, 67n6, 71
dispensational premillennial view, 111n15, 129–31, 144

Eden, 18–19, 43–44, 47–48, 83, 120, 133, 134
exile, 9, 19, 78, 94–96, 97, 107–8
exodus, the, 43–46
   and Abrahamic covenant, 44
   and God's presence, 45, 46, 74–75
   and Israel's life, 48–49
   and Jesus, 50–52, 80, 81, 118–19, 157
   and the law, 31, 56, 57
   new, 50, 53, 110, 112, 115, 157
   and new creation, 18–19, 44
   and the New Testament, 51
   and sacrifice, 74–75, 80, 81

fulfillment, 8–10, 39–40, 51, 62–66, 73, 110, 115, 117–21, 137, 149

God
   as creator, 13–16, 18, 27–28
   dwelling of, 19, 21, 46–47, 51, 74, 100, 120, 129, 136–37, 140, 141
   as faithful, 31, 41, 44, 52, 95–96
   grace of, 20, 31–32, 33n8, 45, 52, 78, 81, 82, 127n11, 129, 147, 153, 159
   judgment of, 16–17, 75–76, 78, 79, 80–81, 112
   as king, 14–15, 87–88, 90, 91, 121
   love of, 30, 52, 81, 95–96, 119
   presence of, 18–19, 21, 46–48, 58, 137, 140, 141, 147, 148
   as sovereign, 3, 8, 13–14, 22n10, 27, 30, 45, 47, 109, 121, 138
   wrath of, 36, 75, 76n4, 78, 81, 81n14, 96, 112, 134

Goldsworthy, Graeme, 7n8, 9n11, 22, 31, 94, 111, 118
gospel, the, 8, 17, 52, 71, 81–82, 112, 127, 129, 134, 145
Grindheim, Sigurd, xi, 75n2, 157n10

historic premillennial view, 143–44
Holy Spirit, 38, 39–40, 41, 100, 112, 120, 127–28, 130, 134, 151
humanity, 15–17, 18, 20, 26, 27, 28, 34–35, 44, 88, 119, 128, 134, 154

Israel
   and exile, 107–8, 110
   and the exodus, 48–50, 74
   and future hope, 110–12, 115, 128, 129–31, 132, 134, 145–47, 148
   and God's promises, 6–7, 30–31, 130n16
   history of, 9, 18–19, 26, 28, 35, 36, 57–58, 78, 92–94, 106–8, 113
   and Jesus, 118–19, 120, 153
   and king, 34, 35, 88, 92, 97, 98
   and land, 15, 19, 60–61, 67, 68n7
   as a nation, 31–33, 37, 40, 57–58, 60–61, 99n12
   and the priest, 78. See also priests
   and the Servant of the Lord, 36, 80, 112, 118n2, 120, 153
   and sin, 36, 57–58, 75, 76n4, 77n8, 79, 88–90, 94–96

Jesus
   and Adam, 20, 21, 119
   authority of, 63–64, 120
   and the covenants, 37, 39–40, 41, 82, 120
   and creation, 21–22, 134
   death and resurrection of, 8, 17, 20, 21, 39, 80, 81, 128, 131, 134, 135n1, 151. See also death
   and the exodus, 51, 52, 53, 81
   and Israel, 118–19, 145, 153
   and kingship, 39, 92, 97–100, 126
   and sacrifice, 80–83
   and seed, 17, 32, 39, 64–65, 88, 118, 145
   and temple, 51, 99–100, 115, 120, 130, 140
   and wisdom, 70–71, 100
Johnson, Dennis E., 136n3, 137n4, 138n5, 140n7
Josephus, 113
Judges, book of, 88–90, 101
judgment, 16–17, 27–28, 33, 36, 109, 110

Subject Index

kingdom of God, 8–10, 87–101, 117–32, 133
  and covenant, 25–26
  definition, 8
  inaugurated, 121–27
  fullness of, 100, 101, 111, 122, 124–25, 131, 134
  mystery, 123–26
  parables, 123–25
kingship, 34, 88, 91, 94, 103, 107

Ladd, George Eldon, 123, 124n6, 125–26
law, 6, 32, 36, 39, 55, 59–62, 63–68, 69–70, 109. *See also* covenant: Mosaic
life, 20, 111, 114, 122, 127, 128, 129, 134, 138, 140–41, 143. *See also* death; resurrection

millennium, the, 130, 142
  amillennial view, 142
  dispensational premillennial view, 111n15, 129–31, 144
  historic premillennial view, 143–44
  postmillennial view, 142–43
Moo, Douglas J., 62n5, 81n13, 128n13

nations, the
  and the Abrahamic covenant, 29–30, 31, 39
  in biblical theology, 15, 17–18, 31, 139, 146–47
  and the Davidic covenant, 34–35, 94, 97
  and Jesus, 39, 80, 97, 98, 100, 115, 130n16, 131
  and judgment, 99n12, 110, 111n14
  and kingship, 88, 91, 93
  and the millennium, 142–43
  and the Mosaic covenant, 32, 57–58, 99n12
  and the new covenant, 36, 58, 61, 80, 111–12
  and the Noahic covenant, 28
new creation, 10, 18–21, 26–27, 38, 44, 51, 110–11, 115, 134–36
Noah, 18, 27–28, 35, 36, 42

people of God, the
  as Abraham's seed, 39, 41, 57
  as bride and holy city, 138–41
  and Christ, 18, 20, 98n9, 100, 127–29, 130, 134, 138, 145, 153
  as secure, 139
  and the temple, 100, 120, 151
  transformed, 138–39
Philo, 157–58
postmillennial view, 142–43
prayer, 71, 84, 152

priests, 48, 75, 77–78, 82–83, 99–100
prophets, the
  and Christians, 114–15
  and exile, 107–8
  and future hope, 36–38, 50, 58, 79–80, 96–97, 110–12, 129–31, 134, 136n2
  and Israel's history, 105–6
  and Jesus, 112, 113–14
  and John the Baptist, 113
  and Moses, 104–5
  and the "silent years," 112–13
  writing prophets, 106

resurrection, 21, 128, 131, 134, 141, 143. *See also* death; Jesus: death and resurrection of
righteousness
  and Christ, 20, 33n8, 52, 59, 71, 72, 100, 119, 128–29
  and faith, 6, 59, 109, 127, 128–29, 134
  and God, 8, 81n14
  and kingship, 35, 90, 97, 100, 110, 112
  in new heaven and new earth, 21, 135
  and wisdom, 69
Robertson, O. Palmer, 28n6, 103n3, 105–6, 110

Sabbath, 6–7, 61–62, 68
sacrifice, 32–33, 73–85, 150–51
  and the Christian, 80–84
  and the Day of Atonement, 74–76
  offerings, kinds of, 77
  on Passover, 74–75
  and the prophets, 78–80
Satan, 17, 21, 52, 99, 118, 119, 123, 142–43
seed, 17, 27, 29, 32, 34, 35, 39, 41, 64–65, 87, 88, 118
sin, 16–17, 32, 36, 37, 75, 128–29
Solomon, 70–71, 87, 92–94
suffering, 27, 117, 124, 131

tabernacle, the, 19, 46–48, 74, 120
temple, the, 19–20, 48, 53, 79, 92–93, 99, 111, 120, 129–30, 140, 144, 151

Watts, R. E., 44n1, 47n6, 49n10
Wellum, Stephen, xi, 26n2, 37n15, 42, 100n13
wisdom, 69–71, 96–97
worldview, 153–54
worship, 84, 99–100, 150–51, 154–55, 156

Younger, K. Lawson, Jr., 88n2, 90n4

www.ingramcontent.com/pod-product-compliance
Lightning Source LLC
Chambersburg PA
CBHW020355170426
43200CB00005B/181